SCREENWRITER
WORDS BECOME PICTURES

SCREENWRITER
WORDS BECOME PICTURES

BY

LEE SERVER

THE MAIN STREET PRESS • PITTSTOWN, NEW JERSEY

To Robert and Elizabeth Server

Published by
The Main Street Press, Inc.
William Case House
Pittstown, New Jersey 08867

Published simultaneously in Canada by
Methuen Publications
2330 Midland Avenue
Agincourt, Ontario M1S 1P7

Cover design by Robert Reed

Printed in the United States of America

Library of Congress Cataloging-in-Publication Data

Server, Lee.
  Screenwriter : words become pictures.

  Bibliography: p.
  Includes index.
  Contents: Charles Bennett—A.I. Bezzerides—
Irving Brecher—[etc.]
  1. Screenwriters—United States—Interviews.
I. Title.
PN1998.A2S44 1987   812'.03'09   87-5510
ISBN 1-55562-018-3
ISBN 1-55562-017-5 (pbk.)

Contents

Introduction

On a hot and dry July afternoon in Los Angeles, California, I went to see a man named John Bright. It was the summer of 1985. Fifty-four years before, with his partner, Kubeç Glasmon, he had written his first screenplay, *The Public Enemy*, based in part on their own experiences in gangland Chicago. Bright wrote scripts for Cagney, Robinson, Bogart, Mae West. He co-founded the Screen Writers Guild. And in the witch-hunt days of the 1950s he was blacklisted out of American movies. There was no comeback. On the phone he sounded ancient and frail. He'd had a stroke, his hip was broken, and his writing hand could barely hold a pen. He was living now in a faded building of small one-bedroom apartments. His faced a patch of vacant lot, and dry grass and weeds grew a few steps from the doorway. A sign on the screen door read, "Late Sleeper." It was one o'clock and the sign didn't lie: Bright was just getting up. He moved slowly, with discomfort but with no show of concern for it. We sat down, facing each other across a coffee table in the tiny living room. The room smelled of the big unkempt dog that curled up between us. It was oppressively hot, and the sunshine glared in through the open door. Bright spoke softly, in a voice like a weary midwestern farmer. He was neither friendly nor unfriendly, but he was reticent, looking past me when he spoke. Small talk died quickly and the room turned silent. I took out my notes, put the tape recorder on the coffee table, and hoped for the best. Bright stoked himself with coffee and nicotine. The dog got up and moved away. I asked my first question.

The conversation that followed was the first of twenty-three—twelve of them collected in this volume—with screenwriters of the 1930s and '40s, veterans of the golden age of the Hollywood studio system. For six months I pursued them, in New York and California and various points in between. Tracking them down was easy and it was impossible. Some, long past their last screen credit, continued to advertise their whereabouts in the Writers Guild's annual directory. But others, even top names, had disappeared without a trace. One Academy Award winner I chased after had resigned his Guild membership, dropped his literary agent, and left town with no forwarding address; he was said to have moved to Mexico. There was no central clearing house for locating the dozens of names on my list. Not even the Writers Guild kept tabs on every person who'd ever pounded out a screenplay forty or fifty years ago. They would all be in their seventies and eighties now, and some, when I found them, were too ill or feeble for me to pester them with my questions. Some had died only weeks or months before I phoned their homes, and reached their widows or disconnect messages. For several days I dialed the San Francisco number of Lester Cole. When somebody by that name finally did answer, it was not the San Francisco Lester Cole of the Hollywood Ten. I got the right number that same night, but never reached

Opposite page: **Board of Directors, The Screen Writers Guild, 1949-50.** *Left to right and up:* **Allen Rivkin, Valentine Davies, Leonard Spigelgass; Edmund L. Hartman, Alice Pennamen, Karl Tunberg; F. Hugh Herbert, M. Coates Webster; Richard Breen, Richard Murphy, Sloan Nibley; Jonathan Latimer, Winston Miller, Carl Foreman; Morgan Cox, Frank Nugent; Howard Green, Oscar Brodney.**

the right man. Next morning the newpapers were carrying his obituary. A sense of urgency began to hang over my detective work.

The interviews were initially intended only as an aspect of my research for a more comprehensive book, a biographical dictionary of the Hollywood screenwriter. At the library of the Academy of Motion Picture Arts and Sciences in Beverly Hills, I spent days knee-deep in film books and periodicals and scripts and studio ephemera of every sort in the library's staggering collection—only to come out relatively empty-handed. The subject of the screenwriter remains, to a great extent, unexplored territory. There are few maps, few charts, few histories. Aside from a handful of autobiographies and the sociopolitical histories of the blacklist period, there has been little published material on the men and women who wrote the movies. Across the decades of critical writing one sees an occasional trail blazed—Pauline Kael's Welles-Mankiewicz face-off, Richard Corliss's essential *Talking Pictures*, Richard Koszarski's cogent case for Jules Furthman—but settlers did not follow. To find even brief biographical material on some honored and very successful screenwriters is dfficult at best. Not so, of course, in the case of the motion picture director. Among the Academy library's vast holdings one can find a volume each on such directors as Byron Haskin and Jacques Tourneur. And, bless them, let such film books flourish and multiply, I say. But look for similar items on the—how shall I put it?—more *mainstream* careers of screenwriters Lamar Trotti, Robert Riskin, Dudley Nichols, Norman Krasna, Michael Wilson, Samson Raphaelson, Sidney Buchman, or Jo Swerling, and you would be looking still at closing time. The director of *Man-Eater of Kumaon* and *Robinson Crusoe on Mars* has provoked a book, but the screenwriter of *The Informer*, *Bringing Up Baby*, *Stagecoach*, *Man Hunt*, *This Land is Mine*, *For Whom the Bell Tolls*, *Scarlet Street*, *The Bells of St. Mary's*, and *Mourning Becomes Electra* (to cite some of Nichols's credits alone) has not. It is an imbalance that indicates how effectively film historians have altered the reality of film history.

Of course, the writer in Hollywood has never had a particularly easy time of it. From the beginning, all he ever got for his troubles, as someone (a screenwriter) once said, was "a lousy fortune." Even the average B-unit drone made more money than all but the most successful playwrights and novelists in literature's "real world." But prestige and independence and artistic integrity, watchwords of most "serious" writers, seldom accompanied the screenwriter's high salary. Like the actors and directors and the other talented professionals contracted to the studios in the '30s and '40s, the writers were shuttled from assignment to assignment, often with little regard for the individual's preferences or strengths. But unlike the actors and the top directors, the movie writer was almost never groomed for stardom. The fact that many of the studio writers were predisposed by nature to being independent, cantankerous, sarcastic, and politically radical (to extremes of left *or* right), and were by and large better educated than the average self-made mogul, did nothing to endear them to the Hollywood hierarchy. The fact that they could and did air their grievances in public forums—ridiculing the studio bosses in plays, novels, and satiric magazine pieces—may have sealed their fate. Whether out of contempt or fear, the studios kept their scribes at arm's length, distanced as much from the publicity machinery as from profit-sharing and copyright owner-ship of their work. No studio could make a film without a writer, but they could *pretend* to. "Audiences don't know anyone writes a picture," says the disgruntled screen-writer hero of *Sunset Boulevard*. "They think the actors make it up as they go along."

And, then, in the 1950s, as if the studio system had not already sufficiently clouded the contribution of the writer, there came the "*auteur* theory." Until this critical approach wafted its way out of Paris, most directors had languished in an obscurity almost equal to the writers'. The few who were generally cited by reviewers and known to the public were either heavy with honors or fueled by De Mille-like self-publicity. In the 1950s, though, a fervent band of French critics at *Cahiers du Cinema* and other small-circulation periodicals began to discern patterns of quality and consistency and identifiable personality in the work of American directors who had previously been considered—if at all—as competent craftsmen with no artistic axe to grind. Unconcerned with the traditional critics' snobbish disdain for low budget or genre films, the French made wonderful discoveries: the fiercely individualistic writer-director Sam Fuller; Howard Hawks, a dominating figure exercising control over most of his scripts and usually acting as his own producer; and others, all rescued from what Andrew Sarris has called "the limbo of cultural disrespect." The more provocative aspect of what came to be known as the *auteur* theory was not, however, the certifying of underground artists, but the notion that some directors made their films "personal" without necessarily having any choice or say in the film's subject or screenplay. These Hollywood directors, according to the theory, could make a film their own statement through sheer style—through staging, visual emphases, camera angles, cutting, and those properties of *mise en scène* indescribably mysterious. Some critics went farther—a director might even express himself best by "transcending" the material he was forced to work with. His personality could become most visible when in a state of tension rather than harmony with the material. What mattered was not the subject an *auteur* filmed, but his technique in filming it. And from this perspective the Cahierist critics would hope to elucidate the "meaning" of a given film by its relationship to the director's style and, therefore, his view of the world. The emphasis on what was seen rather than on what was heard in these American movies was possibly aided by most French critics' inability to speak English.

It was a basically romantic notion of the director as creative artist for whom story, script, and actors were no more than paints in the director's box. It was a notion that held up in the case of some European filmmakers and for another handful of Americans. But the great majority of Hollywood directors were (and are) at best interpretive artists, bringing technical and possibly editorial skills to the service of someone else's material. And in all fairness to the proselytizers of auteurism, they stated as much. Andrew Sarris, the godfather of the theory on American shores, wrote that "Not all directors are *auteurs*. Indeed, most directors are virtually anonymous." And indeed, Sarris's rankings in *Film Culture* magazine and *The American Cinema* probably offended more directors, herded into negative categories, than screenwriters, who were virtually ignored. Sarris's scholarship and enthusiasm were responsible for a new appreciation of American films and filmmakers of the past, however controversial his theories. But although his stated belief was that only certain directors might stand up to auteurist analysis, followers soon broadened this base in favor of an all-out "directors' cinema," junking as well the Cahierists' original prescription for auteurism—all that *mise en scène* mysticism. Discussions of a director's work limited to such quirky considerations as "spatial relationships" were not much fun, and they began to include those old reliable ingredients for analysis of narrative forms: story, theme, metaphor, characterization, dialogue—in other words, those aspects of the film that might conceivably have been created by the person who wrote it.

According to the auteurist critics and historians, the screenwriter, if he existed, was strictly a hired hand. The director brought the ideas, the heart, the soul; the screenwriter brought a keen ability to take notes and type. Despite supposedly shrewd Hollywood producers having hired them by the hundred, despite the producers having paid them weekly salaries far in excess of the national average, despite many of them having by-lined novels and Broadway plays away from their movie work, the screenwriter was, in retrospect, an irrelevant addition to the authorial voice of a film. For auteurists their predilection was self-sustaining in that, since only directors were scrutinized and evaluated, interviewed and fêted, the director's point of view prevailed, uncontested. In any number of interviews with non-writer directors, the only reference to a screenplay might be an offhand "We threw it out," or "I rewrote it all on the set." Such testimony made its way to scholarly monographs where official credits were freshly revised: the screenwriter of record was omitted, the director put in his place.

Some directors in America *were* the primary creative force behind most of their films even without a screenplay credit. A Hawks, a Hitchcock, a Lubitsch usually initiated their projects, nurturing the script from first page to last. Most of the films these men directed would not have been made without them. But other directors exercised this level of creative power only occasionally or not at all. They were contract workers, assigned according to availability or specialty—be it westerns or Broadway adaptations. And even the strongest directors could find themselves in a subservient position. While King Vidor enthusiasts have analyzed at length the place of *Duel in the Sun* in his canon, Vidor actually directed less than half of it. David O. Selznick, the film's producer, found the property, wrote most of the screenplay, and oversaw every frame of it to his satisfaction. Alfred Hitchcock directed *Mr. and Mrs. Smith,* a romantic comedy starring Carole Lombard, but only a naif would see it as anything other than peripheral to Hitchcock, and highly representative of Norman Krasna, the author of the screenplay.

So, a director's cinema, a producer's cinema, a screenwriter's cinema. These are some of the variables of authorship in Hollywood. It is obviously much easier for a critic to deal with a concept of one all-creative figure throughout, than to have to plunge into the deep waters of the collaborative system of studio moviemaking, to research the actual circumstances of each of a director's films, to cross-reference the work of the writer, the producer, the cinematographer, to read original source material as well as the different drafts of the screenplay and any correspondence regarding them. Much simpler, much more romantic to believe that the man with the megaphone has willed it all into being.

Despite Sarris's protest that auteurism was never meant to be a "running advertisement for the Screen Directors Guild," the director as superstar, as sole creator, became a given in contemporary film criticism, whether or not he had shot every last comma in someone else's script, from someone else's story, and that decisions regarding casting, performance, music, camera angles, and editing may have been made by others. Little differentiation was made between the writer-director who created his own material and the director who came onto a project at the last minute. Either one was awarded the appellation of ownership: "A film by. . . . " The director-as-lone-artist theory caught on not just with critics but with producers, the media, publicists, teachers, and people who didn't know "auteurism" from a child's learning disability.

The final blow for an unequivocal cinema of directors may have been struck by the commercial and university presses now publishing current, classic, and not so classic Hollywood screenplays, where it is common practice to give the director possessive credit on cover and title page while the screenwriter is credited in small print somewhere inside (even if the script is an original and no matter the circumstances of its writing). These are not transcriptions of the finished film in most cases, but original texts, written by a particular person or persons, possibly far in advance of the actual production. They may or may not vary greatly from the motion pictures made from them. They may not have been read by their subsequent directors until months or years after completion. They are screenplays, literary entities created by someone, and now, on publication, in obeisance to the throne of the *auteur*, credited to someone else. This is the amazing feat of authorship by hindsight. Consider the possibilities: future editions of Shakespeare will read "Zeffirelli's *Romeo and Juliet*," and "Roman Polanski's *Macbeth*"; the Scriptures will include a by-line for Cecil B. De Mille. Never to write, but to have written—the director, as even the most envious scenarist will admit, has pulled off an astonishing trick.

And so it would seem that the time has come to shine a bit more light in the direction of the neglected screenwriter, to revise the revisionists' view of American film history. There have been, after all, as few unforgotten films made without a screenplay as there are actors who have made a living reading from the phone book. The audiences of the world, from the time movies moved beyond train-pulling-into-station slices of life, have built their fantasies not on directorial touches, or camerawork, or even, in the long run, on stars, but on characters and on stories, and it is writers, whether "hyphenates" as dual-titled artists are known in the trade, or just plain garden-variety writers, who create characters and who tell stories. They have given us heroes and villains, plot twists and jokes, romances and infidelities, and happy endings. And if movies are stories told primarily with pictures, the best screenwriters have written for the camera as well as the microphone. There is almost no component of a film that could not conceivably have come from its script. The great Austrian screenwriter of the silent era, Carl Mayer, author of *The Cabinet of Dr. Caligari, The Last Laugh* and *Sunrise,* described in great detail in his scripts every cut, every movement of the camera, every gesture of each character. It was Mayer, not Murnau, the director, who devised the visual structure that would enable *The Last Laugh* to become the classic of universal storytelling and cinematic "purity," a silent film without a single intertitle of dialogue or exposition. Murnau directed, Mayer created.

And he was not alone. The evidence is there in a thousand-and-one manuscripts moldering in studio vaults and archives. The screenwriter *has* to know what can and can't be done with a lens, an actor, a special effect; these are, like dialogue and structure, ingredients in his work. Writing a movie, and doing it well, is a special skill. Those who have succeeded at it are worthy of attention.

The eleven men and one woman you are about to meet belong to that most productive, colorful, vibrant era of the movies between the coming of sound and the coming of television. It was a time when the big studios turned out nearly a film a week apiece, and audiences turned out for them more often than that. The moguls created dream factories and filled them with salaried dreamers. Playwrights, novelists, journalists, advertising sloganeers and radical pamphleteers all came West for the bright lights and big bucks of Hollywood. The contract writer had to be good, fast, and flexible. He had to create on command, at time-clock hours and at midnight story conferences with insomniac producers. He might be taken off a project that meant much to him and put on another that meant nothing. A current assignment might be interrupted for emergency work on a picture already in production. He might be required to act out—to "pitch"—an entire story for an executive too busy to read. At any given time his career might hinge less on his particular abilities than on friendships, feuds, and office politics. Few who worked in this period were not embroiled in the years of divisive battling to establish a writers' guild, and scores were affected by the subsequent Cold War blacklist.* Some despised Hollywood and left with horror stories of illiterate bosses who mauled their ideas and mangled their work. Others despised it and stayed. But for many it was the eye of the hurricane, a fabulous place to be whether you thought movie work no more than, in Ben Hecht's phrase, "a plush Bohemian vacation," or held Dudley Nichols's belief that it was the "most flexible and exciting" job in the world, its possibilities "enthralling." And for all the turmoil, the frustrations, and the reckless squandering of their talent (the studios spoiled by the abundance of riches at their disposal), the screenwriters of the '30s and '40s created a body of work of dazzling wit and imagination. The scale of their achievement we can not hope to see duplicated.

The screenwriters of this golden age came from everywhere, and the dozen interviewed herein are suitably diverse. There is a novelist, a newspaperman or two, three playwrights, a truck driver, two lawyers, several Ivy Leaguers, an Englishman, a German, and a bootlegger. They cover the spectrum of career possibilities: Academy Award winners and those who toiled on "B" pictures; those who became producers and directors, those who were blacklisted. There are the specialists (in comedy, crime, horror, history), the constructionists, the "gag men," the writers of "originals," and the journeymen for hire, able to patch up an ailing script on any subject. They are a representative sampling of the men and women one would have found in the cubicles and commissaries of MGM or Paramount or Warner Bros. five decades ago, and their words

---

*In the early 1930s the first Screen Writers Guild (now the Writers Guild of America) met with violent opposition by the studio executives. Charges that the Guild was under the influence of Soviet-devoted communists and the New York-based Author's League led to the formation, in 1936, of a conservative—and studio backed—union, the Screen Playwrights. The disrupted Guild held on, covertly, until 1937, when the National Labor Relations Board backed the writers' secret ballot vote for the union of their choice. The Guild won by a wide margin, but it was still three years before the studios, kicking and screaming, would sign a contract acknowledging it. The old idealogical rivalries exploded in the reactionary atmosphere of the late '40s. Congressional committees and self-appointed witch hunters sought subversives among the many activists in Hollywood. Ten of these were sent to jail, and many more, most of them writers, had their careers interrupted or ended.

will, I believe, recapture some of the spirit of that colorful time. In talking with them, in finding out who they were and where they came from and how they worked, I hoped to establish, as well, the possibility of an interrelationship between each writer's screenplays and his personality and philosophy. One could then at least begin to consider to what extent a screenwriter, as much or more than any other creative component, dominated the finished product in the filmmaking process, and not relegate such judgments to the blind faith of theories. To know about John Bright, or Philip Dunne, makes it possible to see the nihilistic crime stories of the one, or the liberal-humanist adaptations of the other, as films "by" these two writers and not their various directors. It is not, however, my intention to offer these two or any of the twelve as the undiscovered sole *auteurs* of the dozens of films they wrote. Such a sweeping assessment would be no more accurate of screenwriters than of the producers and directors with whom they worked. But their testimony will, perhaps, indicate the need for a more generous approach to the history of so collaborative and complex a subject as the American cinema.

My thanks to the staffs at the Margaret Herrick Library of the Academy of Motion Picture Arts and Sciences, the American Film Institute, the Writers Guild of America (West), the Beverly Hills Public Library, and the Museum of Modern Art in New York City; to Ellen Faun for inestimable editorial assistance; to Dean Server for prodigious transcribing at fair market rates; to Terri Hardin for aid and encouragement. Photographs are courtesy of Charles Bennett, A.I. Bezzerides, Irving Brecher, John Bright, Robert Landau, William Ludwig, Nat Perrin, Allen Rivkin, Wells Root, the Writers Guild of America, Larry Edmunds Bookshop, and the stills archive of the Museum of Modern Art. A final thank you to all the screenwriters who generously shared their time and memories.

—L.S.

Overleaf: **Alfred Hitchcock on the set of *The Thirty-Nine Steps* (1935).**

Alfred Hitchcock and
Charles Bennett, c. 1936.

Eighty-six-year-old Charles Bennett, actor, director, writer for stage, screen and television, greets you at the gate of his Los Angeles home with a presence both jaunty and regal. An American resident for much of the last five decades, he is, nonetheless, an Englishman to the bone—last consul, as it were, to Hollywood's legendary British colony of cricket- and croquet-playing, Union Jack-flying exiles in the land of palm trees and back lots.

He began as a child actor some years before the First World War, and by the mid-1920s had become a West End leading man. On the wall of his California living room is evidence of past performances: a poster heralding the 1927 all-star London production of *Othello;* one "Charles Bennett" tops the lustrous cast list of theatrical legends (a fact he quickly dismisses with a deprecating wave, "It's alphabetical, my boy"). Bennett's handsomeness—the sort of good looks old Hollywood's publicists would have labeled "dashing" and "romantic"—could have been no hindrance to a young actor's career. He is, in fact, to this day, a quite handsome man.

But writing, not acting, was to be Bennett's future. He turned to playwriting and had his work produced with growing success. In 1928 the change in professions became a permanent one, and his entry into film work followed soon after his stage hit, *Blackmail,* was turned into an even more successful motion picture. It was directed by Alfred Hitchcock and began perhaps the most important and long-lasting collaboration of either man's career. Together, they created seven classic entertainments of suspense and adventure, including *The Man Who Knew Too Much, The Thirty-Nine Steps,* and *Foreign Correspondent.*

After 1940 the two worked apart, but Bennett's influence would be felt in many of Hitchcock's subsequent films, as the director continually reworked elements from the earlier successes. In *The Thirty-Nine Steps* alone are such perennial "Hitchcockian" ingredients as the double pursuit, the cross-country chase, the handcuffed couple, the icy blonde, the wisecracking hero and the aristocratic villain, echoed in films from *Saboteur* to *North by Northwest* to *Frenzy.* Bennett's and Hitchcock's *The Man Who Knew Too Much* Hitchcock remade entirely, enlarged in running time, budget, and screen size, but losing in the process much of the vitality and pace of the original.

Brought to Hollywood in the late 1930s, Bennett tackled a wide assortment of studio assignments: a prestigious Selznick production (*The Young in Heart*), a Nelson Eddy musical (*Balalaika*), the Edwardian intrigues of *Ivy*, an ill-fated Orson Welles melodrama (*Black Magic*), and three event-filled epics for Cecil B. De Mille (*Reap the Wild Wind, The Story of Dr. Wassell,* and *Unconquered*). In the '50s Bennett's screenplays included at least two minor masterpieces: the dark, relentless *Where Danger Lives,* a brilliant late entry in the *film noir* canon; and *Night of the Demon,* a tense and unusual tale of the supernatural, marred only by the studio's modest attempt to turn the film's civilized shudders into drive-in fodder.

Closing in on his sixtieth year as a working writer, Bennett has barely slowed the pace. In 1985 he completed an original screenplay, wrote his first novel (*Highland Fling*) and by year's end was at work on his second.

Indefatigably refusing to show any sign of what he calls his "extreme old age," Bennett plays host to visitors—old friends and new inquisitors alike—at the small bar in his comfortable home in a Beverly Hills canyon where he has lived off and on since the early '40s. On the wall behind the bar hangs a portrait of the reigning British monarch. Nearby are framed posters and cards from theatrical events of the nineteenth and early twentieth centuries. In one corner is a more personal piece of British history: the opening night program for *Blackmail, "Europe's First All-Talking Motion Picture."* Above that, an early photo of the film's rotund director, inscribed, "To my first and favorite writer, love, Hitch."

Bennett still speaks in the imperious tones of the classical actor, recalling the past with an air of lofty bemusement. He seems to have known every colorful character who ever touched down in Hollywood, from Errol Flynn to Howard Hughes to Bugsy Siegel, and has a well-crafted anecdote about each of them. Some of these he considers strictly off the record and requests my recorder be stopped if I expect to hear his un-bowdlerized version (including tales of the love lives—separate, to be sure—of Alfred Hitchcock and John Gielgud). A genuinely friendly and gracious host, Bennett has made at least one stranger feel like a very welcome guest.

Wine glasses are filled, and Charles Bennett, standing, one arm resting on the bar, is ready to discuss a career in entertainment that began, almost, with the century.

I started out as a poverty-stricken child in Chelsea, England. I was an actor at the age of eleven, which was pretty young to start, but we needed the money. By the time I was seventeen, the war was on with Germany, World War I, so I joined the army. I had a couple of years in the army, in France. And then I came back and there was nothing left for me to do but be an actor.

Looking back, I was a dreadfully bad, lousy actor. I don't know how I held any jobs down at all. But, by the time I was twenty-five, having been with the Bristol Repertory Company, and things like that, I became a good one, just by learning. I even starred, in Paris, at the English Theatre, in Paris, when I was twenty-five or twenty-six. And by that time I was starting to write plays. I had my first play produced in 1927.* I acted in that, but it was almost the end of my acting career, not quite. The first play wasn't a success. Got lovely reviews, and was published in *Contemporary British Dramatists,* but it didn't make any money.

The Return.

Then I wrote a play, during 1927, which A.H. Woods of New York bought an option on, and Tallulah Bankhead wanted to play it, so it went on. That was *Blackmail*. And that was the play which, much later, British International Pictures bought the film rights to, and Hitchcock made it into the first talking picture in Europe. *Blackmail* opened in London in February, 1928, and by the end of the year I had a great success at the Comedy Theatre with another play, a thing called *The Last Hour*. So that was it; I gave up acting. I was a writer from then on. An alleged writer.

Did you work on the script for *Blackmail*?

No. I kept an interest, but I didn't work on the adaptation. In fact, Hitch did it pretty much himself. And due to that project we became very close friends.

Now, British International owned the rights to a famous character in rather cheap British literature, Bulldog Drummond. And I was asked to write a story about him. So I wrote a story called "Bulldog Drummond's Baby," in which Bulldog Drummond's baby was kidnapped. And when Hitch left British International he took the whole thing to Gaumont-British, and it became *The Man Who Knew Too Much*. And from then on I began a long association with Hitch.

What was your first impression of Hitchcock?

At my original meetings with him, I found him a very congenial, little fat man. It was only when I got to know him better that I got to know the darker side of him, the sadistic side—which did come out in his pictures, as you must have noticed over the years.

I must admit we became very close friends. But the trouble was, with Hitch you never quite knew whether he was your closest friend or your worst enemy.

We used to go to St. Moritz together, he and his wife, and my then wife. We'd go to the Palace Hotel in St. Moritz every Christmas. Alma Hitchcock and Maggie Bennett and I would ski while Hitch sat in the Palace Hotel and wouldn't come out at all. This big fat man, and he would just sit, look out of the window.

Together we did *The Man Who Knew Too Much*, *The Thirty-Nine Steps*, *The Secret Agent*, *Sabotage*, *The Girl Was Young*, and in America, *Foreign Correspondent*.

What was the process you went through in scripting a story with Hitchcock?

The usual way . . . let's think of one of them. Somerset Maugham's *Ashenden*, for example, which we called *The Secret Agent*, was a bunch of short stories. It was my job to come up with a story line based on what seemed good in two or three of the short stories. That would then be our basis for a picture.

After that, Hitch and I would sit together and talk about it, talk about it, talk about it. It was a very pleasant life, as a matter of fact. I used to pick up Hitch in the morning. I had a flat overlooking Belgrave Square in London, and he lived on the way to the studio. I'd pick him up on the way, and we'd talk through the morning. Then we'd go to the Mayfair Hotel for lunch—for which he usually paid, by the way. We'd come back in the afternoon, during which time he'd sleep and I'd do a little work. And at the end of the afternoon we'd go back to his apartment for drinks. And that was the working day. A very pleasant way of spending a day, hmm?

One of the biographies of Hitchcock says at that period in the 1930s he held story conferences at home, in his pajamas.

Blackmail (1929): The chase in the British Museum.

I wasn't conscious of that, quite frankly. I don't remember ever seeing Hitch in his pajamas. In those days he *didn't* work at home. When we settled down to cocktails at the end of the day, that *was* the end of the day as far as he was concerned. I can't remember him ever coming in the next day and saying, "What about this, I was thinking about last night," or anything like that. No. So I don't believe the pajama story at all. Ha!

This first series of conferences would be story only, correct? Plot and structure, no dialogue or bits of business.

Fundamentally, it was the story line, the construction. The construction is the most important goddamned thing. It's like building a house—you have to build the outside properly before you put the bits and pieces inside afterward.

As often as not, he would bring in some special dialogue writer much later, to write a particular kind of dialogue for the pictures, which wouldn't have been my type of dialogue. Ian Hay supplied a lot of very good dialogue for *The Thirty-Nine Steps*. But the construction was entirely mine.

Speaking of *The Thirty-Nine Steps*, you didn't think much of the original John Buchan novel, did you?

I thought the fundamental idea, the guy on the run from the police *and* from the heavies at the same time, was a very good idea to base a film on. Our film, though, had practically nothing to do with his novel. His novel had no women in it, or anything like that, for example. And so, we had to come up with an entirely different story, in a way. Try reading the book and you'll see what I mean.

Aside from the female characters you introduced, the business with Mr. Memory is all original to the film, as is the man with the missing finger.

Yes, mine. You certainly never found anything like that in Buchan's book.

Buchan's book was based on something I've always resented, and tried to avoid in every picture I've written. Proceeding by means of coincidences. You find it in many of Buchan's books. A guy is in desperate straits, wandering about a mountain highway in Scotland, and there would be another guy coming along. And of course it would be the one guy he had to meet somehow. Pure coincidences, coincidences. He was a very wicked man from that point of view. I know coincidences happen in real life, but I don't put them into movies.

I understand you would often go abroad with Hitchcock during the writing of the scripts.

If we got stuck we would go away. I remember when I was doing the Ashenden thing. The story had reached a point at which I was stuck and Hitch hadn't any idea of what to do, and we just couldn't talk it out. Now Ivor Montague—a violent communist but a terribly nice guy—was our producer, and he was staying in Switzerland that spring. So Hitch and I just got on one of the very early planes and flew to Basel, and then got a little train from Basel to a small village where we spent the whole day just wandering about in the valley, the three of us talking. And at the end of that talk all of our problems were solved.

Taking a break like that can be extremely useful. But unfortunately, Hollywood very seldom realized it. Some of the studios, like Warner Bros. . . . well, Jack Warner used to expect writers to be checking in at nine o'clock and when they were supposed to leave at half past five. And the result was a lot of bloody good writers checked in on time, all right, but they would spend the day playing canasta or something.

Metro was always tremendously polite, on the surface. I was there for about three years, off and on. When you came in in the morning, through the main entrance of the Thalberg Building, the guys on the desk would say, "Oh, good morning, Mr. Bennett," full of charm. But you'd notice some scribbling going on, and you knew damned well that the guy had jotted down "Charles Bennett came in at quarter past ten," or something like that.

I did have them completely bewildered. My office was on the ground floor, what you here call the first floor. And I soon found that I could open the floor-length window, and, by opening it, I could leave my office in the evening, go across some grass, and get to my car and go home. So for a very long time they knew I'd come in in the morning but never knew if I'd left.

I've always preferred to work at home, actually. I was never under permanent contract to a studio, except to Universal for a short time. I was contracted per picture, and even then I used to frequently work at home because I preferred it. The people, if they were nice, like Sam Wood for whom I wrote *Ivy*, didn't mind if I worked at home so long as I delivered. That was all that mattered. And now in my extreme old age I still prefer to work at home.

I wrote an awful lot of pictures for Irving Allen—*Voyage to the Bottom of the Sea, Five Weeks in a Balloon;* I wrote *The Big Circus,* that starred Victor Mature (who was an idiot, by the way), seven movies altogether. And he would love to do the Jack Warner act. But not with me. I was too strong for him; he couldn't do without me.

Never allow any studio to tie you down to a time you can write. No, no. I've never done that in my life.

And Hitchcock knew this, and there were times when he couldn't work and didn't try to.

Didn't he once stop work and decide he wanted to take a boat ride?

Oh, that was a silly thing, yes. I believe we were working on *Sabotage,* on that occasion. I came to the studio with him in the morning, and with Joan Harrison, who was our secretary. And Hitch absolutely couldn't concentrate at all. I thought, "What the hell's the matter with this man?" He couldn't understand anything I said. He couldn't or didn't want to listen to anything. Finally, he said, "I think the only thing to do this afternoon is go for a little ride. Let's get a little rowboat and go out on the Thames." Well, I looked at him and didn't know what to say. I said, "Well fine, let's do that." So he and Joan and I went down to the pier at Westminster where to our great surprise he had rented a 250-seater Thames steamer, and with a full orchestra on board—just for the three of us. And on board we went and went all the way down to Greenwich. This was supposed to be a story conference, but not a bit of it, not a bloody word was spoken about the story. All the way down to Greenwich, all the way back to Westminster, a lovely afternoon. But that was all that was on his mind that morning. I couldn't get his attention.

Were you aware of Hitchcock wanting to include particular scenes or themes, regardless of the particular story?

Only after we got the story line quite down. He might then come up with an idea, something new. And you'd say sometimes, God, that's awfully good. But then the problem was how the hell to get it into the picture. And equally, if it wasn't so good, how to tell him to forget it. As a general rule, I was pretty adept at accepting good ideas and working them into things, yes. And Hitch was one of the few directors I've met in my life who *could* come up with ideas. Most of the directors I've worked with, men like Sam Wood and De Mille, like that, hadn't an idea in their head.

Hitchcock always stated that everything was done when the script was finished, that he never changed or improvised. Did you find this to be true?

Oh, yes, of course. By the time the screenplay was finished, Hitch would always say, "Well, the picture is finished." He would say, "Putting it before the cameras, putting it on the screen, is nothing." When the script was finished, he knew exactly what angle he wanted for every shot. He always thought very visually, and he could see every scene in his head, see it exactly.

Did he express his attitude towards actors?

He tried to get the best he could. The jokes he made about actors, I think that was a sort of play thing on his part, really. After all, when you're dealing with Jimmy Stewart and Cary Grant—and even when he was in England he was with top people—you can't have much contempt for them, no.

He was actually a tremendously good director with actors. That's the director's real job—to get what the author intended out of the actors. Most directors don't know that, but Hitch did. He was a genius in getting a performance out of an actor. Ninety percent of them out here, all they know really is, "Oh, let's put the camera in here . . . action . . . cut." They know nothing about controlling actors.

I'll tell you another thing about Hitch which I've never noticed in any of the writings about him—and I've got all sorts of books on him in there. He was a tremendously good actor himself. If he hadn't been this great big fat man, he could have been a first-class character actor. There was nothing he couldn't act. When he was directing, if he had a scene with a girl and she couldn't quite get it, he'd play the part out for her perfectly. That was Hitch. He was one of the best actors I've ever seen in my life.

Do you recall the first time the term "MacGuffin" was used?

It was an old joke and referred to the basic plot device. Hitch often referred to the story, but when he got older he forgot how it went. You see, an old gentleman gets into a compartment on a train, and there's a little boy sitting there, and he's got this long, weird package, tied together with weird pieces of string and so on. And the old gentleman can't hold back his curiosity and he says to the young boy, "Excuse me, little boy, I know it's none of my business, but I've been fascinated by that big package you have there. What is it, please?" And the little boy says, "Oh that, that's a MacGuffin." So the old gentleman says, "Oh yes . . . MacGuffin. Well, that's very nice . . . But I don't know what a MacGuffin is." And the little boy says, "Don't worry, sir. That's not a *real* MacGuffin." And that's the story. The MacGuffin was whatever got the story going, revealed—in a suspense film—at the end of the story rather than as it goes along. In *The Thirty-Nine Steps* it was certain plans the heavies wanted to take out of England.

What was your approach to adapting Conrad's *The Secret Agent* for filming?

We made certain changes, of course, going for a more contemporary story. We'd already used the title *Secret Agent* with the Ashenden story, so we used the title *Sabotage*. But it was the basic story—the death of this little boy, the wife in consequence murdering the husband who was responsible for the death. The boy carrying the bomb in the film dies on a motorbus and there weren't such buses in Conrad's day. Things like that were different. The scenes in the movie theatre. Hitchcock did a very good job on that film. The suspense with the boy on the bus was terrific.

But didn't Hitchcock later regret the way he handled the scene? He felt that there was, perhaps, no pay-off to the suspense in having the bomb go off and kill the boy after the audience was identifying with his predicament.

No, he couldn't have made a mistake there. There was some problem with a critic, C.A. Lejeune, the top critic of the London *Observer*, and I think Hitch may have been bothered by her reaction. At a cocktail party after the first showing of *Sabotage,* she came up to me and said, "Charles, I'll never speak to you again." I said, "What's the matter now?" And she said, "Oh, you shouldn't have killed that little boy. It's horrible!" And I said, "I'm terribly sorry, but that's what Conrad's story is about." And it was, the terrible consequences of this saboteur's work. And if Hitch later on said he was sorry he did it, he might as well have said he was sorry he made the picture at all, because he couldn't have done this story without killing the boy.

Funny thing on that picture, when Sylvia Sidney was sailing over Hitch got her on the telephone, and they talked and they thought each other wonderful. By the end of the picture, Sylvia wasn't speaking to Hitch except on the set. She hated him! (Laughs.)

Going back to the audience for a moment . . . did the two of you give much thought to the audience, how they could be manipulated and so on?

I don't think we ever thought about them. I can't remember Hitch ever thinking about them at all. We took it for granted that they'd be there, but we never wrote to a specific audience. You wrote for yourself, mostly. In the days when I was writing so many movies, it would depend. If it was an original, you were writing for yourself. But if it was based on a novel or something like that, then you'd do your best to turn that novel into the movie. You were writing as much for the novelist as for yourself.

Your Hitchcock collaborations are always playing in theatres or on television. Do you watch them when they're on?

Now and then. I saw *Sabotage,* matter of fact, sometime last week. It was on in the afternoon. And it's a funny thing, looking back at a picture from so far away. I can look at a picture I was so heavily connected with back in the '30s, and it's as if I never had anything to do with it. Extremely interesting feeling. I'll watch and think, "I wonder what's going to happen here?" Although I did know—ha—that little boy on the bus was going to be blown up.

Your last film with Hitchcock—in England—was *Young and Innocent* (*A Girl Was Young* in America). Was there a conscious attempt to repeat the elements of *The Thirty-Nine Steps?*

I don't think so, looking back. We never tried to imitate ourselves in any way, no. And no one suggested we do so. I think that's a great error to do, anyway.

Young and Innocent was based on a paperback novel (*A Shilling for Candles* by Josephine Tey). For a great many years Gaumont-British owned this novel and they could never get a screenplay out of it. Nobody could come up with an approach. Eventually they put it in the hands of Hitch, which means it came into the hands of me. And I came up with a good story line for it and a good construction.

This was a case, wasn't it, of changing the original material considerably?

Yes. But I wouldn't dare to say I completely wrote the picture. I wasn't there at the completion of it because I was offered a contract by Universal here in California and I took it. A thousand bucks a week, which was *money* in those days (but not now), more money than I ever had in my life before. So I was not there at the end of *Young and Innocent*. I had the contract with Universal, and I had to sail before the picture was shot.

I left Hitch in England, but he followed presently, under contract to Selznick. And that's a rather amusing story. I was loaned to write a picture for Selznick called *The Young in Heart*, and one night, during one of those all-night story conferences which David loved, and which we all loathed, he said, "It's been suggested I should bring over one of these two directors from Gaumont-British, Alfred Hitchcock or Robert Stevenson. Which should I bring?" I said, "Bring both." And he did. And Hitch came over.

How did you find the difference between moviemaking in England and America?

Appalling.

In what way?

British filmaking was . . . you were working together, having fun, that sort of stuff. Whereas over here it was much more of an industry. And here there *was* a lot of talk of writing down to an audience. Very much so. You thought in terms of the audience first, and the film afterwards. You were to try and make something that a very broad audience was going to like. I was just appalled at the kind of stuff they wanted me to write at Universal when I first came here. And thank God they loaned me—at a great profit to them, which made me very angry— to Sam Goldwyn. So I spent most of my contract time with Universal, away from them. They were fairly bankrupt at the time, and I think they regretted signing me because I was getting more money than anybody at the studio. So they made a profit out of me by loaning me out to Goldwyn. And I was quite happy to leave Universal, I must admit.

What did you do for Goldwyn?

I worked on *The Adventures of Marco Polo*. And although I spent quite a long time on the script, I never took a credit on it, because after I finished it, Robert Sherwood moved in. Very fine writer, Sherwood, but—as so often happens when another writer is brought in—I think my script was pretty well annihilated by him.

Were you also put on scripts other writers had started?

Oh, yes. First time I went to Metro, I was asked by Larry Weingarten to work on a script based on Eric Ambler's novel *Cause for Alarm*. Well, there was nothing in there you could even hang a picture on, it was so bloody awful. A dreadful, very bad novel. All he'd been paid for it was $10,000 and I think he was lucky to get that. But Weingarten had fallen for the first six or seven pages, which did grab you—but after that, nothing. Anyway, this was a difficult thing, because I had to take it and try and create a good story out of it. And thank God, after about six weeks, when I was really struggling, Weingarten said to me, "Oh, by the way, there's a scene in *Balalaika* we need. No writer has come up with anything we like." So, to answer your question, many other writers had been on this *Balalaika* when I came to write on it. About thirty writers had actually tried to write this scene, and been turned down.

So they gave me the scene to write—Nelson Eddy in it, if you will.

So I wrote the scene and made a couple of copies, and brought it into Larry's office. I said, "Here it is, have a look." I gave the copies to Larry and he passed one to a guy who was lying on the couch. This guy on the couch just lay there, never said a word, wasn't introduced to me. And he slowly read this thing while Larry read it in a hurry—he was a frightened little man, Larry Weingarten—and suddenly at the end he threw it down on the floor and said, "I don't get it, I don't get the scene at all. No, Charles, I don't think so." So I said, "Now wait a minute, let's see what the gentleman over there thinks." And the gentleman was still slowly, ponderously reading. And when he finished it he looked across at Larry and said, "*Zis* is a scene! *Zis* is the first scene anybody has written worthwhile shooting in zis picture." And Larry said, "What? What? What?" The man said, "Zis is a scene, I can shoot zis scene." And I said, "Who is this gentleman?" And he was Reinhold Schünzel, the director of the picture. So Larry grabbed it up again, read it again, and then he said, "Yes . . . yes, it's a scene." But he had to be told it was a scene.

So, from that moment on I was taken off *Cause for Alarm,* much to my relief, and I was rewriting the script of *Balalaika.*

They never did make *Cause for Alarm,* did they?

No, never. By the time I came off it I had shaped it into what was threatening to be a pretty good screenplay, I think. Larry was delighted with it, eventually. But I went on to the other picture and then I left the studio to do *Foreign Correspondent* with Hitch, and Larry said, "By the way, there are one or two little alterations I'd like to make. Just some trimmings here and there." He said, "We're going to get Herman Mankiewicz and George Oppenheimer here at the studio to do it. It's not very much." So I said, "Fine." But I knew what would happen. They tore my script to pieces. Herman was a very fine writer, but like every contract writer he wanted to get his name on a screenplay before his option came up at the end of six months or whatever it was, so he wouldn't be dropped. And so, by the time they got through with it, my screenplay was nonexistent. Theirs wasn't any good, so Weingarten passed it to another writer, and another. The last thing I ever heard of it was that they'd spent three-quarters of a million dollars on it in script development—a helluva lot of money in those days. Three-quarters of a million spent, and they never made it. Just writer after writer destroying each other's stuff. (Laughs.) Horrible, horrible.

As you mentioned, you left Metro to work again with Hitchcock. Had his methods changed any since you'd worked with him in England?

No, we worked very much as we had in England. If we got stuck on the plot we'd take a drive to Palm Springs or somewhere.

How much of the story was already done on *Foreign Correspondent* when you were brought in?

That script was an original, to tell the truth. It was my story, no one else's. Of course, there was a book they had brought, memoirs of a foreign correspondent at the beginning of World War II,* but there was no story in it, and no one had come up with one. So Hitch and I worked on it, and Wanger, who was producing it, left us completely alone. I came up with the story

---

**Personal History by Vincent Sheean.

and Hitch helped. We wrote it in a month. Eventually, when I went off, Benchley and someone else came on to add dialogue, comedy dialogue, that sort of thing, which was never my line. It was a good picture, and I got an Academy nomination for it. And that was the last time I worked with Hitch. Never worked together after that time, but we did remain friends. I became awfully busy myself, getting heavily mixed up at that time with a man named Cecil B. De Mille.

You wrote several pictures for De Mille.

Yes, *Reap the Wild Wind, Unconquered . . .* what else?

The Story of Dr. Wassell.

That's right. And, when you work for De Mille, it means over a year of your time. I was very popular with him. He had this terrible reputation for being a bully, but I never noticed it. To me he was a very pleasant person. Occasionally he would get irritated like any producer does.

He used to take me to his ranch in the mountains, a very lovely place 6,000 feet up. Paradise. He had immense areas of the mountains, hundreds of square miles. I remember the first time we went up, drove through these big gates and about two miles, I suppose, before we came to this big ranch house. And as we came to the front of the ranch house, on the big lawn in front there were about two- or three-hundred head of deer. I said, "What is this business with all the deer on your front lawn?" He said, "I'll tell you, Charles, it's hunting season. And the deer know it, and every year during hunting season they come and stay on the front lawn of my house." He said, "I know many of them year after year. Look at that old one there, he's a great friend of mine." And this was the "great bully." He wasn't a bully at all. He was a terribly nice man.

Were these strictly social occasions or would you be working on a film?

Both socially and for story conferences. I did a lot of work for De Mille with a very good writer named Alan LeMay. Alan and I would be summoned on a weekend up to Paradise. You were told to bring your dress trousers and that sort of stuff, but not your dinner jacket or shirt and tie. And on your bed every night were these Cossack blouses of various colors. You dressed for dinner in your trousers and these Cossack shirts, and De Mille dressed the same way. Often it was just De Mille, LeMay, and myself, but dressed this way for dinner, always.

He didn't live in the big ranch house himself; he had his own lower ranch house about a couple hundred yards down the lane with his own pool. It was a short walk down some steps to the pool, and he would go down naked every morning even in winter. And—he told me this himself—there was a big tarantula spider he passed every morning for years, and the tarantula came out and De Mille would say, "Good morning," as the spider came out, and the tarantula would wave back.

How much input did he give you on the development of the script?

Little. When it came to developing a script, he knew nothing. He would get the idea of wanting to do Jesus Christ, or a sea story, whatever it was, but he was entirely relying on his writers to come up with something good.

And when he did try to write something, it was awful. Now and then he would come up with a line of dialogue, and it was what Alan LeMay and I used to call a De Mille "stinker."

Lynne Overman, Raymond Massey, Paulette Goddard, and John Wayne in *Reap the Wild Wind* (1941).

We used to have these long conferences with him, and a court reporter was taking everything down in shorthand. And De Mille would come up with a line. He'd say, "Yes! And he speaks this line . . ." And it was so awful! Then he'd say to the reporter, "Circle that in red!" Then Alan and I would whisper, "How the hell are we going to get this line out?" And we'd manage to get around it somehow, forget to put it in. Not a bit of it. By the time the script came into his hands, he'd read and say, "Yes . . . yes, very good, very good . . . *Hey!* Where's that line we wrote?"

No, De Mille was not a writer. And not a constructionist. I *was* a constructionist, and that was one thing you needed with a big, sprawling De Mille picture.

The critics hated him, of course. But the audiences loved the pictures. And gradually people in the busines had to say, "Hell, all of his pictures make money. There must be something to the man."

Was he really concerned with research and accuracy, or was that just part of his self-promoting?

Oh yes, he had a research department working with him all the time. Everything had to be accurate, even to the kinds of plants that would be in a particular area. He was very thorough in that way . . . and very good.

The Story of Dr. Wassell was a contemporary subject, and the research on that was mainly just talking to Dr. Wassell, and talking, and that was it. He came over here and we met at lunch a lot. He was a very simple and delightful character, a simple soul, and I don't think he cared either way about the film. He found the interest in him very unexpected.

The only thing I remember Dr. Wassell being very forthright about was in insisting that you ate fish twice a week. (Laughs.)

Was a De Mille script considered unchangeable when the film went into production—as with Hitchcock?

You would finish long before production began. Perhaps I'd go away and start on another picture, or come back and be beginning another one for him. As the thing was in production, though, suddenly the call might come from the set, "Come over, we're stuck." They might be stuck on a bit of dialogue, something like that. Usually Alan was around with me in those days, and the two of us would have to go down and do whatever was necessary right on the spot.

But we didn't care to hang about on the set. Only when we were called. And, when we were called, we always groaned. You knew it was trouble.

Jesse Lasky, Jr., has written that your acting ability served you well with De Mille. You'd enthrall him with a scene by acting out all the parts.

Oh, yes, I remember on *Reap the Wild Wind* we hadn't got the climax at all for the picture, and De Mille was getting nervous about it. We had a conference and De Mille was saying, "Well, what are we going to do with the end of the picture? We've got nothing!" I had been keeping very quiet, but now he turned to me and said, "Charles, haven't you got an idea?"

Well, you don't want to disappoint De Mille, and I said, "Yes . . . I have." He said, "Well, what?" "Yes," I said, "I thought it up while I was taking my bath, this morning." He said, "What are you talking about?" And I said, "Well, what if we have John Wayne and Ray Milland down there below the sea, they're about to fight when . . . they are interrupted by *a giant squid!*"

And I began to act a whole scene out for him. I played John Wayne's part. I played Ray Milland's part. I played *the giant squid's* part. And by the end I had De Mille sitting there, completely transfixed, seeing the scene before him. And he breathed, *"In Technicolor!"* He was bowled over.

It was shot, and I think that squid scene was probably half the reason the picture was such a big hit. And I'd thought of it in my bath. (Laughs.)

But, yes, you did do some acting with De Mille.

You came to California in the heyday of the so-called "Hollywood Raj," the British colony. Did they take you right into the fold when you arrived?

Oh yes, automatically. The first thing that happened to an Englishman when you got here was you had to meet Aubrey Smith. It was like meeting the British Ambassador. He lived up at the top of the canyon, a lovely house, still there. On top of the house he had a weathercock—weather vane you call them over here—it was a cricketer and bats, and the bats would revolve. He was crazy about cricket. He had been a player, one of the greatest amateurs in England, an amateur bowler—known as "Round-the-Corner" Smith in his great days.

First thing when you met him, he'd say, "Oh, nice to meet you, my dear boy. Where'd you go to school?" And, after you'd got that over, he'd give you a long look, raise an eyebrow and say, "Cricket?"

And that was it. The whole British colony practically revolved around old Aubrey. A sweet guy, nice old man, but *crazy* about cricket. And of course, he had this cricket team out here, with their own cricket pitch the other side of Griffith Park. But I was never any good at cricket. Never any good at golf. Never any good at tennis, either. Ha! But I played them all.

You wrote *Black Magic* in 1948, which starred Orson Welles. What did you think of the film as it turned out?

Oh, it was a bad involvement with Welles. I had written a script, and then it was decided to shoot the script in Italy. And Edward Small, who was the producer, was afraid of flying and wouldn't go to Italy. The result was that Orson Welles and the director, Gregory Ratoff, got their heads in Rome and did whatever they liked. Orson Welles, who considered himself not only a good actor but a writer, started to mess up the script. The horrible result was, when we got the stuff back from Italy, it couldn't be put together. It was dreadful, and nothing could be done with it as is.

What had been going on in Rome was Gregory Ratoff had been bowing in every direction to Orson Welles, letting him do whatever came to his mind. The film they produced was absolutely impossible to edit.

To make it at all possible to cut the damn thing together, it meant rewriting and then reshooting for at least a week. And I was to direct these new scenes as well as write them. Welles got here and I had to deal with him very sternly. I said, "I'm terribly sorry, Orson, but this is what we have to do. The picture can't be put together as it is." And I remember him saying to me, "Charles, I'm a very good soldier. Just tell me what to do."

Was he accepting the blame for the problem that occurred?

He wasn't accepting anything. Only the fact that something had happened that had to be put right. Oh, I got along with him very well. But the great boy-genius could really mess things up if he was given his head.

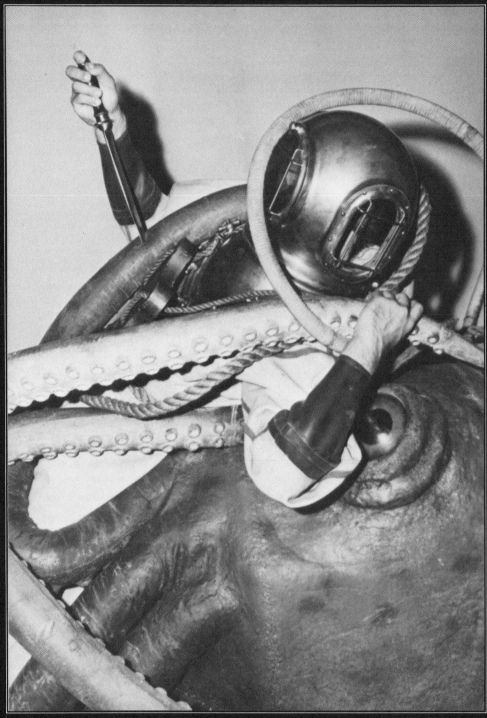

"I thought it up while I was taking my bath." John Wayne and the giant squid in *Reap the Wild Wind* (1941).

You scripted a wonderful horror film called *Night of the Demon*, directed by Jacques Tourneur. What do you remember about that one?

I fell in love with the original very short story, "The Passing of the Runes" by M.R. James. I fell in love with it, bought the rights myself, and decided to make a picture out of it.

I wrote a beautiful script, I know that. But I have never been entirely happy with the picture. I was leaving London in a hurry. The guy who wanted to produce it for Columbia, I remember, came to me as I was leaving England and had me sign something giving the rights to set the thing up with Columbia. And I signed—stupidly, as it turned out. To my horror, the moment I got back here to California, I found out that RKO wanted to make it, with me as the director. Which would have been perfect.

It's still a good picture, and fairly close to my script. But the man who produced it over there in England rather spoiled some of it.

Those shots of the monster seem out of place, as if thrown in after the fact.

Oh, that awful thing. Of course I was against that. I never had any monster. In fact, I was appearing at some film festival where they screened the film, and Harlan Ellison was among the audience. He came up to me afterwards and said, "Charles, did you put that damn monster into the picture?" I said, "*No!* It had nothing to do with me whatever." But, you know, Columbia Pictures in those days, Harry Cohn. They needed a monster.

You never worked with Hitchcock again after 1940. Did you see much of him in later years?

We remained friends. I used to go out and stay with him and Alma at his lovely place near Santa Cruz. Beautiful place in a forest. And I talked with him on the telephone often. We remained quite friendly. And yet . . . with Hitchcock you never quite knew what was up. I would go to his house or perhaps meet him at a cocktail party and he would hardly speak to me.

I remember one occasion Brian Aherne gave a huge cocktail party at his house on the beach at Malibu. Hitch was there, and I talked with him for about three-quarters of an hour, along with Charlie Brackett. And the three of us chatted by the fire for nearly an hour. The next day a case of gloriously expensive champagne turned up here at the house with a note from Hitch saying, "From that stupid man, Hitchcock." So I called him up and said, "What's this *stupid man* business?" He said, "That's what you called me, isn't it?" He said, "You passed me and said to everybody, 'There's that stupid man.' I said, "When did I say that? We were talking by the fire for an hour." He said, "No, we didn't talk. You didn't say a word." He couldn't remember any of it.

You don't think it was some sort of practical joke?

He seemed to have no idea that we'd been talking the night before, or that I hadn't called him "stupid." But it was certainly some of the most beautiful champagne I ever drank in my life.

I remember once, after he'd shown me *Psycho*, and we were drinking in his house, and I said, "Hitch, you're a sadist." And I already knew the many things he'd done, pretty horrible practical jokes, awful ones. And I said, "You're a sadist." He said, "Sadist? How could you possibly say that?" I said, "Only a sadist could have had that bathroom scene in *Psycho*." He said, "Whatever do you mean?" I said, "It was horrible, sickmaking." He said, "Charles, you have no sense of humor. I shot that for *comedy*." Shot that for comedy! Well, that was Hitch.

You've written both originals and adaptations, and stories with every sort of background. Do you recognize any continuing themes in your work?

I've had 8 plays produced, I've written 54 produced movies, I've written, I suppose, over 100 television shows, and I've directed I don't know how many. So it's awfully hard to answer a question like that when you've been . . . very busy. I'm a professional writer and I'll write anything I have to write. Even a good professional writer can now and then be a hack. (Laughs.) I am a professional writer who does the job I'm told to do. When I'm not told, I write what I want to. I've written a novel recently, and I've just finished a screenplay which I hope will sell.

Meanwhile, I push on to the next thing. As regards theme, I don't know about that. I don't know what you mean by theme.

Currently, you're working on a novel.

Yes. It comes from an old script of mine which I love dearly. It's a love story, told against the wild country of northern Arizona and Nevada. When I wrote the screenplay, many years ago, every actor in town wanted to play the lead character. Tyrone Power, Robert Taylor wanted it. And under everybody's eyes that actor—what was his name? A little fellow. . . .

Mickey Rooney?

Oh Christ, no. Tough little guy. Was in *This Gun For Hire.*

Alan Ladd.

Alan Ladd. Well, Alan Ladd bought the rights under their noses. And then Alan died—or committed suicide, nobody ever quite knew what happened. As a result, the rights came back to me after he was dead. I let it go for years and years. And now I'm finishing it, writing it as a novel. And I think it's going to be very good.

When you left England for Hollywood, did you have any idea you would stay for these fifty-some years?

I must admit I didn't like Hollywood when I came here. I didn't like it at all. There were things I loathed. I remember going to a party at Joe Mankiewicz's in my first few days here. It was a huge party and, to my horror, I found hundreds of newspaper photographers there, and everybody was being photographed, celebrities, celebrities. The whole thing was just an advertising stunt. If you gave a party it was for publicity. And that rather disgusted me. You didn't do that in England. A party was a party; you had it for fun, not to see your name in the paper. And there was too much of that in Hollywood then.

But it was also very good to me. I was making, in those days, a very great deal of money, and it didn't stop at $1000 a week, it went up pretty fast. My agent, H.N. Swanson, was very good at pushing it up.

But I remember something said to me by W.P. Lipscomb, a very fine writer indeed. It was my first year here and he said, "Charles . . . be careful. Don't let them push your salary too high." And I said, "Why?" He said, "Because, if you reach a certain stage, *you* are to blame when the picture's a flop." (Laughs.)

Now, I'm going to get myself a real drink. Will you join me?

Opposite page: A.I. Bezzerides with Gia Scala on location in Greece for *The Angry Hills* (1959).

2 · A.I. BEZZERIDES

A.I. Bezzerides is a California native of Greek descent, a former truck driver and electrical engineer, and the author of two hard-boiled novels, *The Long Haul* and *Thieves' Market*, both turned into movies (*They Drive by Night* with George Raft and Humphrey Bogart, and *Thieves' Highway* with Richard Conte and Lee J. Cobb) in the 1940s. He has written thirteen produced screenplays, most of them tough, quirky thrillers with notably anarchic heroes.

His best film, *Kiss Me Deadly*, was inauspiciously derived from a Mickey Spillane best-seller, but Bezzerides, given free reign by producer-director Robert Aldrich, subverted the pulpy source material to create something else again, an unhinged, apocalyptic masterpiece. Its unique style mixed savagery and allusion, allegory and deadpan satire. Praised at the time by the French New Wave, the film was a decided influence on Truffaut's *Shoot the Piano Player* and Godard's *Alphaville* and *Made in USA*.

In his screenplay, Bezzerides takes Nietzschean Neanderthal Mike Hammer on a violent, post-atomic quest for the "Great Whatsit," a Pandora's box of deadly attraction, crossing his path with a dense gallery of the corrupt and the crazy: a dimwitted murderess, a mythology-spouting scientist, a thieving autopsy surgeon, an escaped lunatic, and a nymphomaniac ("Whatever it is, the answer's *yes!*"). The explosive isotopes in Pandora's box is Bezzerides' final, existential punch line: the quest leads only to oblivion.

Bezzerides lives in Woodland Hills, in the San Fernando Valley, with his wife, Sylvia Richards, who has also written for the movies (*Ruby Gentry, Possessed*). Most mornings he heads for a nearby diner, Ryons, where he'll have breakfast and, somehow ignoring the clatter of silverware and conversation around him, will work on his latest writing projects. It's at Ryons where he agrees to meet me one morning, telling me to look for the "good-looking bald guy with glasses."

I arrive a little early and start scanning the tops of heads. A waitress tells me "Buzz" hasn't shown up yet. She offers to point him out when he arrives, but there's no need. Bezzerides spots me as he comes through the door and begins talking at me from across the floor as if we saw each other every day. He is a powerfully built man in his late seventies, grizzled, with thick shocks of white hair sticking out of his open shirt. A ripe Saroyanesque personality, he converses like a force of nature, roaming through subject matter and chewing it up, politics, religion, race, producers, and car repair. His free association—very free at times—doesn't make him easy to interview, and, it's obvious he doesn't have much interest in the films he's signed his name to. Too many compromises, too much interference. Bezzerides had plenty of talent; others had the power. "Obligations," he says, made him take most of his movie and TV assignments. The producers got more than their money's worth out of Bezzerides, a writer with the energy and disposition to give his all to any project. They only occasionally made good use of it. Too often efficiency, not artistry, was all they wanted—"Don't do it good, do it today." But that, any Hollywood veteran will tell you, is an old story.

Writers never understand: producers are the goddamndest crooks you ever saw. And they think that writing is *shit*.

I wrote a book about truckers called *The Long Haul*. Warner Bros. wanted to buy it and they offered $1500. I said, "Gee, that doesn't seem like much to buy the movie rights." I was very naïve. So the agent said, "We'll see if we can get more." And we went to Warners to see Mark Hellinger, the producer. As we walked into his office, Hellinger took something off the table and put it underneath something else. I saw the title, *They Drive by Night*. Well, the agent got them up to $2500. I thought, "Well, if that's all we can get, I need the money." I was working as an engineer at that time. Then I read in the trades that Warners is making a picture about truckers and so forth, based on *The Long Haul*, and it's going into production. So that's when I find out that they'd already done a script. Jerry Wald's written *They Drive by Night* using my novel and using the ending of another story, *Bordertown*. They used it without permission, before they even bought it. A writer at the studio said to me, "You must have made a killing on *The Long Haul*." I said, "I got $2500." "Twenty-five hundred?" he says. "You could have gotten $100,000 out of them." They were about to make a picture called *The Patent Leather Kid*, but George Raft couldn't lose his pot belly and couldn't fit into the boxing trunks. They had a cast ready to go and no picture, so Wald did the trucking story. The script was done before they bought the story. They were lying to me.

But Warners put you under contract?

Yeah, they hired me. I had been working as an engineer, writing on the side. I'd written two novels, *The Long Haul* and *Thieves' Market*. They were based on things I'd seen with my father or on my own. I worked with my father, trucking, going to the market to buy produce. There was corruption and they'd try to screw you. When he was selling grapes, the packing house would screw him on the price and then sell to New York for an expensive price. When I was trucking I wouldn't allow it. A guy tried to rob me in such a blatant way I picked up a two-by-four and I was going to kill him.

I studied to be an engineer and I worked as an engineer at the Department of Water and Power. But then I went to work for Warner Bros., at $300 a week, and that was the end of my working as an engineer.

They put me on a picture called *Juke Girl*. Ronald Reagan and Ann Sheridan. I worked with a guy named Ken Gannett. He didn't like what I did with the thing. He had fallen for all the stereotype forms for "B" pictures. He didn't know the subject. He was a Hollywood character and hadn't gone through anything like this story. But I had been involved in that scene, I knew about people wandering into a town to pick crops. So I could write reality, and he couldn't. He hadn't been exposed to that reality. And we had some problems working together. He couldn't admit that he had something to gain from my point of view. And this is where a lot of writers go wrong, defending their egos.

So you didn't have any trouble adapting yourself to writing in screenplay form?

I had a certain visuality. When I was a kid, before I thought of being a writer, I used to look closely at things. I noticed a lot. I was very observant. And I began taking pictures with a camera when I was a kid, and endlessly took pictures. So I had no real problem writing for the movie camera. Dick Powell, when he had become a producer, wanted me to direct for him. He thought

George Raft, George Tobias, and Humphrey Bogart in *They Drive by Night* (1940).

and Valentina).

I wrote very visually. I turned him down. I just wanted to write. I'm sorry I did now. I think I could have directed all right.

Tell me about the writer's life at Warner Bros. in that period.

Jack Warner thought you had to create from nine to five. He'd be at the window when you got in late and you'd get a note or some such thing. He thought you could create at a certain time and then stop. But it doesn't work like that. You're creative at home, when you're driving in your car, it could be any time. But he could never understand it. I remember him walking in on us shooting craps on the floor in the writer's building. Steve Fisher, Frank Gruber, and me and some of the others shooting craps and we hear Warner barge in. *"Who's winning?"* he'd say. He didn't like it, but he couldn't really stop it.

Jack Warner was always saying something stupid. Warner would make these ridiculous dumb jokes in the executive dining room and all the producers would laugh and laugh and laugh.

The writers ate at their own table. They didn't like to associate with producers. Nobody wanted them around, picking your brain. They'd take your ideas. Even take your conversation. I remember one day at the writers' table sitting next to Jerry Wald. I was working with him and we were talking about it, and Wald says, "Jesus Christ, Buzz, that's a cliché." And I say, "Jerry, everything is a cliché. You're born, you live, die, all clichés. It's what you do with the clichés that's important." A couple weeks later at the writers' table, somebody's talking about a meeting with Jerry Wald. Jerry wants some old bit in the script, and the writer told him it's the oldest cliché in the book. And what did Jerry say? "Life's a cliché! You're born, you live. . . . " That's a producer for you.

Why didn't you get screen credit for *Action in the North Atlantic?*

Because of John Howard Lawson. *Action in the North Atlantic* was basically a piece of propaganda for our alliance with Russia. I was put on it to fix it. There were scenes in there . . . one with Bogart and the girl, and one with Raymond Massey and his wife, that were so out of context in their propagandistic way that the actors couldn't even act them. I polished every scene in that picture. I was entitled to credit. But when it came to arbitration, Lawson was so strong in the Guild that I couldn't get it. They protected their own.

I knew a lot of them working at Warners. The Hollywood Ten guys. I used to drive three or four writers home every day, and one of them was Albert Maltz. We'd start driving and Maltz would say, "Tell me about your background. Tell me about so and so. . . . " And I thought he was interested, and I'd start to tell him some story. But the moment I got to his house, he got out, with my story dangling. He didn't care what I was saying, he just wanted someone to occupy his mind till he got home. But I got back. Next time I'd be telling a story, I didn't let him out of the car. I kept driving around in circles near his house till I was finished.

And I worked with Alvah Bessie on something called *Baby Marine*. They had me break in Alvah. And we had a scene with a truckload of recruits, and a soldier's opening a cake he got from his mother. Alvah says, "Let's do this scene like this. The kid takes a piece of cake and walks all the way over to the one black soldier and gives it to him. We'll show he's not prejudiced." I said, "How about we have him open his cake and say, 'Fellas, dig in,' and you show whites, blacks, chicanos all helping themselves, instead of making a big point of it? Your way is labored." But he couldn't see it. He wanted to do things like that over and over. I couldn't work with him and I quit the picture.

And Alvah Bessie used to be one helluva writer, before the Spanish Civil War. After that he had to prove every day what he believed in.

It was at Warners that you became friends with William Faulkner? He lived with you for a while, didn't he?

Faulkner lived at my house. He was fond of me, considered himself a member of the family. He was making $300 a week and he was starving on it. He was sending the money home. That was one of the reasons why he stayed with me. He'd been drunk so often that no producer would hire him any more. But Warner Bros. hired him, and Warner boasted that he had the best writer in the world for "peanuts."

The first time I met Faulkner I was still working as an engineer. My wife and I were having dinner with some friends at the Pig 'n' Whistle. We saw Faulkner sitting at a table with his girlfriend. I recognized him instantly and I had to go over to him. I said, "I don't usually go around knocking on people's doors, but I've read all your books, everything you've written, and I think you're a great writer." And he shot up and said, "Thank you, suh!" We shook hands and I went back to my table, very embarrassed.

Four years later I'm at Warner Bros. and I'd been there a few months when who do I see coming down the aisle between the secretaries but Faulkner. He had a pipe in his mouth and he had a way of walking leaning way backwards. Well, I see him and he sees me. I say, "Do you remember me?" He says, "Yes, suh, I do. What are you doing here?" I said, "I'm a writer." (Laughs.) I said, "What are you doing here?" And he said, "Uh, I'm a writer, too."

We talked. I asked him where he was staying. He was living at a hotel. He was going to catch a cab home and I said I'd take him home. And then we went to the endless places where he went to get drunk. And he could get *drunk*, man. I had to take him to the hospital, to dry out. Then I'd take him home, and he'd be very shaky.

One time he was in bad shape, asking me to get him a bottle of rum. I didn't want to, but if I didn't he said he was going to drink a bottle of hair tonic he had. So I went to get it. But first I took the hair tonic and hid it in a hole under the sink. I didn't have the nerve to empty it because he'd been snapping the blade out that he used to clean his pipe. I said, "Hey, what are you doing with that thing?" He said, "Oh . . . I'm gonna cut my agent's balls off."

I went out and when I got back with the rum he was passed out on the floor. He had found that goddamned bottle of hair tonic. I got him up and I told him again what the doctor had said, that if he didn't stop drinking like that he was going to kill himself. I left him alone for a few minutes and when I came back he had disappeared with his two bags. I yell, "Bill, Bill, where'd you go?" I ran out to look for him. He was outside the hotel, lugging his two bags up the hill. I caught up with him and said, "What the hell are you doing?" He said, "Gonna have a heart attack." So I held him, knocked the bags out of his hands, took him in my arms and tried to get him back to his room. And he was struggling with himself. I asked him what he's doing. He says, "Trying to get down." But it was his own collar he's pulling on, not mine. So I started laughing and he was laughing. He was something, all right.

He wrote *A Fable* in my house. He'd be typing away in the middle of the night. Worked right on the typewriter, typed all night. I walked in on him, asked him what he was working on there in the middle of the night. He said, "Oh . . . on a novel." "Well . . . what's it about?" He said, "Oh, it's about Jesus Christ coming to earth during the World War." I laughed. I said, "I have to ask you a terrible question. Who the hell gave you entry to write about Jesus

Christ?" Well, he gave me a look that told me it was the last time he'd talk story with me. But he finished the book and it was a stinker, one of his lousiest books.

What did he think of his movie work?

He had contempt for it. Get the pay check, that's all. Sometimes he'd think he would do it for the art. He wanted to do *Pickwick Papers.* And he wrote *The De Gaulle Story,* at 400 pages. And that was a bunch of shit.

Faulkner and I were put together on a script at Warners, to polish a picture called *Escape in the Desert.* We sat in the office and sat and sat and sat. I didn't want to start writing for fear of embarrassing him. I wanted him to start and then we could pitch in together. But he didn't say a word. Finally, I got exasperated and I said, "Hey Bill, we got to write!" And he turned and looked at me and said, "Shucks, Buzz, it ain't nuthin' but a *movin' picture."* So, screw him, I decided to start trying to write. And I started and finally he began to think of things. There was a scene in there where the Nazis are in the desert and he thought of a bit where a rattlesnake jumps out and frightens them. That was Faulkner's scene. And Warner read it and didn't want to shoot the scene. He said it would frighten pregnant women and give them spontaneous abortions. I said to Warner, "If you can guarantee *that,* you'll have a big hit." Jack didn't get it. He said, "No, no, they'll sue us."

But Howard Hawks was always trying to give Faulkner work. And Faulkner didn't do anything with Hawks, really. Bill's contribution would be little bits here and there. But the continuity of a script, he couldn't do it. The screenplay form was alien to him. He was muscle-bound with his talent. He needed prose so he could run off with it.

He loved Hawks, though, got along with him very well. You know why? Because they could sit there together and not say anything. Commune in silence. Hawks would ask a question and they'd have a few drinks. Faulkner would be "thinking" and after a long while he'd finally nod his head and say, "Uh-huh."

What did you do after leaving Warners?

When I ended with Warners I went to Paramount. I was supposed to work with John Houseman. But nothing we worked on ever got made. I respected John but we had trouble getting anything finished. Houseman was the kind of guy who'd tell you what to do and not listen to any of the problems. He only wanted his ideas, even if they didn't work.

At MGM we worked together on a picture called *Holiday for Sinners.* There's a doctor who takes over his father's practice after his father dies. He has a girlfriend and he has his father's patients. One of the people who comes in is this punch-drunk fighter. And I felt that the story belonged to the punch-drunk fighter; there was no story with the doctor. And I kept saying to John, "This is the punch-drunk fighter's story." The fighter owes money to the gansters, he's punch drunk, he can't pay it back. He goes to a priest for help, he goes to a prostitute he knows, he goes to the doctor, and they all turn him down. And he gets killed in the end, and all these characters who turned him down have to examine themselves for not helping him. Where were they when he needed him? And I told Houseman, "The story belongs to the fighter." He said, "Write it the way I told you. It's the doctor's story." I told him over and over again. But they make the picture. We go to a preview in Pomona, and it's so obvious that the audience isn't interested in this thing, isn't interested in this doctor. We leave the theatre and we walk back to our cars in the parking lot. And John is staring at the preview cards, reading them, realizing the picture wasn't going to work. And finally he stops, looks thoughtful and turns to me. He says, "Al. . . . " He didn't call me Buzz he called me Al. "Al . . . What was it you said about the punch-drunk fighter?" I said, "John! It's too late!" Producers, boy, I'll tell you.

We did another one when he went to RKO. I did *On Dangerous Ground* for him and Nick Ray. And they left me completely alone during the writing of that one. But on the structure he wouldn't let me have my way. I told them, "You've got a beginning to this story, and an end to this story that gives meaning to the body of the story. You must use the beginning and the ending." We start with the cop in the city being called up for his violence. He's a vicious cop, vicious to criminals because he can rationalize it. Criminals are criminals to him, they're not people. So he's sent out of the city for his behavior, out to the mountains. And he gets involved with the blind girl and her brother, who has killed someone. And she tells him about her brother, and he gets some insight into this kid who's committed a crime. She's made him think. And when he confronts the kid at the edge of the cliff, he says, "Look, I'm not going to hurt you. I have to arrest you, but don't be afraid." But the kid is afraid, of the policeman's power, of what he represents, and the kid tries to escape and falls to his death. And now we have the end, and the cop must go back to the city, the city filled with violence. And the cop knows that violence is in him and it's going to be a struggle for him. But he's a better cop already, because the memory of that kid and what his presence did to him—made that kid die—has given him insight. But they wouldn't do it. They wouldn't do it that way.

They ended it with him going back to the blind girl.

It ruined the structure. They wouldn't listen.

One critic I read said Ray shot it or cut it to imply a "miracle."

Oh, shit.

But it's still a very good picture.

The beginning and the ending ruined it for me. But it was a helluva picture. Bob Ryan was perfect. Houseman again; he could have controlled the situation, because Ray wasn't that sure of himself. But there was no way to talk to them.

These non-writers think they can do what they want to a carefully constructed script and it won't turn into a piece of crap. They're wrong. But nobody tells them that. Fox bought another novel of mine, a book called *Thieves' Market*. They didn't want to use the original title because "San Francisco objects to it." So, *Thieves' Highway*. So who cares? I said okay. Then the director, Julie Dassin says, "For the prostitute, I want Valentina Cortesa, so rewrite it for her." He was going with her. We were going to have Shelley Winters, who would have been perfect. This Italian, Cortesa, what would she be doing in this story? I said, "But . . . Julie!" But I rewrote it. And we go to the meeting with Zanuck—and already the picture is getting fucked up before that.

So we go to Zanuck's office. He's got a yes-man standing there, lips puckered to kiss Zanuck's ass. And Zanuck goes like this—holds his hand out, and the flunky immediately puts a Coke in his hand. I said, "Hey, how about me?" (Laughs.) And Zanuck said, "Get him one too."

Now in my story the father is dead at the beginning. The kid starts trucking because he's trying to make his father's life valid. The first thing Zanuck says is, "I want a new beginning.

Robert Ryan, Ward Bond, and Sumner Williams in *On Dangerous Ground* (1950).

George Raft and Edward G. R

I want the father still alive. He's crippled, that's why the kid's trucking." It was bullshit. But I said, "Yes, Mr. Zanuck." I write another beginning, this revenge business. The picture didn't do real well. There were good things in it, but it wasn't the picture I wanted to do, it wasn't the story I wanted to do. I had the producer's chickenshit changes, the director's girlfriend, and Zanuck's ideas. I only knew that story from my life, my book, my script. But that didn't matter. Oh, I tell you, once you give in a little bit you're finished.

What about when you were brought in to rewrite an existing script by somebody else? Could this ever be as satisfying as a story you originated?

I did a picture called *A Bullet for Joey* with George Raft and Edward G. Robinson. Robinson wanted me to polish his dialogue. He gave me $5000 to do it. Just his dialogue. The hell with George Raft. And I went through the script and polished his dialogue. But what it did to the other guy's dialogue they couldn't believe. And Raft got wind of it and he said, "Hey, how about me?" So I shrugged and said, "More money." Raft said, "I'll pay." So I did his. It was a low-budget picture; there wasn't a lot of money around. But I worked on it, and then I said to the director, an Englishman, Lewis Allen, "Do you mind if I write one scene just for me?" He said, "I would welcome it."

So I rewrote this scene at the end. The girl is having a love affair with this spy and she realizes he's the one stealing the secrets. In the original script, she tells him she knows who he is and he pulls out a gun and shoots her. I built it up so that, as she backs away from him, he aims the gun but he's reluctant to shoot. He realizes what she means to him, that in all those nights getting information he was also falling in love with her. And it's traumatic for him as he says, "I'll have to kill you. . . . " And he pulls the trigger.

Well, I thought it made for a better scene. And the girl liked it, and the director liked it. But the actor wouldn't do it. "I'm a big spy. I wouldn't do that." He just wanted to pull the gun and shoot her. The director said, "You see? You think a director's job is easy?" But we got the actor to go home and think about it overnight. And the next day he'd decided to do it. He *overdid* it. By the time he agreed to shoot the scene, he had the character crying like a baby.

But to answer your question—it can be fun or involving, but it's not the same as writing your own story.

I worked on a lot of things people wanted fixed or rewritten. I did a lot of things with Bob Aldrich. I did *Sirocco* for Bogart. There was a script that was no good, and Curt Bernhardt asked me to rewrite it. It was for Bogart's production company. Bogart and Bob Lord were partners. So I start rewriting the thing. And three days into it, as I'm turning in pages, Lord calls me in. He says, "I'm firing Curt." I said, "Why?" He said, "Don't ask me why." I said, "Look, I'm on this job because of him. So I don't know if that'll work out with him fired. I'm upset about this." So Lord kept him on. And then Bernhardt got some guy from Germany in to work with me. And he did nothing. But he'd lie back, and as I finished a scene he'd say, "It's wonderful how you can take my ideas and put them in the script." But I didn't care. The picture got made. I worked with what I had. This was one of—what's his name—Zero Mostel's first things, and there were scenes between him and Nick, the little Greek, and how could you resist writing a comic scene for them?

It's a pretty depressing picture, though. Especially the ending, Bogart knowingly walking to his death, the Arab throwing the hand grenade in on him.

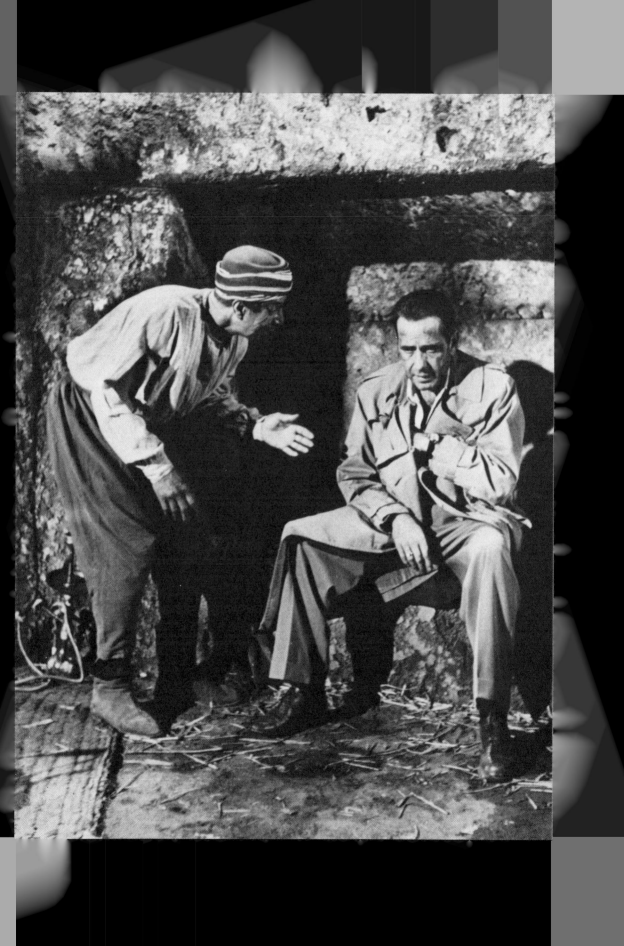

It was that character's fate. You knew he was doomed. They didn't give me any problem with it. I got along okay with Bogart. He wasn't very involved creatively. He knew me, trusted me because I'd worked on *Action in the North Atlantic* that he was in.

***Track of the Cat* was an unusual film. Also very depressing.**

William Wellman gave me this book to read and I loved the book.* I told him, "Let me write the script and then we'll talk and we'll see what we have to do." So I wrote it. He loved it. I had a big drunk scene in there. Wellman and Wayne and all of them were big drinkers, bottles all over the place. And Wellman came in after reading the scene and said, "You're one of us!" He thought, to write it as I did I had to drink like they did. And, boy, did they drink. I said, "Bill, I wrote a scene. I don't drink." Well, that was the last I heard from him for awhile.

So then I finished the first draft of the script. And John Wayne called me in—it was his production company doing it—and said how wonderful it was, and if he was younger he'd have liked to play the part. I said, "It's just the first draft. It needs cutting." He said, "I understand." But Wellman didn't want it changed. I said, "Bill, it needs cutting. It'll take a couple weeks." He said, "No, I like it. Any changes, I'll do them." I said, "Don't you understand? It's overwritten. The scenes have to be worked on." Wellman said, "No, it's perfect." He had so fallen in love with the script that he wouldn't touch a word of it. And he didn't. He didn't touch a word. And, my God, that's going too far. I'm not untouchable. But he wouldn't listen. And then, on top of this overwritten script, he had another pretense he put into it. He said, "I'm going to shoot it in black and white in color." It's in color but everything in it is black or white.

Wellman was a good director, scene-wise, camera-wise, but he lacked a writer's ability to cut and revise. The film is very overwritten. But he wouldn't listen. I should have grabbed him by the collar.

Bob Mitchum, though, was fantastic. He carried scenes that needed to be polished, and his performance made some of it work. I got to know him very well and I thought he was a wonderful guy. But cynical. God, is he cynical. We did another picture together, with Aldrich, *The Angry Hills*. I asked him, "Why are you doing this piece of shit?" We were on location. He said, "I've never been to Greece."

I was with them in Greece, writing this thing while they were shooting it. The producer and Leon Uris had worked for a year on a script and it had to be thrown out; it was no good. The whole thing had to be rewritten, and that producer didn't like that much. We're on location and Mitchum went for some local Greek girl. So his wife, who thought I was tremendous, started to go for me. I excused myself from that one and one of the crew says, "A gentleman never turns down a lady." I said, "I'm no gentleman."

Can we talk about *Kiss Me Deadly?* I think it's your best screenplay.

I knew Bob Aldrich when he was an assistant director. We were going to do a picture, a western, for Burt Lancaster. I had just started working on it. And we're going to lunch, Lancaster, Aldrich, and some other people. And Burt was grabbing my arm, telling me all sorts of shit that had to be in the picture. And there was so much crap. He didn't know his ass from a hot rock. So I said, "Burt, why don't you stick to acting and leave the writing to the writer." Well, he looked at me. And after lunch I went to my office and packed my stuff. I knew I was fired and I wanted to beat the message.

Track of the Cat by Walter Van Tilburg Clark.

Robert Mitchum in *Track of the Cat* (1954).

Robert Aldrich (with gun) directing Gaby Rodgers and Ralph Meeker in *Kiss Me Deadly*

Bob called me, asked me, "Why'd you do that?" I said, "He's telling me what to do and I can't write with somebody doing that."

And later, when Bob was directing and he wanted me, he knew the best thing was to let me alone. He gave me the Mickey Spillane book, *Kiss Me Deadly,* and I said, "This is lousy. Let me see what I can do." You give me a piece of junk, I can't write it. I have to write something else. So I went to work on it. I wrote it fast, because I had contempt for it. It was automatic writing. You get into a kind of stream and you can't stop. I get into psychic isolation sometimes when I'm writing.

How long did it take to write?

About three weeks. I wrote at home, day and night. On some things I'm fast. On some things I'm slow. I do a lot of drafts, over and over. I copy and then I edit, cross out. Writing is hard, and sometimes you only discover what you're looking for by hard work, writing and rewriting.

What made you decide to change the contents of the Pandora's box from drugs to radio-active material?

People ask me—or they asked Aldrich—about the hidden meanings in the script, about the A-bomb, about McCarthyism, what does the poetry mean, and so on. And I can only say that I didn't think about it when I wrote it. These things were in the air at the time and I put them in. There was a lot of talk about nuclear war at the time, and it was the foremost fear in people's minds. Nuclear arms race. Well, I thought that was more interesting than the dope thing in the book. The Pandora's box references related to these characters, and the same with the poem by Rossetti.

I was having fun with it. I wanted to make every scene, every character, interesting. A girl comes up to Ralph Meeker, I make her a nympho. She grabs him and kisses him the first time she sees him. She says, "You don't taste like anybody I know." I'm a big car nut, so I put in all that stuff with the cars and the mechanic. I was an engineer and I gave the detective the first phone answering machine in that picture. I was having fun.

It's a truly nihilistic film . . . every character seems intent on self-destruction.

It was not too long after Hiroshima. The threat of nuclear war hanging in the air. And we did it. It didn't come from the cosmos. My mother—not a political animal—listened to the McCarthy hearings, and she shook her head and said, "What are they doing to this beautiful country?" Look at it today, where you don't dare drink the water or walk across the soil. You can't breathe the air. You can't eat the food they're growing. Man's doing it all to himself. He'll go around killing millions of innocent people and rationalize it. I think man has been programmed long, long ago so that he self-destructs. And it's finally paying off. But there are certain shits in our society who don't care because they think they will be above it all when it happens. They think they can escape their destiny, but they can't.

Anyway, I was just writing. The Pandora's box was just a substitute for the dope. When you opened the box a little, it radiated. When the girl flings it open, it blazes. Dramatic.

The Mike Hammer character is unusually brutal for a Hollywood movie of that time.

The character in the book is that way. I just heightened his natural violence. I tell you, Spillane didn't like what I did with his book. I ran into him in a restaurant and, boy, he didn't like me.

But the brutishness seems typical of several of your protagonists—the Ryan character in *On Dangerous Ground*, Mitchum in *Track of the Cat*, Richard Conte in *Thieves' Highway*. Their violence is obsessive, unsympathetic.

Those characters fit those stories, that's all. I don't sympathize with their violence. But it is more interesting to write. Violence, traumatic events, these are the feelings that go deep. Under hypnosis, you don't remember pleasant things, always tragic things. Joy passes. Fear and anger don't pass. They sink into your genes.

***Kiss Me Deadly* was considered another "B" movie here. Were you aware of how well-received it was in Europe? It made Aldrich's reputation with the critics there.**

I hadn't realized how seriously they had taken it. Somebody from one of the French movie magazines tracked me down in my hotel in France. I don't know how he found me. And he wanted to know about *Kiss Me Deadly* and about Aldrich. They asked me this, that, how certain things got into the picture. I told him, "I *wrote* it." He couldn't believe it wasn't Aldrich. The poem, the bomb. I laughed. I said, "Aldrich directed it, but I wrote it." I was embarrassed. He said, "For many years we have thought of this New Wave picture as Aldrich's. But it is you." I couldn't believe what went on there. Truffaut, for Christ's sake, thought it was one of the best pictures made. I was awed.

One time I went over to visit a friend of mine, Nancy Nicholas. There was a big camper sitting outside her house when I got there. And in the kitchen there was a young guy drinking coffee. He was French. Nancy introduced me, said I was a writer. He asked me what I wrote. He wasn't too thrilled by it all. And I said I'd written a picture some of the French seemed to think was all right. "Oh yes?" he says, "What's that?" I said, "Oh, it was a crappy little picture, *Kiss Me Deadly*." And he shot up fast. *"Kiss Me Deadly!"* And he goes out and gets his friend, and they both come back and stare at me. I said, "What are you so excited about? It's a piece of junk. I heard you French liked it, but. . . ." They just kept staring at me with their mouths hanging open.

Aldrich took credit for everything, of course, when they asked him about it. But it's funny . . . a couple of months before he died he called me. He told me he'd been wondering how the hell he had shot *Kiss Me Deadly* in twenty days. So he had taken out the script and reread it. He said, "Now I know. It's all there. It's in the script."

Overleaf: **Lucille Bremer and Fred Astaire in *Yolanda and the Thief* (1945).**

3 · IRVING BRECHER

Irving Brecher.

S.J. Perelman once called Irving Brecher one of the three quickest wits in America (the other two, in alphabetical order, George S. Kaufman and Oscar Levant). A radio *wunderkind*, Brecher had followed Milton Berle to Hollywood in 1936 and stayed to take the only solo writing credit for a Marx Brothers movie, not once but twice (*At The Circus* and *Go West*). In the '40s, still at MGM, he scripted a series of musicals for the Arthur Freed unit, ranging in quality from highly entertaining (*Best Foot Forward, Yolanda and the Thief*) to high art *(Meet Me in St. Louis)*. In show business circles he is known to have more than held his own trading quips with such caustic colleagues and longtime friends as Groucho Marx, Milton Berle, and George Burns.

On the telephone he is quick-witted, all right, and a tad suspicious. "How did you get my number?" he says.

"Well, I've been doing some research. . . . "

"From the Guild? They're not supposed to give out home phone numbers."

"No, no. Let's see," I dither, "how *did* I get your number. . . . "

"How do I know you're not a burglar? Who else have you talked to?"

The names of several screenwriters, his contemporaries, are mentioned.

"Him I know," Brecher says. " . . . Him I don't know. Who else?"

I give him another name.

"Is *he* still alive? Who else?"

"Nat Perrin," I say.

"Nat Perrin's a very good friend of mine. Where did you talk to him?"

"At his house, off Wilshire? I spent an afternoon with him."

"Hm. Well anyway," Brecher says after a moment, "I'm not doing any pictures right now. What do you want to talk to me about?"

"It's the pictures you've done," I tell him.

"I'm pretty busy. I have some business deals I'm in the middle of. I don't know about this. Give me your number and I'll call you in a couple of days."

He never calls. I try again a few days later. He is still suspicious, but bordering on merely dubious. He tells me to call him later in the week. Two calls later he abruptly makes an appointment for nine the next morning. "I can only give you one hour."

"I'll see you then," I say, knowing it won't be enough time.

Brecher lives now in a tony high-rise between Beverly Hills and Westwood. It is a wealthy, but not particularly pleasant, stretch of Wilshire Boulevard, all canyons of new condos, "for sale" banners dangling, the traffic noisy and ceaseless. Visitors to the building are carefully screened and announced by a pretty Englishwoman, and a healthy-looking security guard is summoned to unlock the elevator door before the visitor can ascend.

Standing in the doorway of his spacious apartment, Irving Brecher is tall, white-haired, commanding. He has an aggressive presence, a sharp, no-nonsense intelligence to his face, and he smokes big cigars. One might take him for the hands-on president of a large company, even for one of the old studio moguls, in the days before moguls were computers and conglomerates.

After the intimidating phone conversations, I'm pleased to find Brecher, in person, delightful company, friendly and open—though not without the occasional Groucho-like barb. He is a wonderful raconteur, and our talk will end up going long past the agreed-on hour.

He takes me into his small office-study. On the bookshelf I see video cassettes of his two Marx Brothers movies, on the wall photos of Brecher with Jack Benny, George Burns, and other cronies. As I set up my tape recorder, I jokingly ask how I'd finally convinced him I wasn't a burglar.

"I did some checking," he says, settling into an armchair. "I called Nat Perrin and asked him if you were all right."

"He okayed me?"

"He . . . " Brecher pauses, lights his cigar, "never heard of you."

"Oh. . . . "

"Don't worry about it. Nat's memory, you know . . . a burglar's about the only thing he would remember. And, speaking of people not getting any younger, what's your first question?"

You came to Hollywood by way of New York radio, didn't you?

I was writing a radio show starring Milton Berle called *The Gillette Community Sing*, forty-five-minute show every Sunday night on CBS. I was writing it by myself, for fifty-two weeks a year. I didn't realize that was impossible. When you're young, nothing's impossible. In the course of writing that, Milton Berle was signed to take the leading role in a movie being made at RKO in Hollywood, *New Faces of 1937*. To make it possible for him to continue his radio show, the whole crew and cast were moved to the Coast while Berle shot the movie.

When we got here the producer decided that the script was not usable and wanted a new script. Berle, or his agent, suggested that I do it. I had tremors about it. I had never been near a studio, plus I was writing the radio show every week. But they convinced me it was the thing to do and that became my first experience at screenplay writing. I would be writing the radio show, and writing the screenplay, running between the producer, Edward Small, and the director, who were generally at odds about what the script should be. There had been a number of scripts—I did the final script—and I shared credit with a man who had been on it earlier and who is now my very good friend, Nat Perrin, and Philip Epstein, one of the Epstein brothers. Unfortunately, Philip died very young.

Eventually the script was finished and the picture was shot. Most of the script was actually written during the shooting of the picture, and the picture, if you don't know of it, was not really successful. The basic story was the idea of a phony Broadway producer who sells investors more than 100 percent of the production with the hope that it will flop and he'll keep the rest of the money. Sound familiar?

Mel Brooks' *The Producers?*

Yes, he didn't originate it. I think the original idea was in a *Saturday Evening Post* story. Anyway, that was my first experience. And while I was in Hollywood doing the film and the radio show, my agent came to me and said that a producer at Warner Bros. named Mervyn LeRoy was impressed with the material on the Berle radio show and was interested in signing me if we could work out a deal. That name meant a good deal to me because I had just seen a masterpiece he produced and directed called *They Won't Forget*, with Lana Turner being introduced. I always felt that if I'd been built like Lana Turner, I'd have been a star, too.

So I went out there. I was quite nervous, because even though I had had a taste of studio life, the names LeRoy and Warner sounded much more important to me, very exciting. I went to LeRoy's office at Warner Bros. in Burbank. The secretary buzzed and told me to go in. She said, "Mr. LeRoy is on the phone, but he'll be right off." And I walked across his long office toward his desk. I saw this smallish man sitting there, and behind him was a large photograph I recognized of Irving Thalberg—Thalberg had recently passed away. And as LeRoy swung around in his swivel chair, still talking to his wife, Doris, and discussing their new baby, he stared at me and said into the phone, "Doris, this is amazing, a young fella has just walked into my office who is the exact image of Irving." I had never realized I looked like Thalberg, but later I looked in a mirror and thought there might be some resemblance. So LeRoy hung up the phone and—he was an impulsive man—said, "Let's make a deal."

I said, "Mr. LeRoy, don't you want to know whether I can write or not?"

He said, "Oh, I think you can write." And we talked for a few minutes. He was a very charming and warm man, and became a dear friend of mine over the years. He worked out a deal with my agent for me to come back in November when my contract with Berle to write his radio show would be over. I signed the contract. I went back to New York with Berle, and I had a difficult time telling Milton that I didn't want to go on with him. It strained our friendship somewhat, but it picked up again, and Milton and I have remained very good friends for many years.

Did LeRoy have a particular project he wanted you to work on when he signed you?

No. It was a personal contract with him, not with Warner Bros. I was getting $650 a week, but I'd been getting more than that on the radio before I left. It was a phenomenal amount of money in 1937, though, and when I came back in November, he asked me if I would do him a favor. I liked the way he put it. He was paying me $650 a week. So I said, "What do you mean, a favor?" And he said he had a sick script they were in the middle of shooting,

Fools for Scandal, with Carole Lombard. He said, "The screenplay's just not funny enough. I need you to punch it up." That was the expression they used then. "But you can't have any credit." So, of course, I did what I was asked to do, and wrote some material which added some laughs to the film. And I *did* receive a credit, for additional dialogue.

Six weeks after that, a wonderful thing happened. LeRoy came to me, very excited, and said, "We're moving to MGM, January 1st." He had signed what was then the biggest contract that any working man in films had ever gotten. Six thousand dollars a week—only L.B. Mayer at MGM was making more money. He was a hot article in the opinion of Mayer and MGM. And he went there and took with him the people under contract to him: Lana Turner, Kenny Baker, and a very talented man named Robert Rossen, and myself.

LeRoy's first assignment at Metro was to produce an existing script for *The Wizard of Oz.* There was no assignment for me, and I was asked to write part of a new radio show that MGM was putting on, Maxwell House sponsoring, called *MGM Good News.* They wanted me to write for a contract actor, Frank Morgan, and I developed his character as a kind of wild, Baron Munchausen.

Then LeRoy called me in for *The Wizard of Oz.* It was like the earlier job at Warners—the script was finished, the numbers were in place, everything was all set, but they needed some more laughs for the Tin Man and the Straw Man and the Cowardly Lion, and for Frank Morgan, who was playing the Wizard. So I did some polishing, unbilled, and enjoyed it. The picture, as everybody knows, turned out to be a classic. Judy was absolutely wonderful in it, and so were the three comedians.

Can you remember some of the bits you wrote for it?

I wrote some amusing stuff for the Cowardly Lion, and the exaggerations, the silliness of the Wizard. I don't have a script from it to remind me. The Bert Lahr part, I remember, intrigued me the most. I made, overall, a small contribution, not a great contribution. *The Wizard of Oz* would have been successful without those laughs.

And after that LeRoy assigned me to what was my life's dream: to write for the Marx Brothers.

To me they were the funniest men in the world, right up there with Chaplin. As a kid in Yonkers I used to make up like Groucho with a rubber cigar, a burnt-cork moustache, and steel-rimmed glasses, and I'd do his material or some that I thought of myself at parties—our parties might be three people. And I was a big fan of their movies and . . . it just never dawned on me that somehow I would end up at MGM with them. I really went into shock. The idea of writing for the Marx Brothers seemed too huge even to contemplate.

They had just made two very good movies for Thalberg, *A Night at the Opera,* which I think was their best film, and *A Day at the Races.* Thalberg, as I mentioned, had died, and now LeRoy was asked by Mayer to make another Marx Brothers film. He called me in and told me I would do it and said it would have a circus background. I was taken to meet the Marx Brothers, and I quickly learned that Groucho would be the one I would have to deal with on the script. Harpo had total distance between himself and the script. He was only interested in what he was going to do in the film, and had no ideas about story, only about his own bits. And Chico was interested in making movies for one thing—his salary, because he was a gambler and he was always broke.

Groucho and Harpo and I became very close. Harpo was an angel. But Groucho was tough, ascerbic—he was not well-liked by many people in this town. He was not a very secure person, and he always feared making a movie, that it wouldn't turn out right, that it wouldn't be funny enough. He was very concerned with the quality.

Would he do any actual writing on the script?

Groucho, who could write and wrote books and great letters, was not a great contributor to the films. People naturally believed that he was making a lot of it up—he had the gift of sounding like he improvised. But in my experience, and, I think in that of most of the writers who worked on Marx Brothers films, there was very little that Groucho would put in. He would read what you wrote and tell you what he couldn't do and influence it. And Harpo would come in with ideas and improvisations for his pantomime, and that was helpful.

Everyone would go over each piece of the script as you finished it?

I would think and write and then go to the producer. LeRoy was really not Marx Brothers-oriented. I think, looking back, he might agree this was not the ideal project for him. He was more interested in and better at drama. There was very little input from him. I'm not minimizing him as a talent, but compared to other producers—and I remember with great respect Hunt Stromberg—Mervyn was quite accepting. I would read scenes to him and he would love them, and say, go ahead, write. Then we would read it to Groucho and Groucho would nod, "Pretty good . . . well, I'm not sure." Then there would be a week or two of limbo, before Groucho might come in and say, "Don't you think this section needs something?"

Didn't the Marxes usually have several writers working on their scripts at the same time?

I am the only writer to ever have a solo credit on a Marx Brothers picture. At one time another writer was assigned to work with me, Dore Schary. He worked for about a week, and we weren't getting anywhere, and he was either removed or asked to be taken off. And then Groucho's friend Arthur Sheekman worked for a little while. I think maybe he didn't get along with LeRoy. Anyway, he threw in the sponge and went on an around-the-world trip with his wife.

It was a tremendous, laborious job to write a Marx Brothers movie.

Did they have you adding or rewriting things while the filming began?

LeRoy wanted me to stay with it, to go to the set when necessary and all that. And there was one interesting story that came out of that. If you remember *At the Circus*, Groucho is a half-assed lawyer investigating the theft of $10,000 from Kenny Baker, the owner of the circus. The money's been stolen by a rough guy who gives it to Eve Arden to hold onto so he's not caught with the money. And she has it under a pillow in her dressing room as Groucho stalks in, bent over, looking around. He's making sweet talk to her and she's playing it cool. That's the scene.

And I get a call from LeRoy. He said, "Eddie Buzzell says, in the scene with Eve Arden they need a line to make a blend. Go down and find out what the hell he wants." So I went down there, and Buzzell, the director, explains to me what they need. And he says, "See what you can come up with. Meanwhile, I'll shoot something else." So I went back and thought up a line for Groucho to say. I told it to LeRoy and he said, "That's great, go down and tell Buzzell to shoot it."

Now, what I wrote was that when Groucho turns away for a moment, Eve Arden grabs the wallet with the money and slides it down her cleavage into her leotards. And Groucho catches it out of the corner of his eye, walks up to the camera and says, "There must be some way I can get that wallet back without getting into trouble with the Hays Office."

I went down to the set, told Buzzell the line, and he said, "That's ridiculous, nobody will understand it. What the hell are you talking about? I won't shoot it." I said, "LeRoy heard the line and he wants you to shoot it." And he said, "Fuck LeRoy, I'm not going to shoot it." And LeRoy heard about his attitude and, to inflict a little discipline, he sent another director down to shoot the line, a fellow named Sylvan Simon. Now, I said to Simon, "You know, Buzzell doesn't think this is going to work, what do you think?" He said, "I don't know, I don't know if anyone knows the Hays Office." But anyway, we used it, and Groucho loved the line because it was nihilistic. And the result was that at the sneak preview Groucho said that the line was not only the biggest laugh he ever got, but the biggest laugh he ever heard in a theatre. And it showed something, it told us all something, that the audience was way ahead.

How long did you work on *At The Circus*?

One year.

Were you at all reluctant when you were told to write their next picture, too?

I don't know how I survived it. LeRoy asked me, I tried to refuse, but goddamn it, I did it again. So I wrote *Go West*. *At the Circus* had some funny things in it, but *Go West* overall I think was a better picture.

On *Go West* didn't you test some of the comedy scenes before live audiences?

Yes. They had done it before with *Opera* and *Day at the Races*. They didn't do it with *At the Circus:* the scenes were too hard to contain for the stage. But my script for *Go West* we broke down into five block comedy scenes to play live, to break it in. And the story would be threaded together by a master of ceremonies, and in between the sketches there would be a dance number or a girl would sing a song.

Our first stops were Chicago and Joliet, and just before we left I got a phone call early in the morning from Harpo. He said, "Get over to the studio as fast as you can." I said, "What for?" He said, "We need to make some publicity stills so they can print some twenty-four sheets to advertise the Chicago show. Groucho has a cold, and you know Groucho when he has a cold: he won't come out of the house." I said, "Why are you calling me?" He says, "You said you used to do Groucho. Come in, they'll make you up, and you can be Groucho for the stills." And they made me up to look like Groucho, and my picture went up on twenty-four sheets all over Chicago and Joliet.

We go to Chicago, we open in Joliet, and after each show I worked on the script, changed some things, trying to improve it, to take out anything that wasn't playing. The problem there was that Chico could never remember the new lines. It was tough enough to get him to remember the old lines. But it was exciting, terribly exciting to work that way, and very helpful. It was a great education in comedy, getting instant reactions to what you were writing.

We were in Chicago, and one day Chico took me for lunch at a famous restaurant there. Chico was a gambler and knew all the mugs in any city, and we're sitting there and in come three guys with broken noses. Real goons. And they slapped Chico on the back. One says, "Hey, Chicky baby, hey boy!" They've all got heavy, Italian accents. "Hey, what are you doing in the old burg?" Chico and the Marx Brothers were all born in Chicago and grew up there.

And Chico tells them what he's doing there. And he says, "I want you to meet this guy; he writes some of our stuff." The guy slaps me, almost broke my shoulder: "Hiya buddy." And one says to Chico, "Hey Chicky, while you're here why don't you come out and visit the ranch—we got a ranch in Wheaton." Now if you don't know Chicago, Wheaton is about eight miles from there, and it's about as much ranch country as New York City. But they say, "You've got to see the ranch. We'll take you hunting." I said, "What do you shoot?" And the fella says, "Chickens, dogs, cats." Chico says, "Well fellas, I think I'm busy, you know, I'm working."

Anyway, so we broke the script in on the road. Nat Perrin worked with us briefly, came to Chicago and spent some time. Those were very black days and it was hard to keep your mind on the work. Hitler had invaded Poland while we were in Chicago. We played Joliet, Detroit, and then we came home to Hollywood and shot the picture.

What kind of traveling companion was Groucho?

I had traveled with Groucho before and Groucho was a threat to travel with. He was a danger.

I'll tell you a story about that. *At the Circus* was released in 1939. My wife and I decided to go to Europe. I had never been to Europe. Groucho was then single and decided to come with us. We got to New York and it was in the papers that Groucho Marx and his writer were on their way to Europe. He got a telephone call at the hotel, the State Department telling him that it was dangerous to go to Europe now with the threat of war. And there was a lot of amusing banter, with Groucho saying, "I'm beginning to think these Nazis don't like Jews," and so forth.

So, Europe was off. My wife said, "Well, we're here, we should have some sort of vacation." I said, "What do you suggest?" My wife had been born in Virginia, and she said, "What about White Silver Springs, the Greenbriar? It's magnificent, you can play golf." Groucho said, "Okay, let's go." I said to my wife, "I understand they don't like Jews down there." She said, "I never had any problem." I said, "Well, you don't come off as a Jew." Her name was Bennett and she looked like Myrna Loy. She wasn't used to looking under stones for anti-Semitism. I had been brought up with it; Groucho too. But she assured us everything would be all right, and told me to book the reservations. I said, "All right, we'll go tomorrow." But she couldn't go, she had some business in New York, she'd join us down there. So I sent a telegram reserving two rooms and signed it Irv Brecher. I received a telegram confirming our reservation and we head down there.

The ride down on the train, Groucho can't sleep, he's upsetting people, and when we arrive at the depot at White Silver Springs on a cold, crisp morning, I begin to again realize that he could be very difficult. And I said to myself, Here we are in this WASP country, where they have lynchings and God knows what, and I've got this guy with me, and I hope he doesn't do anything. And as we set out in the taxi, I'm thinking of all the things he's done when I've been with him. We get there and I say, "Groucho, why don't you take care of the bags? I'll go check in." And he says, "Why don't you do that, youngster?" But as I start toward the door of the hotel, I hear his feet behind me and I look, and he's walking like "Groucho" and I say, "Oh, God, cut it out, will you?" He says, "Oh, yes!" I go through the door and start for the counter and there are three men in shiny black suits. They looked almost like triplets, thin-nosed, blue-nosed. They're standing at the counter and I walk up and start to say, "You have a reservation for. . . ." And before I finish, Groucho sidles up and says, "Is it true you people run a chain of brothels?"

Groucho and Chico Marx *At the Circus* (1939).

Lucille Ball in

One of the three men says, "You don't have a reservation." I said, "I didn't tell you my name yet." He says, "You don't have a reservation." And we were there for two hours, and I pleaded almost with tears to the manager. And they finally relented and gave us a room—a broom closet with pipes running through it. And we sat there and I said to Groucho, "Well, you made your joke. . . . " And he said, "I'm beginning to think it was undiplomatic."

But the topper is, the movie they were showing that night in the hotel was *At the Circus*. They wanted to keep him out, this Hollywood Jewish actor, but they ran his movie. My wife came down the next day, and with her southern charm got us our two rooms.

What did you do after *Go West*? *Shadow of the Thin Man*?

LeRoy recommended me to a man who I thought and still think was the most able producer of my experience, Hunt Stromberg. I was assigned to do the script of *Shadow of the Thin Man* with a friend of mine, Harry Kurnitz. The story was by Elliot Paul, but there wasn't a helluva lot of story and it had a lot of problems. Kurnitz and I worked together for a little while, and then Kurnitz left to do something else and I worked alone.

Stromberg was an education. Here was a man who made you write better than you thought you could. He was indefatigable in terms of taste. He was never in a hurry, always encouraging. If he disapproved of something, he didn't just say, "It's no good," he told you why. He was a sick man, in great pain all the time, but a wonderful man. I wrote that for him, and I think that one made me feel more of a writer than just, you know, a comedy man.

After that you began working for Arthur Freed.

I was asked by a friend in the studio, a writer named Fred Finkelhoffe, if I'd like to work with him on a picture from the Broadway show *Best Foot Forward*. My experience with that was harrowing. Arthur Freed was the producer, and Fred was a favorite of Arthur Freed—he had done *For Me and My Gal*. Fred was a character. A dear man, but he was not . . . steady. He always had something else to do while he was working, another project, sometimes a secret project. We worked for a week on *Best Foot Forward*, and then Fred had to go home to Bucks County. So I went on alone.

I found it difficult to work with Freed. He, really, was more interested in the musical numbers than the book, and he never seemed concerned about listening to the scenes as they were being written. Sometimes he'd ask you to leave what you'd written, and he'd read it and send it back and say, "Good, keep going."

I was due to go on vacation for twelve weeks in January of '43. I had a play opening in New York, *Sweet Charity*, which I had written with another fellow. The play turned out to be a failure, but I was excited about doing my first Broadway show and I had planned to go east with my wife and our baby daughter. I was all packed to leave a couple days later, after I turned in what I thought was the final shooting script. And Freed called and said, "This is the worst shit I ever read." He'd been okaying it right along, but he had never really read any of it before. I said, "Really?" He said, "Yes." I said, "Well, I don't agree with you." And he said, "I'm not asking you to agree," and he got very rough. I said, "Then you better get somebody else." He said, "No, you're going to do it over." I told him, "No, I'm going to New York." He said, "No, you're not." I got scared. I was not a fighter and he was a great power at the studio. He was Mayer's best friend. I said, "I don't know how we can settle this. I'm supposed to go to New York." And Freed said, "I'll prove how lousy it is. You're going to read it to Sam Katz."

Now, Sam Katz was the head of what was called the "unit." They had so many producers and directors that they divided them up like an army, into brigades. Sam Katz was in charge of one. He used to own theatres, Katz and Balaban. I had found him an admirable man. I knew him slightly, but I had never worked in his unit before.

I had the worst night of my life in anticipation of going up to Katz's home in Bel Air, on a Saturday morning, with Freed present, and reading this script—a script that Freed had condemned as "shit." It looked like I was going to have a serious confrontation about my so-called career, because I knew that they couldn't stop production of the play in New York. I was terrified.

I sat on the lawn at Katz's home and I read the script from line one. Katz and Freed are sitting there, and Katz started to chuckle. Every once in a while Katz would say, "I love it." And Freed starts saying, "Didn't I tell you it was great, Sam?" So help me God. It was one of the most disgusting exhibitions I had ever seen. Katz liked it and that was enough for Freed to switch sides. He wasn't going to tell him, "You're wrong, Sam." I got through the script, and at the end Katz said, "Arthur, start to shoot this." And they did.

And I went to New York and had my flop play.

Did Freed try to explain his behavior to you after you left Katz?

He went on like nothing happened. He wore armor, armor. Now this is not to say that he didn't have certain talents, he must have—he was connected with some fine movies. But my experiences with him were strange.

Best Foot Forward was a hit—the Broadway show was good, but the picture naturally was better because it had more to it. Now, Finkelhoffe had worked on it with me for one week, but when the credits were announced as recommended by the producer, it said "Screenplay by Brecher and Finklehoffe." I expected when Finklehoffe saw this he would say, "I'm not entitled to this." But he didn't. My instinct, my ego, indicated that I ought to say, "For Christ's sake, he didn't do anything on it." But we were friends. I didn't do anything.

And like somebody who returns to the scene of the crime, along came a picture called *Meet Me in St. Louis*. And Finklehoffe and I were assigned to it.

There had been about five scripts for *Meet Me in St. Louis* by different writers at Metro. None of them was judged right. Freed asked Finklehoffe to try it, and he said, "I will if you put Brecher on it." Freed could do without me, but he agreed to put me on it. I didn't want to go, but I went.

Fred was working on a show with Paul Small, the brother-in-law of Dore Schary. They had a vaudeville show going up in San Francisco, and Fred was there most of the time. We worked for six weeks at my home in Bel Air but most of the time he was in San Francisco. And Freed would call my house once in a while and ask for Fred—because he adored Fred and he didn't like talking to me—and I had to tell him Fred just left, went out for cigarettes or something. He'd say to have him call. So I'd call Fred in San Francisco and tell him, "Freed wants to talk to you." And he'd call. It was a pain in the ass, but I didn't mind. Fred worked for six weeks, and when Freed read the script, he said, "It's the worst. It makes no sense." And Fred went away again.

I worked for seven months on it. They were not really interested in this picture. I never would hear from Freed, and I would just write and expect to be taken off it one day. I didn't think they would even make it.

Here's what made them put the picture into production. In 1944 we were in the war. There were no Technicolor cameras available. Metro had a commitment to Technicolor for a camera and had nothing to shoot that lent itself to color. They finally concluded that the only thing that might work was this *Meet Me in St. Louis* crap. They assigned a friend of mine, Vincent Minnelli, to direct. Freed called me in and said, "Minnelli's going to have to shoot this thing. You better be ready in a month." I said, all right. I was dispirited about the whole thing. But Minnelli and I worked together. I would read scenes to Vincent, and he would challenge me, and I would make them better. And he made certain suggestions. I would say he made a definite contribution.

Anyway, we worked together, and finished it, and now it comes time to plan to shoot. Judy Garland didn't want to do it, turned it down. She was having an affair with a director at the time. . . .

Joseph Mankiewicz?

I am not mentioning any names—and he advised her not to do the picture. For the first time, I was called up to L.B. Mayer's office. I liked him and he was very nice to me. He also thought I looked like Thalberg. And he said, "Arthur . . . ", meaning Freed, "thought I should talk to you. I understand you *read* very well." I said, "I read better than I write." He didn't laugh. He said, "It would be a nice thing if you would read the script to Judy Garland. Read the script and convince her that her part is good. We need to make the picture. We have nothing to shoot and we have this camera." I said, "I would be glad to do it, Mr. Mayer. I hope it does some good." I was led into a room with Judy. She had been to our home a few times at parties, and my wife and I loved her. She was very sweet. They left us alone now, and she was very tense. She said, "I don't know why they're doing this. I really think it's wrong for me." I said, "Judy, I know there's a little girl in the picture, Margaret O'Brien. I know she's got some good scenes. But your scenes carry the story. Let me show you what I mean." And I started to read to her. And when it was over she was saying, "Maybe you're right." And I suppose, after that softening up, they leaned on her, and she made the picture. You know the result.

Once again I had the same fucking thing with Finklehoffe. Freed did it. The credits came down "Brecher and Finklehoffe." I went to Minnelli for advice. He said, "I think the only honest thing to do is to go to Finklehoffe and tell him he's not entitled to a credit, and fight it out." So I called Finklehoffe in Bucks County, and he says he's glad to hear from me. His wife is sick; he's having lots of problems. I didn't have the heart to say it. So I let it go again.

When Finklehoffe learned the credits were both of us, he sent me a fancy cigarette holder from Cartier and a note—he used to call me Ivan—"I love you dear Ivan, your coat is so warm." Signed with three F's. The picture had a sneak preview. All along the studio executives had sniffed at this project. "There's no story," they always said. The sneak preview was phenomenal. They came out on the street, Eddie Mannix and Bennie Thau, amazed at the audience's reaction. They were very nice about it. I was happy about it, and, of course, Freed was taking bows and it raised his proceeds 100 percent. The next day I went into the hospital for a hernia operation. When I picked up the trade papers a day later, there's a full page ad: *Meet Me in St. Louis,* screenplay by Fred F. Finklehoffe." Just him now, no collaboration. I couldn't believe it. When I got back to the studio, there was a chorus of protests from friendly writers, guys saying, "What kind of shit is this?" But, that was him. I never got over that one.

The songs for *Meet Me in St. Louis* were written after you had done the script, right? Would you indicate where you thought a musical number should be?

Yes. For instance, in the script I had a scene where they're all going to see the fairgrounds, and they're going out on the trolley. Esther is looking for the boy next door, having a yen for him. And I wrote in the script, "at this point it would be a good idea to have a mass number on the trolley." And Martin and Blane wrote "The Trolley Song." Jesus, what a song.

After the great success of Meet Me in St. Louis, did your relationship with Freed improve?

Yes, after *Meet Me in St. Louis* Freed began to smile at me because it won all sorts of acclaim. He assigned me to do a screenplay with a man whose work I admired, Ludwig Bemelmans. Freed had bought his story, *Yolanda and the Thief,* and Bemelmans came out and became a center of attention in the Freed unit. He was a charming Austrian, a great raconteur, and had written and illustrated some lovely books. He was a wonderful artist, and I've got a lot of his drawings here. There was something about his art—he couldn't draw an egg that wasn't funny. He painted my whole office with murals, telling the story of *Yolanda and the Thief.* The only thing I hated about leaving Metro was having to leave that office.

Anyway, I'm assigned to do the screenplay with him. And he's charming, and we talked and talked and we dined together, and all we talked about was restaurants and things like that. We got along very well, and he liked my humor, and so on. And nothing is happening. The story was nothing. I didn't like it. But Freed wanted to make it . . . and to star Lucille Bremer, who had been in *Meet Me in St. Louis,* and, if she was not having an affair with Arthur Freed, was at least being coveted by Freed. In any case, I didn't want to work on *Yolanda.* Nothing was happening with it, and I didn't think there was a picture in it that I could do that would be worth anything. And then Bemelmans goes away, leaving it just Freed and me. Minnelli is supposed to direct, but he's busy shooting *Ziegfeld Follies*—to which I had made some contributions—and he can't be involved in *Yolanda* at this point.

I go in and tell Freed. He says, "You're gonna work on it. It's gonna be great." He builds up my ego, telling me how great I am. And I still say I don't want to work on it. He calls Sam Katz on the intercom and says, "You're going to have to talk to Brecher. I can't handle this guy any more. He says he doesn't want to do the assignment." Then he says, "Katz wants to see you."

Now at this time I had a little more confidence in myself. I'd saved some money. I had a big hit radio show, *The Life of Riley,* which was in the top ten. I was the only one Metro let do anything on the outside, because Mayer and Eddie Mannix liked me, and they made me promise not to take a writing credit. So I was feeling pretty good. I had "fuck you" money.

I go to Katz and tell him, "Sam, I don't want to work on this shit." He says, "Kid, close the door." He says, "You know, we made a lot of money with Arthur. We owe him something. This one is for Arthur." I said, "You're going to make a lousy picture and give him a present?" He says, "Yeah." He said, "He likes this girl. What can you do? You know, *this* (tugging his crotch) is stronger than anything." I said, "But why should I get cursed with this?" He said, "Let me put it another way. What's your salary?" I said I had a contract for so many months, $1250 a week. He says, "What did you say?" I said, "$1250." He says, "What did you say?" I said, "$1250." He said, "Did you say, $2000? Four firm years at $2000, with twelve weeks off with pay?" And that's what happened, and I went back to work.

I do *Yolanda* as fast as I can and turn it in. And they play with it, Minnelli and the rest, and they do the best they can. But the girl never had it. She just never had it. She was a pretty girl, but she did not exude anything. The film had a couple of good songs in it, which Freed wrote. He was a good songwriter, I have to give him credit for that. But *Yolanda* turned out,

Mary Astor, Lucille Bremer, and Judy Garland in *Meet Me in St. Louis* (1944).

as expected, not a profitable picture. Oddly, now it's become something of a cult picture, and many people think highly of it for some reason.

Summer Holiday was your final film for Freed, and for MGM?

Yes, that marked the end of my relationship with MGM. And it was the low point for me in terms of this particular battle.

Freed brought in a great, talented director named Rouben Mamoulian. He said, "We're going to do *Ah, Wilderness* as a musical." I said, "That sounds very good." And he said, "You work with Rouben. I don't want to hear about it. I trust you guys." Words to that effect.

So I started to work with Rouben Mamoulian, whom I liked very much. A decent man and a very fine mind. I was writing what Mamoulian wanted to direct, but I wasn't compromising myself; I was doing things that I liked. But if he didn't like it, I would change it. Some of the concepts were a little too surrealistic, but they were right, I think, as the numbers emerged.

One day Mamoulian says, "I think you ought to turn some of this stuff in to Freed now; let him know where we're going." Which I did. And Freed calls me in and says, "I read this *shit*. I don't believe this. What kind of . . . ?" I said, "This is what Mamoulian and I agree on." He said, "Mamoulian and you? Who the hell is Mamoulian?" Freed had apparently become aware that he had employed a man whose name was bigger than his. At any rate, he started to scream at me for daring to think of Mamoulian as the leader in this production. And he finally said, "Get out of here, you sheenie bastard!"

I went outside. I can't tell you how I felt: here's a Jew calling another Jew something like that. I went down to a friend of mine who was the head of a unit, L.K. Sidney. Now at that time the studio was going through some serious changes. Nick Schenck in New York was out after Mayer's head. There were great divisions of loyalty, people in factions. I went to L.K. Sidney and told him what happened. He had a tremendous temper, and when things like this happened he got red with anger. And Benny Thau, who was Mayer's right-hand man, said, "Would you mind telling this story to L.B. Mayer?" I gathered by now that they were eager to put a zinger into Freed. I said, "Well, I won't enjoy it, but I'll do it." And I had a check in my pocket for $18,000 for a retroactive increase in salary from a deal Sam Katz worked out. "By the way," I said, "I'd like you to take this back because I'm leaving the studio." Thau said, "Put it back in your pocket; I don't want to hear about it."

We went up to L.B. Mayer. Mayer said, "What's wrong, son?" I had tremendous trepidation telling Mayer the story. Freed was a notorious sycophant to Mayer, and they were very close. They used to joke at the studio, "If you want to shave Freed, you've got to lather L.B. Mayer's ass." Freed had enough talent *not* to be a sycophant, but he was.

When I finished the story, Mayer said, "That son of a bitch." He pressed a button on his desk and says, "Arthur, come up here." Freed says, "Yes, Chief!" That's the way he'd respond: "Yes, Chief!" When he walked in he did a take, seeing me there with Thau and Eddie Mannix, the honchos. Mayer said, " I heard about this 'sheenie bastard' business. Is that what you said to him?" "Well . . . what the hell did? . . ." "*Did you say that?*" He didn't answer. It was perfect. Mayer said, "Are you going to apologize to him?" And this *king* had to apologize. And the other guys were showing such joy watching all this. Freed says, "I'm sorry, I lost my head, that's all." Mayer says, "Okay." And Freed ran out.

Eddie Mannix said, "What are you gonna do? That's the way it is." And Mayer said, "It's pretty bad, isn't it?" Mannix and Thau went out, but Mayer asked me to stay. He said to me,

"I understand you want to leave." I said, "Yes." He said, "You know, this is still a great studio." I said, "I can't come here any more. You've been wonderful to me, but I don't want to be any place where I have to see this guy." Mayer said, "Well, promise me if you make another deal someplace else at least you'll talk to me and tell me what it is, and maybe I can persuade you by matching it." He was wonderful. I said, "I promise, L.B." And he put his arm around me and walked me to the door. It was a long walk. And then he said to me, "You know, I wish I were going with you." It was like he knew something was going to happen. And a few weeks later they zinged him.* He was out and Dore Schary was in. Dore Schary had fucked him—and he had brought Schary in. At any rate, that was 1947 and I left the studio.

You had been doing the radio series you created, *The Life of Riley,* all this time? You wrote as well as produced it?

I was producing it, and writing without credit—Metro had asked me not to take writing credit because they wouldn't have been able to live with the other writers at the studio. I would write movies during the day, and at night or on Saturday or Sunday I would work with the other radio writers on story lines. They would do a draft and I would generally do a rewrite—because a writer finds it very difficult to accept anyone else's writing. But I did appreciate that they were good writers and had a lot of good material.

In '48 my agent made a phenomenal deal for me to produce, write, and direct a film of *Riley,* and it was very successful. The picture came out in '49, and—at forty cents a ticket, not $5.50 like today—it made about $2 million. That gave me a lot of security.

Pabst Blue Ribbon was my sponsor on radio, and in '49 they said they wanted to go on television with *The Life of Riley.* Live, from New York. I said I didn't want to do that. And they said, if you don't want to do it, we'll have to cancel the radio show. I was making a lot of money on the radio show, so I agreed to do the television version. But William Bendix, who played Riley, wasn't available. They said they didn't care, get anybody. I didn't realize at the time that they were just filling the time slot so they would have it for Madison Square Garden boxing the next fall.

So we made a ridiculous deal for me to do the radio show from Los Angeles and the television show from New York. I went to New York and found this guy named Jackie Gleason. My agent says, "Don't touch this guy, he's unreliable." But in desperation we took Gleason. It got closer to the time of shooting and I realized I couldn't live this way, shuttling back and forth on airplanes all week. I was sure the planes would crash. NBC was going to carry the show, and I went to a friend there and told him I wanted to put the show on film. He said it was against their policy, that they couldn't afford it, and if we put it on film we didn't need *them.* But on the basis of my personal plea they said, you could put it on film but *you* have to pay the difference. Now, do you know what a half-hour program costs today? Maybe $400,000. The price Pabst was giving me for the production was $8,200. That's what a prop man gets today. To put *Riley* on film cost me $2,000 a show. We shot it in a little store on Melrose Avenue. I made twenty-six of them, and it won the Emmy. The day it won the Emmy it was canceled.

Later, I licensed the show to NBC, and they produced the big series with Bendix.

In '52 I wrote and directed *Somebody Loves Me,* the story of Blossom Seeley, with Betty Hutton. For a time I fooled around with a play that never went on, and in '58 the head of Universal

*Mayer was ousted in 1951.

called me in to do the script for *Cry for Happy,* a funny picture. A couple of years later, Fred Kohlmar, a wonderful guy who has since passed away, asked me if I would do *Bye Bye Birdie.* They had a script by the guy who wrote the play, Mike Stewart, but they didn't want to film it. I said I would do it on the condition that they would let me direct, and that was fine with them. We made a deal, and after I finished the script they came and said the studio wants George Sidney to direct. They had advanced Sidney a lot of money and he owed them a picture, and he was going to do it for nothing.

What were some of the changes you made from the stage version of *Birdie?*

In the play, the Dick Van Dyke character was an English professor. I couldn't get him to do anything in the picture. And then I decided to make him a chemistry professor who invented a thing called "Speedup." That led to the whole ending with the Russians rushing around on the stage. I always thought in terms of big laughs. And I got Ed Sullivan to work in the picture. Fred Kohlmar asked me to woo Sullivan, and Sullivan was terrified, but I convinced him. He was an old friend. I told him it would be a cinch, and his presence in the film helped so much.

And then, in the play, there was no actual song, "Bye Bye Birdie." I said to Strouse and Adams, the composers, "Why don't we have the title as a song right at the very beginning?" And they wrote a good song.

Were there any projects you worked on that didn't end up getting made?

Yes, and there's a story. It was announced that Bill Goetz is buying *Guys and Dolls* for the screen and he wants me to do the screenplay. It happens that they never got the rights; Goldwyn got them. But before that, my agent, Abe Lastvogel, went to see Harry Cohn, the head of Columbia, about making a deal. Cohn says, "Brecher, do I know him?" And Lastvogel says, "Yes, he was in here after *The Jolson Story* and you wanted him to write and produce a sequel. And he didn't want to do it." And it was true. I had said to Cohn, "I'm flattered, but I can't do a picture as good as the first one, so please. . . ." And that was the end of it. He was a brusque guy.

Lastvogel explains this, and Cohn says, "Yeah? Well . . . there's something funny about that guy. You better go down and talk to Ben Kahane." Ben Kahane was their right-hand man on business affairs. He was a friend of mine, I thought, had come to my home for dinner and I went to his. So Lastvogel goes to Ben Kahane and says, "Cohn wants to know what's *funny* about Irv Brecher?" Kahane opens a drawer and pulls out a dossier, hands it to Lastvogel. It's from Red Channels and it says, "Irving Brecher . . . Loyalty questionable."

Now Lastvogel tells me this and I'm shocked. I said, "What the hell are they talking about?" And he shows me a copy of a page listing my "affiliations"—the Hollywood Democratic Committee, Bundles for Russia, and so on. It was submitted by Sol Lesser and Jack Tenney.

I said, "The only thing I know about Sol Lesser is he wanted me to do a 3-D picture for him, and I said, 'Maybe I'll do it,' and a week later we called it off." Lastvogel explained to me that Lesser, playing the Hollywood game with the witch hunters, had submitted my name through channels, to get a clearance. And it came back that I was "hot." And Kahane never told me and Lesser never told me.

I was absolutely sick. I wanted to kill these guys. I said, "Abe, for two years my phone hasn't rung. I've been working on a play and I've had the money from licensing the TV show, so I didn't need anything. But nobody ever called me." He said, "Well, this must be the reason."

You were blacklisted for two years and didn't even know it?

I said, "What do I do now?" Abe said, "I know you're going to get mad, but you'll have to write a letter to Ward Bond and Roy Brewer."

Ward Bond, that prick, and Roy Brewer of the Carpenters' Union. You had to write them a letter explaining your past associations. They would either clear you or condemn you to death. And I wrote a letter—the worst job I ever did. I didn't have to mention any names, but what names could I mention? I had sent twenty-five or fifty dollars to a charity. And I was somewhat facetious in spots—I wrote, "I joined this group because Mrs. Roosevelt joined, and I think she can't get a job either." It must have gone over their heads. The day after the letter was delivered, I was off the list. That's Hollywood.

Opposite page: James Cagney makes a sale in *The Public Enemy* (1931).

4 · JOHN BRIGHT

John Bright at
seventy-seven.

© Robert Landau 1986

I ain't so tough," says a bullet-riddled James Cagney, stumbling into the gutter in the 1931 screen sensation *The Public Enemy*. It is a statement nobody would ever apply to John Bright, the co-author of that and thirty or so other scripts from Hollywood's heyday. Bright didn't just write hard-boiled, he lived it. A flamboyant iconoclast, rebel, brawler, self-described "uncompromising radical," Bright challenged the big studio bosses not once, but over and over. His life, like those of the Chicago gangsters he once knew and wrote about, is the stuff of which movies are made: violent, glamorous, filled with a cast of characters including mobsters and movie stars, con men and communists, squealers and martyrs.

It was late 1929 when Kubec Glasmon and twenty-one-year-old John Bright breezed into Hollywood, a Chicago druggist (and bootlegger) and his literary protégé down to their last dollar but determined to cram their store of gangland knowledge into the "definitive" novel on the subject. Warner Bros. and Darryl Zanuck, looking for a follow-up to the studio's ground-breaking crime stories, *Doorway to Hell* and *Little Caesar*, had other plans for the manuscript titled *Beer and Blood*. It transferred to the screen as *The Public Enemy*, and the writing team of Glasmon and Bright went under long-term contract, creating Cagney's next four pictures, each one a racy, slangy, freewheeling hit.

Following a breakup with Glasmon, Bright took on Mae West's first starring vehicle, *She Done Him Wrong*, contributed a memorable episode to Paramount's *If I Had a Million,* and put Bogart behind bars in *San Quentin.* But factors other than creative would derail his later career again and again. In February 1933, Bright and nine other screenwriters created what would become the Screen Writers Guild. It was the beginning of a long series of battles with the moguls, the producers, and the right wing of his own profession. Along the way, Bright joined the Communist party, becoming one of the most principled and adventurous activists in Hollywood. The in-fighting would culminate in Bright's blacklisting and a long exile from the studios and from America. The writers' union, which he had helped to form and make strong, looked on and did nothing.

John Bright in 1985—seventy-seven years old and weakened from recent illness—lives in a small apartment in West Hollywood he shares with a young woman and a likable if scraggly dog. Inside it is cluttered, books and magazines all about, volumes on politics, cinema, psychology, and combinations thereof. On the wall is a yellowing poster for *Brooklyn USA,* his play produced on Broadway in 1941, the opening coinciding unfortunately (for the box office) with the attack on Pearl Harbor. There is a photo of Bright and Dalton Trumbo, inscribed by the latter, *"For John, who started it all."*

If he is bitter about the setbacks and adversaries of the past, he doesn't let it show. He has a hard shell; it isn't likely to crack at this late date. However deeply held his political ideals, Bright is a realist at heart. He reminisces, remembering encounters with foolish or horrid behavior, with a wry expression, a quiet, cynical laugh, as if to say, *"What do you expect?"* He has known the Hollywood circus at its best and worst, known the clowns, the ringmasters, the few brave lions.

As we talk, Bright chain-smokes, crushing the butts into a black enamel ashtray. Printed around the rim are the words, VOTE FOR BIG BILL THOMPSON. It's an authentic souvenir from Bright's past and youth in the violent Chicago of the Roaring Twenties. Thompson was the town's notorious mayor and the subject of Bright's first published work.

Yeah, I wrote his biography. In shameless imitation of Mencken.

Did you know him?

Yeah. Although I wrote an unauthorized biography. He sued me, but he dropped the suit.

He was in the pocket of the gansters.

He had a finger in all kinds of corruption. (Laughs.) I was only nineteen when I wrote the book. It was the first thing I wrote.

How did it do?

It sold well in England, not too much in the United States.

The English loved reading about our corrupt politicians?

Yeah. They were astonished at his demagoguery. He'd once threatened to punch King George in the snoot . . . to get votes from the Irish and the Germans.

You worked on a Chicago paper as a kid?

That's right. *The Daily News.*

One of Ben Hecht's papers.

I was Hecht's office boy. He was the star reporter on the *Daily News*. A middle-aged man of twenty-eight when I was a kid of thirteen. We became good friends afterwards, here in Hollywood.

When did you meet Kubec Glasmon?

I was his soda jerk. I became a writer at his behest. He was, at best, semiliterate. But to me he was a sophisticated man. I was a kid of sixteen, seventeen, working at his drugstore.

That's where you got to know some of the Chicago mobsters?

His drugstore was a hangout for gangsters.

He was a bootlegger, wasn't he?

Yes. I delivered the booze for him.

He was able to get liquor legally, as a pharmacist.

Yeah. It worked as follows. He would use prescription whiskey, which he got legally. Then he cut it five or six ways, diluting it. He rebottled it and sold that to the gangsters. I peddled the bottles around, to clubs and places.

You met Al Capone, among others.

I met Capone. He was the underworld mogul in Chicago. I saw a good deal of him then. He owned several nightclubs in Chicago. His story was a fascinating one. I should have written it. I had a fascination with underworld characters at that time. It was during Prohibition, and he was a glamorous figure. Always had a lot of people, bodyguards, around him constantly.

I was present at a particularly dramatic incident in which he ordered the death of two Sicilians who were getting too big for their britches. They were illiterate Mafiosi. At the Commonwealth Hotel, Capone ordered them assassinated. And they were beaten to death with baseball bats. Caved in their skulls. I was present at that time.

You saw it happen?

Mm-hm. I confess to being a little shocked.

I take it Capone wasn't worried about witnesses being present?

No, not at all. It was at a banquet. It was the waiters whom he hired to do the job. It was in the middle of a speech, accolades to him. He gave the signal, and the job was done. Seems . . . unreal to me now.

You say Glasmon encouraged you to be a writer.

He subsidized me for the Thompson book.

Warner Bros. writers Robert Lord, John Bright, Wilson Mizner, and Kubec Glasmon, 1931.

Was the book his idea?

It was my idea, done with his encouragement.

How long did it take to write the book?

I worked about six months on it. Then took it to New York. Glasmon went with me—after what they called a "Jewish bankruptcy" fire at his drugstore.

He set fire to it for the insurance money?

Yeah. He hired a couple of pros to do it and he picked up the insurance. We took the book to New York to find a publisher, and Cape and Smith published it. And that was the beginning of my literary career. We came out to California then to write the definitive novel about the underworld.

I heard you left New York chasing some woman.

Yeah, I was chasing a girl. I subsequently made the mistake of marrying her.

Why was she going to California?

To get away from me. But I followed her out to California. Glasmon and I took a slow boat, through the Canal. And we spent all the money from the Thompson book. The total advance. (Laughs.)

You spent it in the ports along the way?

We had several ports of call. Panama . . . saloons with hookers . . . and . . . I arrived in California with twenty-nine cents on the 29th of October, 1929.

It was fated, huh?

(Laughing) Yes.

Had you been thinking of writing for the movies?

I had no intention at all of going into movies. I was just chasing this girl. And we got married at the Wee Kirk o' the Heather, at Forest Lawn. We got married in a graveyard. Symbolic of the marriage.

The two of you and Glasmon rented a house in L.A.?

We rented a small house and went to work on the underworld book. We were running out of money and hocking everything when we were called on by some criminals we knew from Chicago.

They had a racket. They sold a lot of worthless property. They made a profit out of just the down payments. They collected $50,000 in down payments, which was a lot of money in those days. It was very colorful circumstances. They would look for suckers and their whole gimmick was getting a down payment for this worthless land on top of a mountain.

What did they want from you?

A "mooch cabin."

The mooch was the sucker?

Yeah. They wanted the little place we had as a residence, as a front for them. They'd bring the customers into the house and give them the pitch. They paid us six month's rent, which enabled us to get by and for me to finish the underworld book . . . and they paid for a lot of booze and groceries and so on. The bunko squad came by, but they couldn't prove anything. (Laughs.)

You were writing the novel *Beer and Blood*, which eventually became *The Public Enemy*. Was Glasmon involved in the writing of the book?

He was sort of a critic on the book . . . I couldn't have written it without him.

You planned on getting it published in New York, but what happened? The Warners bought it first?

I had a deal for a second book with Cape and Smith. At that time there was very severe censorship, and we were quarreling with the publisher. They wanted the book edited severely. We had tried to make the book accurate, and the dialogue was pretty much the way I heard it in Chicago. The publisher refused the book unless it was edited. They wanted to hire Morris Ernst as the editor, and I wouldn't tolerate it.

Morris Ernst was a celebrated lawyer at the time?

Civil liberties attorney. They wanted him to rewrite it. Glasmon agreed. I refused. I wasn't going to have any lawyer redo my dialogue. And while we were quarreling about it, we sold the book to Warner Bros.

Who did you deal with at the studio in the beginning?

It was largely the work of Rufus LeMaire, who at that time was dickering for a big job and wanted to produce the picture. Darryl Zanuck took it away from him and made him casting director and produced the thing himself, which made Zanuck into a celebrity.

I know you didn't get along with him later. What was your initial impression of Zanuck?

He was a tin-pot Mussolini. But he was a very talented person, as evidenced by his rise to fame and glory. I worked with him for three years before I tried to throw him out of a window.

What did they give you for the rights to *Beer and Blood*?

They gave me $2,000. The money was then seized by the Bank of Hollywood when the bank failed. I got ten cents on the dollar about ten years later.

So you lost what they paid you for the book. The two of you were put under contract?

Yeah, for $100 a week.

And you began working on a script for *Beer and Blood* or *The Public Enemy* after the title change?

Yeah.

Your original story had a much broader canvas than the film that was made, didn't it?

It included every aspect of the Chicago underworld, Italians, Irish, Jewish, Polish, with each group's particular methods and interests specified. Zanuck wanted to cut this down to one story. At our first meeting with him we determined which story to use. He thought that the Tom Powers story was the most commercial and easiest to adapt.

What happened to the novel? *Beer and Blood* **was never published, was it?**

Warner Bros. bought the publishing rights as part of the deal. I thought they were going to find a big publisher for it. Instead, they published a book called *The Public Enemy* as a movie tie-in by Grosset and Dunlap. It was a swindle, a hack job knocked off in a hurry. It had nothing to do with my book. And I lost the right to my manuscript. They own it. Still do.

Your dialogue in *Public Enemy* **and the subsequent films got a lot of comment. What was your approach to writing tough dialogue?**

It was street talk. Within the boundaries of censorship.

Minus the obscenities, in other words?

Yeah. The way it differed from phony. . . . The key to underworld dialogue was understatement. You didn't spell out your meaning.

When did you first notice Cagney?

Well, I met Jimmy when we started working. He was a nobody, making $100 a week. He became a star as a result of the picture. Cagney was not supposed to be the lead.

He had been cast as the friend of the main character, right?

Yes. We thought Cagney should have the lead. Eddie Woods had the lead and he wouldn't have been right for the part. It demanded an extrovert actor. The director, William Wellman, convinced Zanuck to switch the actors, to give Cagney the lead. The picture was rewritten to accommodate him.

Was the Tom Powers character based on a real person?

Uh, yes. An Irish hoodlum of our acquaintance.

Were you happy with the way the film turned out?

I didn't think it was a great picture. But it was regarded as . . . pioneering. On the whole I was happy with it, considering censorship.

There were whole scenes the censors made you change.

Yeah.

Your original ending was different, I believe.

Yes. They reformed the brother for the movie. Originally he went bad as a result of what happened to Cagney. We indicated that the brother was going to take his revenge.

On the guys who killed Cagney?

Yeah.

Edward G. Robinson and James Cagney in *Smart Money* (1931).

Mae Clarke and James Cagney

And they shot it, but it was cut. Do you know why?

They had to have a moral ending in those days.

Were you on the set for the grapefruit scene?

The grapefruit scene was the last scene shot in the picture. The picture was shot out of continuity. And Mae Clarke, the actress playing the part, had a cold and her nose was sore. After reading the scene, she arranged with Cagney to fake it. Wellman overheard this conversation and said to Cagney, "Look, kid, this is your big chance. This scene is going to be talked about in a talked-about picture. And I think you should really give it to her." So the scene was not faked. As a matter of fact, Cagney added an aspect to the scene. He *twisted* it when it hit her, and the grapefruit cut her face. She was furious at this. The moment the scene was over, she called Cagney a double-crossing so-and-so, and the same for Jack Warner, and us. Then she stormed out of the studio. All hope for a retake was gone. She had a rich husband and didn't need money. And so we waited for the development of the film with prayer and with hope because a retake was impossible. But it turned out all right.

The grapefruit scene is the most famous in the picture, and everybody seems to have taken credit for thinking it up. What's the real story?

The real story is that it was in the book. It was based on something that had really happened. It was an incident that involved a character by the name of Hymie Weiss. He got mad at his girlfriend and shoved a grapefruit in her face. The scene made history, film history. Zanuck took credit for it, Wellman took credit for it. All of which was denied by the widow of Harvey Thew—he was assisting us with the screenplay.

What was Harvey Thew's contribution to the script?

He was an old pro Zanuck gave us to help with the technical aspects of a screenplay.

He did little of the actual writing on it?

He knew nothing about hoodlums.

They put you on your next picture before *Public Enemy* came out?

Yes, *Smart Money,* with Edward G. Robinson.

That was another original story by you and Glasmon?

Yes.

There was some difficulty getting Robinson to do it, wasn't there?

Yes. He was playing prima donna. An original by a couple of unknowns was not to his taste. It was after *Little Caesar*. He was scheduled to do *Five Star Final,* which had been a Broadway hit. Our picture was in between. Hence, Robinson played hard to get. But Zanuck convinced him, with his extraordinary capacity for convincing people. Zanuck was really an extraordinary person in some ways. He gave Robinson a real sales pitch on the picture. When we had a scene at a crap game, he would get on his knees and talk to the dice. An aspect of his salesmanship. To get Robinson, part of what Zanuck sold him on was that he'd design his own clothes for the picture.

Zanuck knew that would appeal to Robinson?

Yes. And then Robinson insisted on an expensive pair of shoes, custom-made. Zanuck granted the request. And in the picture, Robinson was seen only from the waist up.

Star's vanity.

It was just too absurd.

It was a very good script, but poorly directed.

Yes, it was.

That was Alfred E. Green.

He was a hack. I had contempt for Green. It wasn't 'til much later that Zanuck began to respect directors. During his initial reign, he was the boss, his directors were stooges.

And how did he feel about writers?

He had respect for writers.

He fancied himself something of a writer.

He fancied himself a writer and had written a book we all looked at secretly, and gloated at its absurdity. *Habit and Other Stories.*

He wouldn't have liked you looking at it?

No, not at all.

What were the working conditions for writers at the studio? Did you have to maintain certain hours? A specified amount of material per week?

It was the only time clock that existed for writers at the time. We had difficulty maintaining it.

You'd get in late.

Yeah.

The Glasmon-Bright team was a great success, right? The films were all hits. You were often mentioned at length in the reviews.

Everything we did was respected.

Were they still paying you $100 a week?

I went on strike and got raised to $750.

Glasmon too?

Yeah. Although he didn't join me in my strike.

What was management's reaction to your going on strike?

Well, I was officially sick . . . enjoying Palm Springs.

Who would you negotiate with, Zanuck or Warner?

In matters of money it was Warner.

Did he try to talk you out of it?

Yeah. With threats.

But they gave you the money.

Mm.

Your next picture was *Blonde Crazy*.

Yeah. With Cagney and Joan Blondell. That wasn't our title. Our title was *Larceny Lane*, after the famous corridor for gangsters in Chicago, at the Congress Hotel.

In that one Cagney gets slugged a lot by the leading lady, instead of the other way around. Was that an attempt to turn the tables after the noise over the grapefruit scene?

Umm, yeah. Blondell was a trouper.

An underrated actress.

Very much so.

Where did all the scams you have in the picture come from?

Oh, out of life.

How long were these scripts taking you to write, story to finish?

Six weeks.

And they'd begin filming as soon as you finished writing?

Right away. It was a conveyor belt.

Next came *Taxi*, a great film. It was strongly pro-union. Considering the moguls' opinion of unions, did you have any problems there?

Curiously enough, no. That was the first pro-union picture made. And when it was reviewed, Zanuck commented to me, "Did you know about any 'social significance'? I thought it was cops and robbers." (Laughs.)

There's a funny scene when Cagney starts speaking perfect Yiddish. Like the grapefruit scene, it looks improvised. Was it?

Cagney had once told me he spoke Yiddish, that he had swapped Yiddish lessons for tap-dancing lessons with a guy he knew as a kid. I thought it would be funny to use it in the picture—to have Yiddish coming out of this very Irish face. So the scene was indicated for him in the script.

Loretta Young seems a little out of place in *Taxi*.

We wanted Blondell. That was the original beef I had with Zanuck. He wanted to break up the Cagney-Blondell team, and also he was stuck with Loretta Young on a contract and wanted to use her. She was supposed to play a Brooklyn cab driver's wife. And Loretta Young was very much a finishing school lady. I got into a very severe argument with Zanuck about the casting, and I enlisted the support of Kenyon Nicholson, who wrote the original. He was a very celebrated writer at that time and working at Warner Bros. on something else. This got me into trouble with Zanuck. There was shouting. He called me a stool pigeon. So I threatened to throw him out of the window. And that was the end. I survived two or three more pictures, but. . . .

Somewhere I read that you punched him in the nose.

Not quite accurate. I threatened to, but I was overpowered. His secretary, male. He was in the room at the time . . . taking notes. (Laughs.)

Why didn't he fire you then?

My option wasn't due . . . for six months. But it was bad blood between us from that point on.

You worked on *The Crowd Roars* with Howard Hawks. What did you think of him?

A good director. He had his problems with Zanuck on that picture.

You went with Glasmon and Hawks to Indianapolis to get material for the script, didn't you?

This was the first illustration in my life of a classical double-cross. We had gone to Indianapolis for the races and lived with the racing drivers. I listened to their dialogue and decided the whole picture that had been planned was a phony. I lived in a whorehouse with the racing drivers, who were interested only in women and booze and racing, in that order. I was at a twenty-four-hour crap game, and in the middle of this game there was an incident discussed that caused the rewrite of the whole picture. Billy Arnold referred to this pal and what his best friend did to him. I questioned him some more about it, and as a result I saw how to take the picture in an entirely different direction. I called Hawks and told him about it.

Was Hawks staying with you at the whorehouse?

No, he was staying at the home of Fred Duesenberg. Because he was a fake Englishman.

Hawks was? He thought he was an aristocrat?

Yes. And what happened was, I called him up at three o'clock in the morning, in great excitement about the necessity to revise the script. He subsequently told Zanuck, who called us and ordered a rewrite. And Zanuck took credit for the incident, for having gotten an "inspiration."

So you tell the idea to Hawks, he tells it to Zanuck, and Zanuck tells it to you as his own idea.

Right. (Laughs.) My first introduction to Hollywood double-cross.

In general, did you get along with Hawks?

He was a distant person.

You did two more pictures then, before your contract was up.

I did *Union Depot*, with Douglas Fairbanks, Jr., and *Three on a Match*. That was my last picture.

And you left Warners because of the feud with Zanuck?

Zanuck told me I'd never work again. And I wound up getting the cream picture of the year, the Mae West picture, *She Done Him Wrong.*

How did you get *She Done Him Wrong*?

My agent, Myron Selznick. He hated Zanuck.

When you left Warners, you and Glasmon called it quits?

Yeah, we went our separate ways.

Why did the team break up?

It had been coming apart. I was a kid when we first started. And I grew up. I began to assert myself as an equal. I had met him when I was seventeen and began to write with him a couple of years later. He was always the senior partner. When I grew up, came into my twenties, there was friction between us as I asserted myself more and more. And then we had political differences. I was a left-winger, he was a conservative. He chose his friends in his own circles and I chose mine.

What was your first impression of Mae West?

Well, Mae West was Mae West. She was convinced that she had written a classic, and I disagreed.

What did you think was wrong with it? As *Diamond Lil* it had been a success on Broadway, hadn't it?

It was successful because of Mae West's astonishing personality, and not because it was a good play. People went to see it because of West's personality. She didn't see that. She thought it was a great work of art and insisted that the picture follow the play. I quarreled with her consistently, all through the picture.

She resented you being put to work on her script?

She didn't resent me at all, at first. Until I told her the artistic quality of her play . . . which she stole from a drunk.

How did she do that?

I was told that by James Timony, her long-time lover and close friend, who got drunk and told me the lowdown on it. She stole the play from a drunk and then became convinced that she had written it.

It must have been difficult trying to write for her.

It was . . . very difficult. I was working on the final scene of the picture when she had me fired.

What reason did she give?

That I was too much trouble. And the studio gave in to her.

How much of *She Done Him Wrong* would you say is your work?

About half. But you had to play a game with her in order to get your own lines into the script. You had to pretend that you were using something you heard her say. As long as you admitted

James Cagney and George E. Stone in *Taxi* (1932).

it was originally her idea, she would go for it. And she always agreed with you that she had said it.

Did you feel she was close to her screen persona in real life?

She was . . . earthy. She fucked everybody. That was the be-all and end-all of any association with her. But she justified it, humorously.

What kind of men did she like?

Mostly black prize fighters . . . and muscle men.

She didn't try to keep those activities secret?

No.

What did the studio think about it?

As long as she didn't hit the papers, why, they didn't care.

What was your contribution to *If I Had a Million?*

That was an interesting assignment. It started with seven different directors and seven different writers. Bud Lighton was overseer of the whole project. We sat around and criticized each other's work. An interesting experience for me. The directors included Lubitsch, who came up with an idea for Dietrich that I voted for, but I was in the minority. It began with Dietrich in a bed, waiting for her husband, who was played by Lubitsch himself, a splendid actor. He came home drunk and went through the motions of undressing, with Chaplinesque comedy. She pretended to be asleep while he made a pass at her and then went to sleep himself and started to snore. She got out of bed and went by his clothes and discovered the million-dollar check. Then her whole manner to him changes and she gets back in bed and says to him, characteristically, "*Dahhling. . . .*" And fade out.

Which episode did you write?

The George Raft.

The check forger who can't cash the real check when he gets it?

Yes, I came up with that one. And I was outvoted for the finish of it. I wanted an ironic finish. I wanted Raft—who couldn't act—frustrated at being unable to cash the check because he was a forger, needing a shave, hungry, and he sees a child who is crying because his toy airplane had been run over by a truck. And Raft says, "You think *you're* in trouble." And he fashions the million-dollar check into an airplane for the child and goes off into the morning light. An ironic ending. They wanted a violent ending, in the flophouse, which was how it was made.

Who directed your episode?

A man by the name of "Lucky" Humberstone.

You were one of the founders of the Screen Writers Guild.

Yes.

Did you already have a strong interest in politics at that time?

I began being interested when I picketed for Sacco and Vanzetti in Chicago. I was an uncompromising radical. Even in those days.

What were the goals when you began organizing a writers' union?

To get fair treatment from the producers.

Things like credit arbitration, royalties, minimum wage?

Yeah.

There was no other creative union at that time, was there?

We were the first.

The producers were against the Guild from the beginning? They were afraid of you.

Yes.

And tried to destroy it with a company union.

The Screen Playwrights. They finally wound up with a majority. But we, the Guild, finally defeated them by invoking the Wagner Act. That's when they capitulated and dissolved the Screen Playwrights. It was rough. They had the backing of MGM, the producers, and we were mavericks on the outside, from the industry point of view. I was at Metro at the time, and we in the Guild had the third floor, and the Screen Playwrights had the second floor, and we didn't speak at all.

I know there were all sorts of charges hurled at the Guild, but was the Screen Playwrights politically motivated or just kowtowing to the bosses?

John Mahin, he was my ancient enemy. He was the president of the Screen Playwrights. I had been a friend of his when he was a nobody and a contract writer at Metro. I had just had my successful strike and gotten my big raise. And I was trying to convince him to do the same, because he was my opposite number in the profession. He got quite drunk and said, in effect, "Thalberg will take care of me." Subsequently that was true.

So his politics weren't really a factor?

No. He became a reactionary later.

Your partnership with Kubec Glasmon had dissolved. What was he doing then? Which side was he on?

He had joined with the Screen Playwrights, at MGM.

So you two were no longer friends?

That's it. But just before the Guild won with the Wagner Act, we were fighting in the courts; and we decided, at a Guild meeting at Phil Dunne's house, that we should try and recruit the borderline cases. And—to everyone's surprise—I said I'd try Glasmon. And I went to see him downstairs, at Metro. He greeted me very cordially and after I explained why I'd come to see him said that he would consider rejoining the Guild. We reminisced about our past together. And then he pointed to the window, and mentioned that the sun was very *uncompromising*.

And he said that I had been one who didn't compromise. That he, as a Jew, had been *raised* to compromise. And he felt that he had been wrong to have compromised in this . . . subservience.

Two weeks later he was dead. A heart attack.

How old was he?

Late thirties.

When did you join the Communist party?

I joined up in 1936 and stayed with it until I went into the service. After which I intended to rejoin but I had my misgivings about the Party and never did rejoin.

What were your misgivings then?

Partly with the Soviet Union. I never became anti-communist in the jingoistic sense, but I had qualifications about the Party and the Soviet Union being a worker's paradise. And any qualificiations in loyalty to the Soviet Union made you *persona non grata*.

What were your reasons for joining when you did?

The usual . . . ideals. And the campaign against Hitler and the Nazis.

How much Party interest was there in influencing people through the scripts the writers wrote?

That was the absolute bullshit line . . . the old wives' tales of Robert Taylor and Adolph Menjou. It was impossible for any writer to have any influence at all in that respect. It was impossible to influence Hollywood movies in that way. The Party was interested in influencing society, people, not production.

But wasn't it a goal of someone like John Howard Lawson to work party ideology into his scripts?

His credits, like *Blockade* for Walter Wanger, may have been anti-Nazi, but they weren't pro-communist particularly.

Lawson seems to have been the most devout of the Hollywood Communists.

He could never admit that he was wrong. Up until the time of his death, he was still a member of the Communist party. He was a very rigid man . . . but a good friend. Personally I got along with Lawson fine.

In the late '30s it became chic for young people to join the Party. Did you feel that a lot of members were dilettantes?

I had a sophisticated hunch that a lot of them weren't really interested. Including Robert Rossen.

A lot of the ones who later informed?

Yes.

But people forget that of the Hollywood Ten, for instance, only three—including Lawson—were members of the Party. All of the others had dropped out for reasons of principle. They didn't like the way the Party was going.

Dalton Trumbo joined the Communist party, resigned, rejoined, and he was not a member of the Party at the time of his death. He was much too bright to swallow the horseshit so rigidly and obsessively.

In the mid-'30s you got another writing partner, Robert Tasker. He's an interesting character. He went to San Quentin for armed robbery, didn't he?

Yes, for five years, seven months. He started writing while in prison. Became the editor of the *San Quentin Bulletin*. He wrote a novel, *Grimhaven*, which he smuggled out of prison to a publisher. We met later, through a mutual friend, and became partners.

He learned how to write scripts from Frances Marion. She kept him . . . at $300 a week. She was his mistress. She liked football player types, and he was a great big guy, bigger than you are.

She wrote the great prison movie, *The Big House*. Was Tasker involved with her then?

He ghost-wrote the Frances Marion screenplay for *The Big House*. Word for word. A condition of his parole had been that he couldn't write any more about prison life. She took the sole credit. It was a very bitter day for him.

Didn't he marry a famous heiress?

He married the girl they called "The Shit Pill Heiress." She had inherited Fletcher's Castoria.

What was the attraction for her—marrying a screenwriter or an ex-convict?

Ex-con. He was exciting to her. She was a horror. They had a stormy time together. They divorced eventually. I think she's still around somewhere.

Tasker got into a lot of brawls?

Well, he wasn't a professional brawler. . . . (Laughs.) But he always took care of himself. We shared a house together while we were between marriages. Our place was a stop-off for guys just out of San Quentin. Tasker liked to help them out.

He knew a lot of shady people.

An amusing incident occurred once . . . as a result of his connections. He got a sure-fire tip on a fixed race at Santa Anita. It was a terrific long shot and so the odds were enormous. The only people who would conceivably bet on the horse were those who knew it was fixed. I gambled all I had, $1200 on the nose, and Tasker bet the same amount. We were all set to move to Europe on our gains.

We went to look at the horses and check on our interests. There was no doubt the fix was in. The fix horse was so goosed up on drugs that he was practically flying. It was such an obvious fix that all the insiders and the bookmakers had gone to bet on the race.

Damon Runyon and Mark Hellinger had the box next to us, and this was the one race they wouldn't show us their tickets on, so we knew they knew it was a fix. Well, the race was run—after several false starts by the drugged horse. It took off, finally, three lengths ahead at the start, looking insane. The other horses were held back by their jockeys anyway, all in on it.

But there was a horse in the race, Black Gold, the favorite, and he was a horse that wasn't raised to lose. And although his jockey, who was in on the fix with the rest of them, tried to reign him in, that horse only knew to win a race. He shot past the fix horse, and he won.

And as soon as he won he was so mad at his jockey that he turned his head around and bit him!

It was a great upset for the underworld. And for us. Runyon and I agreed to toss a coin for who'd get to write the story. He won. He sold the story to Columbia and it became a big hit directed by Frank Capra.*

In 1936 you and Tasker went under contract to B.P. Schulberg, who'd been set up with his own studio, right? He was trying for a comeback?

Adolph Zukor set him up with his own studio, for old time's sake. He had a sweet deal: pictures budgeted at $800,000, access to Paramount talent, all the stars. But he blew it. He was self-destructive, there's no other explanation for it. He was a compulsive gambler and womanizer. He lost $500,000 at one gambling house alone in one year. Sylvia Sidney was his girlfriend and that broke up when Schulberg invited her to come out to him at Malibu, and she walked in on Schulberg in bed with two whores. He did it on purpose. He was a male chauvinist extraordinaire.

He was very old-fashioned in his conception of Hollywood and stories, and he was completely inconsistent and contradictory, but he was a maverick. He hired Tasker and me, Clifford Odets, Bill Saroyan was another, *because* we were radicals. *He* wasn't. But he thought that we were writers with some guts and that's what he wanted.

It was a pretty good writing stable that he had. But it didn't last. It was a mad studio, under his influence. There was a crap game in the lobby, to begin with. All kinds of fucking going on, hookers in and out. It degenerated . . . Hollywood at its most corrupt.

He hired me and Tasker, and our first assignment was to do a script that would be the glorification of Pinkerton, the corporation detective and union buster. We were very upset about that assignment.

He didn't consider your personal sympathies on that one?

He didn't see the contradiction in hiring us for such a script. It was an example of his inconsistencies. But we got out of the Pinkerton assignment. I'll tell you how.

Schulberg called us into his office. The great man was in tears and he was holding a letter, addressed to him. It was from a woman in Madera, California, and written in a tear-jerking manner. She told how she had read in the paper that he was making a movie glorifying Pinkerton. And she said he could not be *serious*.

Pinkerton was a terrible man who had murdered her husband. And "if you made such a movie that would make you a murderer also."

Schulberg finished reading the letter and then he said, "Do you two think that I would knowingly contribute to the death of this woman's husband? Or glorify his murderer? I'll be goddamned if I will! Cancel the picture as of now! And you sons-of-bitches have got to come up with another story."

Well, *I* had written that letter and had my wife's mother in Madera, California, send it in her own handwriting. And that's how we got out of that assignment.

I was with Schulberg for two years. He was a drunk and a gambler and a wonderful guy. He died a few years later, broke, at his son Budd's farm in Bucks County.

You and Tasker wrote the Bogart movie, *San Quentin*?

*Whoever won the toss, Hellinger wrote the story that became *Broadway Bill*.

Yeah, we did that freelance, for Warners. There was a different regime in power.

Can you tell me what happened to Robert Tasker?

The war was coming on, and the draft. Bob looked on military service as a variation on prison and he wasn't going to go back to prison. So he lammed and went to Mexico. He got in trouble down there. Beat up a man, his wife's lover. He happened to be the son of a Mexican police chief. Tasker was framed for blackmail. He was tipped off that he was marked for jail. And Mexican jails are not very pleasant. Rather than go to jail, he killed himself.

He once told me, "I should have killed myself in San Quentin."

It was a prophecy fulfilled.

Yes.

How did he do it?

Seconals and tequila.

After the reformation of the Writers Guild did the feuding cool down?

It cooled down, due to the war.

You went into the service during the war?

The Coast Guard. I wrote propaganda films and other things. It was the equivalent of the Signal Corps. My life in the service was not exactly idyllic. I was always in danger of getting shipped out to Greenland.

Why?

I was a bad boy.

What sort of problems did you have?

I got into trouble by my telling the truth in a Navy film about Barney Ross. He'd been serious-ly wounded and was drug addicted. He was a Jew and insisted on being labeled as a Jew. The Navy cut that out and he was furious. He was on a bond tour at the time.

The Navy didn't want the film to say he was Jewish?

The Navy didn't want to say he was Jewish. And I tricked them, by having him shown with his rabbi. The Navy was so furious about having been tricked that they demoted me.

What other projects did you work on?

The only film that I wrote that I was proud of was a V.D. picture.

My commanding officer had been briefly in Hollywood. He had played Clark Gable's brother in *Gone With The Wind*. And he'd been dropped quickly. So he hated Hollywood and he hated me as someone with some success in Hollywood. So he had it in for me and was always look-ing for assignments that would hang me. One of them was a V.D. picture.

Now V.D. pictures, everywhere they were shown, had no effect at all. None of these films. So I had a doomsday assignment. I ran about twenty of the V.D. pictures in Washington. They were divided into two categories: fright pictures, showing lots of chancres and so on; or the

Gene Tunney, the moral approach. Neither worked. I got real drunk one night while trying to figure out a new angle on V.D. I ran into a warrant officer in a bar. He took a liking to me and told me a story of venereal disease that I hit upon as a way of doing a picture. It had a valid angle in the sense of curbing the spread of the venereal disease. It was based on a true story of a destroyer, a very tight ship where a number of guys got the clap in some port, and, when they went into action, these guys were out of commission and in sick bay. And that became the thesis of the picture, the crime of endangering your mates and your ship by being laid up with that disease. Esprit de corps. And everywhere that the film was shown, V.D. dropped off a little. I became promoted to Chief by virtue of having written the only successful V.D. film of World War II.

What was *We Accuse?*

That was a film I wrote while I was in the service. I wrote it on my own time.

It wasn't done for the Navy?

No, no, no. It was for the Soviet Union. It was Soviet footage and captured German footage. An anti-Nazi theme. It detailed Nazi war crimes. It was a good picture. But I took a big draw, in retrospect, writing for that, with my name on it.

It was used against you in the witch hunt years?

Yes.

You went back to Hollywood when you got out of the service? Did you sense that it had become more reactionary?

It was. And still is.

Did you have trouble getting work?

No. I was working for Arthur Freed, writing a script for Lucille Bremer. Freed was pleased with the way it was going. The CSU went on strike and I supported it, refused to cross the picket lines. The bosses didn't like that. They wouldn't let anyone work at home. They were making a point. Freed tried to convince me, but I wouldn't cross the picket line. So Metro fired me.

Your last credit before you left Hollywood was *The Brave Bulls,* directed by Robert Rossen. Were you a bullfight aficionado?

I had lived in Mexico at one time and I knew quite a lot about bullfighting. It was fairly accurate. Based on a novel by Tom Lea.

Rossen contributed to the script, but he gave me a solo credit. We were friends for some time . . . until he became an informer.

When did you realize that the blacklist was coming, and that you would be on it?

People testifying to the committees mentioned my name. Very frequently. And I knew it was inevitable that there would be a mass blacklist. I was writing a picture called *Dynamite* for Alan Ladd, and the producer was very friendly with me. He liked my work very much. This was 1949, and I knew that all the signs were in the close offing. This producer offered me a chance to recant. I played dumb and prepared to leave for Mexico.

Did some of the people who were subsequently blacklisted feel that it was all going to blow over soon, that it wouldn't go any farther?

Yes, consistently. The boom didn't drop on a mass basis until later, when I was in Mexico.

Since the studios had been working with all these people for so many years, it seems unlikely that they would have cared about any of this, had it not been for the politicians.

They didn't care. They capitulated. They chickened out. Dore Schary had promised that nothing would happen. A phony liberal. He was sincere, in that sense. He protested the Waldorf Agreement and then capitulated.

What was your feeling toward witnesses who felt they had to name names?

Contempt. Briefly and in a word.

What was your plan when you decided to go to Mexico?

I had had a Mexican wife before that, and I spoke Spanish. Mexico seemed a logical place for me to lam to.

Some of the other blacklistees followed you down there?

I was the second one. Gordon Kahn was first. Subsequently, Trumbo and Albert Maltz and the others came down. Ring Lardner.

You settled in Mexico City?

Yes.

The writers socialized with one another down there?

Yeah, sure. We got together frequently. One by one they left and went other places. Europe, mainly.

Did the situation in Hollywood stay foremost in everyone's mind all this time?

There was considerable bitterness. Which still exists among those who are still alive.

What happened to Robert Rossen?

Robert Rossen came down to Mexico when the blacklist was on. He had just won the Academy Award for *All the King's Men*, for all the good it did him. He was on the list.

We were sitting around in Mexico and Rossen decided he was going to go back to Hollywood and make headlines telling off the committee. He was going to stand up to them the way Dimitrov challenged the Nazis at his trial. He said, "I'm going to do a Dimitrov!" And he went back and talked to the committee. But he didn't tell them off. He told them names. He capitulated. And I sent him a wire: "*How do you spell Dimitrov?*"

Did you ever hear from him again?

There was no reply.

What were your plans in moving to Mexico?

I hoped to get into the Mexican picture business, and I subsequently did. Under a different name, I wrote the first four pictures that were made in Mexico in both languages. I had a deal with a friend of mine who was on the board of the actors' union in Mexico. He maneuvered a deal for me to work on double-language pictures. Of those pictures I wrote four out of the only five that were made. My first picture for them was *Rebellion of the Hanged*.

That was by the mysterious B. Traven. Did you see any sign of him down there?

Oh, sure. I worked with him. At that time he was Hal Croves and denying being Traven. But I was instrumental in exposing him. We were shooting on location and he was there apparently as the secretary of B. Traven, but there were many clues that betrayed him. One in particular. He denied speaking German, but when a boom fell on the set he warned someone in German. That was proof he was a liar. Then he protested that a crucial scene in the picture be played differently and argued, *"I was there."* And he couldn't have been *everywhere* with Traven without being Traven.

I argued that the climax scene with the vicious drunken overseer threatened by the revolutionaries, *his*—Traven's—version, should go out the window, and I argued that it was a possible comedy scene ruinous to the drama of the thing. I justified my change in the script in that respect. Traven was very angry about it and stalked off the set. I was sustained by the director, the producer, and Gabriel Figueroa, the cameraman, for my position.

Then the producer ran out of money for the film and tried to borrow it from various places. His name was José Cohen; he was a Czech refugee. He would have been a Nazi if he hadn't been a Jew—in Pedro Armendariz's expression. I suggested to Cohen, "What if the real Traven is *not* Hal Croves? Then everything has a questionable legality." He could question any contract that was signed. So, with characteristic Mexican corruption—a payoff—I got the file, his *imigrante* file. It seems that he had come into Mexico at the time of the revolution in 1916. He had been very active in Germany, with Bert Brecht and others, very active in the German revolution. So he kept his anonymity in Mexico and maintained it when he found out that it paid off.

What was he like?

Terrible, nasty. A curmudgeon. I didn't like him at all. He lived in Acapulco, and he had three savage dogs. He cultivated these dogs for security, and they killed, ate his maid. I thought he was a very distasteful person. A *vicious* man . . . with a revolutionary justification.

During your stay in Mexico, were you—like the other writers who passed through—just waiting for the blacklist to blow over so you could go back?

I was determined to live in Mexico permanently. But I couldn't make a living.

The pay down there, I take it, was a fraction of Hollywood's?

Yeah. When I was introduced to Cohen at the time of *Rebellion of the Hanged*, he said, "You're blacklisted in Hollywood; you can't *afford* to dictate money to me." And I capitulated.

What was the pay?

I got $5,000 for the script and to be there.

Expenses were a lot lower, though, in Mexico.

Yes. But there still wasn't enough to go around.

Did you try to sell any scripts on the Hollywood black market?

That was done by others, Trumbo mainly, and Maltz and Lardner. I didn't attempt it at all. I washed up all Hollywood traces. But on my return from Mexico, I did three pictures for a producer under a different name.

What producer?

Frank . . . ah, I forget.

What were the scripts?

Nero, which wasn't made, and two others.

And the pay was low? Did you feel some of the producers were just taking advantage of the blacklist at that point, to get things cheaper?

Yeah. The producer attempted to justify it, that he was sticking his neck out.

You came back to the U.S. after how long in Mexico?

Ten years.

You did some TV work when you came back?

Yes.

In the late '60s you worked for a time with Bill Cosby's production company?

Yes. I was responsible for them shooting Trumbo's *Johnny Got His Gun.* I recommended it to Bruce Campbell and Bill Cosby.

You and Trumbo were good friends, weren't you?

He was my best friend. He was my oldest friend in Hollywood. I knew him when he started, after he quit working at a bakery. He was a reader then. He was a great man. I remember when Herbert Biberman, one of the Hollywood Ten, was dying of cancer of the bone. They had been in jail together, and Herbert was very admiring of Trumbo as a screenwriter. He had a script that he had high hopes for and he gave it to Trumbo to read. Trumbo read it and gave it to me for my opinion. I agreed with him that it was awful . . . dreadful, mechanical. Everything was wrong with it. But here was a dying man with a dream of one last good piece of work done. So Trumbo told a big fat lie. He said the script was hot, it was wonderful, would put Biberman back on top. And Biberman died with the feeling that he had at last reconquered Hollywood. Trumbo wasn't going to tell him the truth. I admired him for things like that.

As the blacklist lifted, were the writers looking for revenge, compensation of some kind?

It varied. There were those of us who were inclined to forget. Others, like Lester Cole . . . as recently as last year he heard Budd Schulberg on a call-in radio show and called him up . . . (Laughs) . . . *insulted* him.

What's your feeling now about someone like Schulberg?

I have mixed feelings about Budd. He was reluctant to be a fink. But he yielded under pressure. I'm not bitter about him at all. He was a victim, too, as Trumbo said. I knew him when he was a kid. He joined the YCL at my insistence, and then the Party subsequently. He was a shy stutterer in those days. Still is shy and a stutterer.

He made the one artistic justification for informing.

On the Waterfront. Yeah.

Did you know his wife Jigee?

His wife got a bad shake in Hollywood. She was once arrested as a prostitute—a frame-up by the police because she was a Red. She was a beautiful woman, fascinating. I knew her until the later years, when she fell apart.

And any change of feelings toward the instigators, people like Mahin?

No . . . that would be going too far.

Do you stay in touch with many of the people from the old days?

Yeah. Most of them are dead. Maltz died recently. I was very friendly with him. Jack Lawson. I was Trumbo's best friend. Cole. He's teaching in San Francisco and working for the Communist newspaper. He's probably the last unreconstructed Stalinist in the business. Most of us have qualified our enthusiasm for the Soviet Union. But he hasn't. Just a few months ago he defended the Soviet Union's attitude about Jews. He said, in *The Nation*, that he had *proof* of the absence of anti-Semitism in the Soviet Union . . . I've quarreled with him off and on until recently, when we sat at the same table at the Guild dinner, the fiftieth anniversary. The table of honor. He and I were the only original members of the Guild left.* Fifty years ago now.

Ahh . . . ancient history.

---

*Lester Cole died shortly after this conversation was taped.

Opposite page: On the set of *The Robe* (1953): director Henry Koster (in cap), producer Frank Ross (with camera), and Philip Dunne (right).

5 · PHILIP DUNNE

Morning in Malibu and a light fog is blowing across the Pacific Coast Highway. Up the road somewhere a pop star and her actor boyfriend are being married and helicopters strafe the beach in pursuit of aerial wedding pictures. Hidden from the tabloid commotion, set back from the road and high above the Pacific, is the home of Philip and Amanda Dunne.

It is a tall, modernist house the Dunnes built in 1947, when Philip, returned from wartime government service, resumed his position as one of the three (with Lamar Trotti and Nunnally Johnson) stalwarts of Darryl Zanuck's writing staff at Twentieth Century-Fox. In that year he scripted *Forever Amber, The Ghost and Mrs. Muir,* and *The Late George Apley.* Fox, under Zanuck, was Hollywood's "writers studio," where the script was a bible, not a suggested blueprint, allowing Dunne—of whose thirty-three screenplays only six were filmed at other studios—a remarkably consistent body of produced work. Though he prided himself on an ability to mimic the styles of the novelists he was often adapting, a Dunne "voice" is clearly heard—in the authenticity and intelligence of his many historicals and in his scripts' literary tone, dry humor, and progressive and humane values.

His father, Finley Peter Dunne, was a renowned humorist and editor in the early part of the century, an intimate of presidents and Broadway stars. Philip grew up in the gilded world of Eastern boarding schools ("hatcheries for the progeny of millionaires"), of polo ponies and sail boats. Ethel Barrymore was young Dunne's godmother. Upon leaving Harvard, he headed for a respectable career in banking, but the Crash of '29 altered those plans, and, fleeing the falling bodies of Wall Street, Dunne found himself in the readers department of Fox Studios, on Western Avenue in Los Angeles. Despite a lack of literary credentials, other than having edited his school newspaper, he soon moved up from reading to writing. After a few seasons of freelancing, and his name on at least one hit, *The Count of Monte Cristo,* Dunne returned to Fox (now merged with 20th Century) as a screenwriter, and stayed for the next twenty-five years. He would write many of the studio's most prestigious and money-making films, including *How Green Was My Valley, Pinky, The Rains Came,* and *The Robe.*

In 1955 Zanuck made him a director, his first assignment *Prince of Players.* Dunne enjoyed the new position and directed nine other films, writing most of them as well. The results were uneven—erudite but stolid. He has the distinction of making both the first Elvis Presley vehicle to lose money (*Wild in the Country)* and the best screen version of a John O'Hara novel (*Ten North Frederick).*

With Fox's descent into chaos in the '60s, Dunne's career lost momentum. His last screen credit, for Universal, was *Blindfold,* an amiable spy spoof. Ronald Reagan wanted a part in it, and therein, as you'll read, lies a story.

Since then, Dunne has not been inactive. Movies and politics (his other lifelong pursuit) have occupied him in numerous ways—as a lecturer, speechwriter, lobbyist, memoirist (the excellent *Take Two),* cogent book reviewer and scourge of inaccurate biographers and historians, fervent opponent of auteurists, Zanuck-bashers, and Malibu land developers. In the Hollywood community, Dunne is a man held in high esteem—as a distinguished screenwriter, a fighter for worthy causes, and in times of crisis a voice of reason and compassion.

Meeting him, one is struck first by his startling youthfulness for a seventy-seven-year-old—one suspects, at the least, a Dorian Gray pact in operation. He is patrician-handsome, tall, bespectacled, white hair in a boyish cut. His conversational tone is lightheartedly academic, prone to literary and Latin quotation, historical and political allusion—the "Harvard slant" his first Hollywood employer called for.

His attractive wife, Amanda, fixes us coffee, then Dunne leads me outdoors and along the eastward side of the house to a small cottage that serves as his study. The wall behind his desk is covered with a lifetime of awards, honors, photos of celebrated friends and collaborators. A scroll from the New York Film Critics is secondhand, but holds a place of honor. It pronounces John Ford winner of the 1941 best director award for *How Green Was My Valley;* across it in red crayon the winner has scrawled: "Thanks, Phil . . . Affection, Jack."

A combination of doctor's orders and unemployment brought me to California from New York. I arrived with a couple hundred dollars my father gave me and a letter of introduction from a man named Quinn Martin. My brother edited the theatre page of the old New York *World,* and Quinn Martin was the theatre critic. He was finishing out his watch at the *World* before he went out to begin his new job as the story editor at Fox Studios. So his was a very good letter to have. I took it to Winnie Sheehan, the head of production at Fox, and he hired me as a reader, saying that I could give them the "Harvard slant."

So I started working there at Fox. Leonard Spigelgass, who was a sort of senior reader, and had been there about a year, had the office next to me. Lennie taught me the ropes — how to analyze these manuscripts we were given. And he also tried to teach me how to type, without much success.

That first day I had my first encounter with a Hollywood screenwriter. It was near the end of the day and I was sitting in my office with Spigelgass when a man named Gene Towne burst in. He'd just finished a script and he was really excited. He was a big, strange-looking man with a bald head. And I'll never forget, he was spitting from excitement. And he told Lennie and me, "This'll kill 'em! They'll piss, they'll shit, they'll fuck!" This was the way he talked. And he said, "I just showed it to Winnie . . . and Winnie pissed, he shit, he fucked!" And at that moment a messenger came in and handed him a pink slip. He was fired.

How did you do as a reader? Did you recommend anything that was filmed?

No. Nothing.

I had that job for less than a year. This was 1931 and Fox Studios went into one of its usual convulsions. They were in all kinds of trouble. The executives were scattered. Sol Wurtzel, the second in command, had been locked out, and he was out on the sidewalk saying, "You can talk to me, fellas, I haven't got leprosy." And Winnie Sheehan was up in San Francisco, I was told, talking to a priest. And the efficiency experts had come in and taken over the studio. There was a fellow named Dick Carroll, who was a very successful freelance writer and magazine editor, and somehow he was the ranking executive left at the studio. Jack Ford and Raoul Walsh and others were gone and suing the studio for their salaries. And Dick Carroll said to me, "How would you like to be my assistant? You and I are going to run the studio." And, with no higher mountain peaks to be found, for a moment we were it. That lasted for about two weeks and then we were fired, too.

At that point I decided I could just as well be an unemployed writer as an unemployed reader, and I started writing short stories and original screen stories. As a reader I had found that writing a synopsis was not unlike writing a short story. I sold a few things with collaborators, including Dick Carroll. Then I was hired as a junior writer at Metro-Goldwyn-Mayer. I think it was 1932.

You wrote *Student Tour* there?

Yes, that was my first one.

What did you think of the results?

I never saw it.

***The Count of Monte Cristo* is what you consider the real start of your career?**

Yes, that was the first important assignment.

Rowland Lee, the director, and Dan Totheroh had done a wonderful job distilling a compact story out of this enormous book. You know, Dumas wrote the way all nineteenth-century authors wrote, in installments. They collected paychecks every month, and they would go on as long as they could. So they had done a treatment from this very long book. What I had to do was work this into scenes and then do the dialogue.

I never did read Dumas's book. I didn't have time. We had to go into production in, I think, six weeks. So there wasn't any of Dumas's dialogue in there. Only seven words, "One . . . two . . . three," and, "the world is mine." And the critic for *The New York Times* wrote that it was "wonderful how the Dumas dialogue had stood up so well over the hundred years or so!" Obviously he hadn't read it, either.

You continued to work for the producer of *Monte Cristo,* Edward Small?

Yes, he kept me on. I worked on something called *The Melody Lingers On,* and then I was assigned to collaborate with John Balderston on *The Last of the Mohicans.* John was an extraordinary man. He was a good writer and knew the eighteenth century better than anybody. His play, *Berkeley Square,* was a classic on the eighteenth century. We did a very good screenplay. If they'd shot the script that Balderston and I had written, they'd have had a classic. But they didn't. Sometimes they just can't keep their hands off a script. They started rewriting it, and the film ended up being a cheap western.

Who was doing the rewriting?

It was supposed to be secret, but I was told it was a very high-priced Metro writer, moonlighting. The producer was impressed, I suppose, that he could get this very big writer. But this stuff wasn't any good. The writer wasn't any good. I won't mention who it was because your tape recorder is running. Let's just say he later became a pillar of the Screen Playwrights.

John Mahin?

No. John Mahin was too good a writer. He'd have done a good job.

Johnny Mahin had been my brother's roommate at boarding school. And we'd been good friends. Then, all of a sudden, we were on opposite sides of the fence. He became president of the Screen Playwrights.

The Screen Playwrights nearly wrecked your career before it really got going, didn't they? I'm thinking of the P. G. Wodehouse letter.

Yes. It was such a silly thing. I had known "Plummy" Wodehouse at Southampton, but I had no idea what his political leanings were. They came out later, to some extent. The Screen Playwrights were very bold as a company union. They boasted of their villainy. They published a list of their members, and practically all their members were big names. And I saw P. G. Wodehouse on there. So, knowing him slightly, and being ardent—and stupid—I thought, "Well, I'll tell him what he's mixed up with and I'll get him out of this bunch." So I wrote him a letter in which I described the Screen Playwrights as I thought they were. And it was not inaccurate. It may have been a little hotheaded, but it wasn't inaccurate.

Wodehouse turned the letter over to the Screen Playwrights and they took it and printed it in a trade paper along with a story attacking the Guild.

Printing your letter was to show how underhanded the Guild was acting, or something to that effect?

That's right. From their narrow vision that must have been what they saw. It was 1937, the year after the sit-down strike and all that, and unionism was the hot political issue in the country.

There was a meeting called at Charlie Brackett's house, to decide how to deal with this. I had been sued, the Guild was sued, the Authors' League of America was sued. I walked in and the first thing I saw was Marc Connelly, the president of the Authors' League at the time. Now I had written in this now-public letter of mine to Wodehouse that Marc Connelly had written an "earnest but characteristically dull reply" to something. And now I walk in and here's the guy. So I said, "Marc, what can I say?" And he said, "Oh, don't give it a second thought. It's perfectly all right; it proves there couldn't have been any collusion with the League. I don't mind at all. *Forget it. It's great.*" And he never spoke to me again.

The letter led to your first meeting with Darryl Zanuck, didn't it?

I was shocked and startled to see it printed. And, when I arrived at the studio, I got a call from Jason Joy, who was administrative head of the writers. He told me that Zanuck wanted me out of there, lock, stock, and barrel. I thought, "My God, I'm going to be the Dreyfus of this thing." And I didn't want to be a Dreyfus at all. So I said to Joy, "If Zanuck wants to fire me, he'll have to do it in person. I have a contract." And Joy said, "Well, he won't see you." And I said, "Well, I won't leave. If you want to, you can call the sergeant at arms and have me removed, but I won't leave." Joy had been head of the American Red Cross before he took this job, and he subsequently became a very good friend of mine.

So Zanuck did see me. And it was a memorable meeting. I went in. He was very irritated. He said, "What's this all about?" I said, "It has nothing to do with my work. It's just . . ." And he said, "Go on, go on, get back to work." And that was the end of the meeting. Later, the next time I saw him, he said, "I don't believe I've met Mr. Dunne."

What was your role in the Guild at that time?

Robert Donat (left) as Edmond Dantes in *The Count of Monte Cristo* (1934).

George Sanders and Lionel Atwill in *Lancer Spy* (1937).

I was chairman of the membership committee for the Guild. I was keeping lists of the members at each studio. Many of them were undercover, you know; they couldn't admit they were members. And I kept lists of the Screen Playwrights, trying to see if this one looked soft so maybe we could win him over to our members. I was describing my duties to Harry Bridges, the labor leader, and some of his people at the time, up in San Francisco. And one of Bridges' people said, "You're the chairman of the membership committee? What does that mean?" And Bridges said, "He's the organizer." And the man said, "Oh. How much do they pay you?" And Bridges said, "They don't pay him, stupid. He's a *writer!*" I liked that accolade.

What was your first assignment for 20th Century-Fox?

Lancer Spy was the first assignment. That was from a book. I don't remember the book very well, but there was one.*

You're listed as working on *Under Pressure*.

I think Lester Cole had much more to do with rewriting that. My brother and I were called in, I forget why. That had to do with sandhogs in the East River. It was very short, whatever we did.

Cole has said that Raoul Walsh had thrown out the original script and was rewriting it on a paper bag.

That one I don't remember.

Can you tell me about Zanuck's relationship with writers at Fox?

It was an ambiguous relationship. His was called the "writers' studio," and it was, because the script was always the star. Nunnally Johnson said that anybody who changed a script after Zanuck approved it was guilty of insulting the American flag and womanhood or something. And that was true. And when I changed a line in my own scripts, when I became a director, he came down on me like a ton of bricks. He'd say, "For twenty years I've been protecting you from other directors, and now you're forcing me to protect you from yourself."

On the other hand, he went along with the public recognition for the director. Public credit— the size of type and so forth. Writers were not invited to premieres and all those things. So even with Zanuck it wasn't all that great for the writer, because there was no more credit for him at Fox than there was anywhere else.

And often the writer was the one person who should have been consulted in some instances and *wasn't*. They'd have a sick picture and decided they wanted the ending rewritten. This was a "doctoring" job and I did quite a few of them. I'd be brought in and they'd already have it all worked out. They'd say, "We want this scene and then we want this scene." And I said, "Have you got a budget on these changes?" They said, "Yes, it's going to be ten days' shooting and cost such and such money." And I said, "Well, if you do this and this you can do it all in one day." But nobody had thought to ask me first. All the non-writers had put in their ideas on the problem.

What would go on during a story conference with Zanuck?

They changed over the years. When I first went in, there were about ten stooges—Zanuck's

*The book was written by Marthe McKenna.

retainers. This is typical of someone who's on the way up; he's insecure and surrounds himself with yes-men. I directed Elvis Presley in a picture, and he always had his gang of sort of semi-ruffians. They would be doing karate motions at each other all day on the set, and their job was to get beat by Elvis at karate.

But later on Zanuck simply got rid of all the stooges. They weren't there any more. He might have one, Jacques Cermonde, his Frenchman. Zanuck worshiped anything French—that was the top. Jacques was supposed to talk French with him. He still had a horrible accent; the Nebraska was there ineradicably.

But in the early days there were stooges, and it could be kind of funny, the way he dealt with them. One of their jobs was to submit notes and criticism of the scripts. There was one fellow named Henry who had been a very successful comedy director once, but had gotten on his uppers. Zanuck had thrown him one of the stooge jobs. So we were in the conference, and this man read a memo criticizing a script of mine. And it was quite a savage criticism of the middle part of the script. Then Zanuck threw the memo down and said, "This is the stupidest goddamn memo I've ever read! Here is a brilliant script, there's nothing wrong with it at all, and this ridiculous memo comes from Henry here who's trying to tell us . . . " And he went on and on, building it up. And then he looked at me and he said, "Well, what do you think?"

I said, "I think Henry's right." I would have said it even if I hadn't thought so—it was too big a setup. A big, fat pitch coming straight at me. And Zanuck knew this was what he was doing. This was the way he operated. And then he would get down to real business.

He loved to play games. And sometimes they were cruel, with the stooges he could kick around, people like Mike Curtiz. But he wouldn't play this sort of game with me, or with Nunnally, or any writer. He would never kick us around the way he kicked around Curtiz and others.

The great thing about Zanuck, I think, was that he had the first attribute of a successful executive: he was a great judge of character. He knew how to handle people, to get them to do what he wanted them to do. He might have a different approach for everyone, and they would all work. Except for this ability of his, I never would have undertaken to write something like *Forever Amber*. He'd convince me the studio was depending on me—there was a "crisis." And I'd fall for it every time.

What would happen if you had a real creative difference with him on some script?

We had them all the time. We had fierce arguments. And that was the other great thing about him. He didn't want you to "yes" him at all. He'd throw out an idea, and the fur would fly. Or I'd have an idea and he'd say, "God! No!" And then you'd be off. And you'd come around or he'd come around to accepting something. That sort of thing happened all the time. And I remember a few occasions when I'd start out arguing black and he white, and we'd end up on the other side. Pursuing a logical argument, this often happens. And he was a very logical man.

But some projects got his approval very easily, didn't they? I believe you got the go-ahead for *David and Bathsheba* by telling him the three words of the title.

Yeah, but there was a whole lot that went on before the three words. Everybody was interested in making another *Gone With the Wind*, something BIG. And we were going to have a trilogy in one film: the boy David fighting Goliath; the mature David, the friendship with Jonathan, finishing with the Bathsheba affair; and then the old man and Absalom. It was to be a gigantic

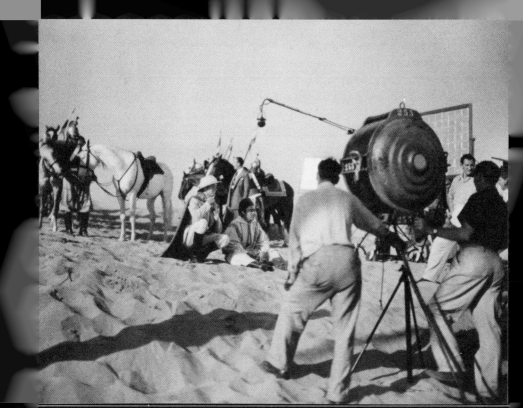

Tyrone Power and J. Edward Bromberg on location (a sand-covered golf course) for *Suez* (1938).

four-hour movie. I turned in the treatment. It was something like 120 pages. It would have become a 400-page script. It was a monumental job, and I wish I had a copy of it. A lot of it was very good, and you could still make the other stories.

Well, this became the damndest conference I ever had with Zanuck. I sat there and he sat there, and he looked at the ceiling and I looked at the floor, and then I looked at the ceiling and he looked at the floor. Nothing happened for ten minutes or so. It just dragged on for what seemed a very long time. And usually Zanuck was very verbal. Finally, he just put the script down and said, "I'll send you another assignment."

So I was, let's say, crestfallen. I came out here to Malibu. It was Friday. And I was thinking, "My God. . . . " I had a big investment in this thing, an emotional investment. I'd fallen in love with the character of David, as who wouldn't. He was a marvelous character. At least *my* character. I don't know how marvelous *his* character was, but the one I'd invented was a marvelous character. My David. And I think it could have been accurate . . . except my David never would have danced naked in front of the Lord. But almost everything else he *did*. I just had him with a much more modern mind.

So I was here at Malibu for the weekend thinking about this, and I got the idea, why not just tell that one story, David and Bathsheba? It could be told as a tragedy, or as a French farce, when you think of it.

And on Monday I sent him a memo. He typed in red ink on your memo, that's how he answered you—so he didn't clutter up *his* files with *your* memos. And I knew that the way to his heart was brevity. So my memo said, "*David and Bathsheba.*" And his reply came back: "Write it."

You wrote many films with a historical setting. They tend to be among the more literate of that type. Of how much concern was authenticity?

In historical pictures the thing that always bothered me was the kind of anachronisms you'd find in De Mille pictures, for instance. People saying, "I'll *contact* you tomorrow." Things like that. That had to go out. Just won't work.

Tom Stempel, in his book on Nunnally Johnson, spoke about my "relentlessly literate scripts." And Tom made the point that Nunnally couldn't write these things because he was afraid to be literate. Nunnally preferred to write very colloquial. But I felt there was nothing wrong with being literate as long as you continued to be dramatic.

With their anachronisms and purple dialogue, biblical films tended to be the worst offenders. How did you avoid that trap in *David and Bathsheba*?

I used the King James Version as a reference point. I would try to get something of the cadence. Parts of *David and Bathsheba* are in blank verse. I didn't tell anybody that. I just found that the pentameter kept creeping in. It's not the words; it's the style. Although sometimes you tried to get the slightly offbeat word instead of the obvious word.

Would you have to hear your dialogue spoken aloud to know if it would "work"?

I would play out the scenes up and down in this room. And I found out later that I might have an audience. My middle daughter and her friends used to hide out there behind the hedge and watch (laughs) . . . watch me emoting.

No applause followed your performances?

No! But you can imagine them giggling away while I'm going, "Blah, blah, blah. . . . " Acting away. You know, you want to know how the scene plays, how does it sound. And all writers are hams, suppressed hams. They seldom get a chance to express their—what would be the word—their *jambonerie* or whatever it is.

Until *How Green Was My Valley* your scripts for Fox were all collaborations?

Many were not actual collaborations. I was put on something after another writer had been taken off. Some were doctoring jobs. I collaborated on several scripts—*Suez, The Rains Came, Stanley and Livingstone*—with Julien Josephson. After that I usually worked alone.

What about *Johnny Apollo*? You're co-credited with Rowland Brown.

Yes, he wrote the original.

What happened to Brown? He was obviously very talented, a writer-director before anyone thought there were such things, and then it all seemed to go downhill from there.

I don't know for sure what it was. In the early '30s he directed a brilliant picture, *Quick Millions,* with Spencer Tracy. A wonderful picture. Brown had this affinity with the underworld, broken down prizefighters, pathetic characters. He wrote about them, understood them, understood gangsters, all kinds of lowlife. He had an affinity with the underworld and a wonderfully graphic way of expressing it. His screenwriting was very good. I remember he had one scene in the script—I don't know if it was ever filmed, but it was in the script he showed me—a man is being carted away to prison to be hanged, and they drive him past a great big billboard that says, "*In All The World No Trip Like This!*"

What happened to him?

I suppose one thing was he just didn't get along with the brass. He was very tough. I saw him again much later, around 1960. He came to my office, and he was looking for a job, any job at all. It was just shocking to see what had happened to him. He'd been a big, sort of round fellow, and now he was old, skinny, a beaten man, totally beaten. Those things are always a terrible shock, to see somebody who'd been so proud, so tough.

Can you tell me how *How Green Was My Valley* developed? It went through several stages and changes, didn't it?

The first problem was selecting and compressing the material that we had. The story was really rich with incident and characters. Then there was the political aspect to the story. Zanuck was not going to go for any socialist manifesto, and I was not going to twist the story into being anti-union. So there was a degree of shading necessary with some of the characters, such as Mr. Gruyffydd, the preacher, who was more of a firebrand in the book. We made him more a voice of reason.

Originally, the film would have been much longer. It took the boy Huw into manhood. Tyrone Power was going to play Huw from about the halfway point. Willie Wyler was going to direct, and I had worked with him for several weeks. Then, after the studio found Roddy McDowall—he'd come over from England as a refugee—we decided to do the entire thing with the young Huw. I reworked the scenes from the later sections to have them experienced by the young boy, which made it much more effective, in fact. The search for the father after the disaster in the mine, and so on, much more effective this way.

Willie did not direct it, of course. There were delays and he went to something else. John Ford was hired for it, on the guarantee that he would bring the picture in for a million dollars. Otherwise he wasn't allowed to shoot it.

The script was finished when Ford came on?

Yes.

Did he shoot the script as you wrote it?

Yes, with very few changes.

And yet the feeling of the film is entirely "Fordian"—the sentiment, the humor, the nostalgia, the family setting—and not "Wylerian." Is this just coincidence? What do you feel Ford did with the material that made it different from what Wyler would have done? Or am I wrong in assuming you even think there'd be a difference?

Oh, there were all kinds of things that he did that Willie would not have done. For instance, when the postman brings the invitation from Queen Victoria, he has him hold out the envelope and throw a big salute, you know, all that stuff. And the bit with the doctor saying, "*He'll never walk again.*" He had the doctor, Freddie Waller, playing such a ham job. My wife, Amanda, was very distressed when she saw it. She had been in *Tovarich* with Freddie and she liked him, you see, and she said, "What have they done to Freddie!" Ford let him overplay. Willie would not have done that.

So, things like that. These broad strokes. . . . There's *no* reason in the scene where they're washing up after the mine, in the first sequence, for the wife to pass her husband who's smoking a pipe and dump a pail of water on him. That is not motivated, and I never liked unmotivated actions. I watch it and say, "Well, it is funny, it's a laugh. Yes, Jack would go very broad, much broader than I wrote it.

There was a love scene in which Mr. Gruffydd is trying to explain to Angharad why he can't marry her. Ford played them very close together. And I always felt this was a scene which should have been played apart, that he would be retreating from her as she would be advancing on him. But Ford even had him take hold of her by the shoulders. And I don't think he would have ever touched her . . . because why make it worse?

Then there were other things I thought were just hurried. When the boy presumably had his back beaten to a pulp by the teacher and his brother picks him up and swings him right around to the camera and you see the back and there's not a mark on him. I thought, you know, they could have swung him or photographed it another way. So I think Jack tended to hurry. But he was under duress. Had to bring the picture in for a million. It was all "camera cut" with no protection at all.

So a few things like that I disagreed with. But certainly I couldn't have disagreed with the overall effect. He did shoot the script, but he did all sorts of wonderful things in it. I had the boy calling for his father at the end, and it was his idea to have him sing. And that really made that ending. That was a real directorial touch.

Ford referred to whatever script he was discussing as "this crap"?

That meant he *liked* it.

What happened the time Ford called you down to rewrite a scene?

I was just giving him back the famous Ford joke. A producer was supposed to have complained that he was behind schedule, so Ford grabbed the producer's script, tore out five pages and said, "Now we're on schedule." They were shooting and Sara Allgood had said the scene "wouldn't play." So I did his gag and tore the page out and said, "Now it plays." So Ford said, "See? The sonofabitching writer won't do anything to help us, so we'll have to shoot it the way he wrote it."

I always wanted it to be good. Zanuck had to play it two ways. He wanted it to be good, too, and he would go way out to make something good. But he had to think in terms of a profit or he would be through. He wouldn't have a studio. And we all had to make pictures that made money—everything depended on it. We did not set out to make classics. We set out to make successful entertainment. But, then, so did Molière and so did Mozart.

You had to be careful that some private enthusiasm didn't affect your judgment in a negative way. Clarence Brown's favorite of all the movies he ever made was *Night Flight* by Saint-Exupéry. It had a wonderful cast, Gable, Montgomery, Barrymore. But it was not successful. It was a lot of little stories, and it just didn't work for the audience. But Clarence was a very passionate and able pilot—he had what we used to call a "transport" license, the same as a commercial one. Clarence loved flying, and he was blinded by his private love when he made the film.

You've written that film writers are considered a low form of animal life. No other ingredient in a film is any *more* important. So how did this happen? Why didn't screenwriters have the same clout as the directors?

Well, in the silent days directors had made themselves very visible. They were often complete *filmmakers,* and did a lot of improvising. Many films were really created during the filming. Writers might be gag writers, or title writers, and were fairly insignificant. They sort of trailed the director.

When sound came and the New York playwrights came out, people said, "This is going to be the new era of *the writer*." But it didn't pay off. The director was still the visible figure. And people like Frank Capra were very happy to push that and wear the crown. And I think critics had a lot to do with it. By glorifying movies as an art, and writing the way Pauline Kael does, everything's an art that connotes an artist. So they have to find an artist, and the director was the visible figure. And that led to the *auteur* theory.

I remember one of my daughters invited a young writer friend of hers to the Academy to see some screening, and he was saying, "I don't know why writers needed a guild," and so on. I said, "Let me show you why." Up in the Academy theatre they have one-sheets of all the award winners. I said, "Do you remember *How Green Was My Valley*? Well, you can see from this that it was produced by Darryl F. Zanuck, and you can see it was directed by John Ford . . . and then down there, if you have very good eyes and a magnifying glass, you'll find out who wrote it." I think the minimizing of the writer's credit had a lot to do with his lack of recognition. The real revolution was when the writer and director merged into one person. So now the writer sets out, instead of writing something on assignment, he says, "I'm writing something that *I'm* going to direct."

Were there good scripts you felt were mangled in the actual filming by bad direction or other factors?

I won't quote myself but Tom Stempel. He called *The Egyptian* one of the best scripts he'd ever read. And he said, "After the script, everything went wrong." And I think that's true. It wasn't only the direction; it was the casting. I do feel it was a good script, sort of a grand, moody, powerful script. And if we'd *had* Brando, as planned, and if we *hadn't* had Bella Darvi, we might have had a good film.

That was one thing Zanuck was bad at—casting. He had simplified ideas. High-class characters, kings, popes and so on, should be played—always—by English actors. We were casting *The Egyptian*, and we were looking for the Pharaoh Akhnaton. He was a sort of epileptic, and he insisted on being drawn as he looked, with a pot belly and scrawny, a very strange man. One day there walked into my office an actor who looked like my idea of Akhnaton—sort of unhealthy looking, scrawny, strange-looking. And I talked to him and I said, "Would you mind reading a scene?" And he read the scene and I called Zanuck, and I said, "I've got the perfect actor for Akhnaton. His name is John Cassavetes and he'll be absolutely great for it." Zanuck said, "No, no, no. We've got Michael Wilding, an Englishman, to do the part." And he had no idea what to do with it.

Then, later, into my office walked a swan-necked, sloe-eyed beauty, Dana Wynter. I said, "My God, she's Nefertiti, she just walked in!" But Zanuck let Mike Curtiz cast some lumpish girlfriend, who looked about as much like Nefertiti as you or I do.

So I always thought casting was Zanuck's weakness. And then, you ask about bad direction, and *David and Bathsheba* was an instance, although I was partly to blame because I gave in on it. In the ending when David puts his hands on the Ark, there's a big clap of thunder—which later we find out was "the rain" starting (laughs) you know. But to him it's doom. And now his past flashes back, and I have two scenes—I wrote it to be very impressionistic—one was a very little boy and a terrible man pouring oil on his head, saying, "I annoint you. You will be King of Israel"; this was Saul, a dreadful man. And the other scene from the past is Goliath coming out of a sort of mist, an apparition, like the ghost in Olivier's *Hamlet*. Well, that's the way I wrote it, and Henry King, the director, got to Zanuck, and King was very literal. He wanted it all explained. I was called in and had to write all this trashy exposition, explaining who Goliath was and all this stuff. And they cast Francis X. Bushman as Saul, for God's sake, and Saul would have been thirty-five years old at the time. But they had this poor old actor propped up there. I should have put up a fight, you know, but the pressure was great. And I think it was an error on their part, that long-winded treatment of it. The audience would have gotten it without everything explained to them—just to say, these are the two important things in his past. The whole thing would have taken, maybe, thirty seconds of screen time instead of five minutes.

In the '40s you got into a debate in print with Joseph Mankiewicz on the question of why there weren't more good original screenplays, as opposed to adaptations.

Yes, it was in the old *Screen Writer* magazine. Joe wrote this piece on "Why Aren't the Writers Turning Out Glorious Original Screenplays?" And I answered him that "they aren't writing them for the same reason you're not writing them. You're such a good writer that you always get assignments." As Zanuck said to me once, "If I can have a best-selling novel, and a script by Nunnally Johnson, I've got a hit, and I don't care who directs it."

Metro, say, had a star system to fall back on, but Fox had to depend on the property. So the reason there were not a lot of *great* original screenplays was that the top writers who were capable of writing them were the ones who were kept busy adapting proven material. Having

Susan Hayward in *David and Bathsheba* (1951).

Jeanne Crain and Ethel Waters in *Pinky* (1949).

been a reader, I knew that the originals floating around were mostly the despairing efforts of out-of-work writers. That was largely the originals market in Hollywood. In those days an original was what a writer did when he was out of work. I used to tell young writers who were out of work, "Don't write a screenplay; write a play or a novel. Then you can sell it to the movies and write the screenplay later on."

But I'm absolutely in awe of people who can think up stories. And I never could. I'm not very inventive in that way. I'm a good adaptor and I'm good at dialogue and can write in different styles, but I don't think up stories.

There were very good writers, weren't there, who just couldn't write for the screen?

My friend John O'Hara was just *not* a screenwriter. I know he tried hard, but he just didn't seem able to master the medium. It might have been the necessity for being brief that bothered him. You couldn't ask audiences to sit still for too long for a talking head. That's one of my own weaknesses, too much talking. But I don't think that John was suited to writing a screenplay. And I don't think Faulkner was, either. Howard Hawks—I don't know why—kept bringing Faulkner out, probably hoping something would rub off on him, but it didn't do any good.

Scott Fitzgerald was another example. Everybody talks about how *Hollywood* ruined Scott Fitzgerald. But Scott had written a very lousy and unsuccessful play before he came to Hollywood, and nobody ever said that *Broadway* ruined Fitzgerald. Actually, he was just written out.

The image persists of a lot of top writers being contemptuous of screenwriting and the people they worked with here. Let me put it this way: How often did you perceive a writer deliberately doing second-rate work?

I can't conceive of it. You said "perceive" and I say "conceive." I can't conceive of anyone doing that.

Ben Hecht was the foremost proponent of the idea, and yet his screenplays were always first rate.

Yes. It was an image he had to keep up.

Didn't you once stumble in on Hecht and MacArthur while they were writing a script?

Oh, yes. It was at Charlie's and Helen Hayes's house. Hecht was sitting at the typewriter, and his head was clamped in place with one of those clamps they used to photograph criminals. MacArthur was beside him, lying stretched out on a couch. When Hecht would finish a page, he would hand it over to Charlie. Charlie would look at it, and if he'd say, "*Very good*," Hecht would take the page back and tear it up. He'd write another page, and if Charlie would say, "*Mmm . . . I don't know,*" Hecht would take the page and add it to the finished pile. But I'm sure they were showing off.

You wrote three films for a tyro director who'd been a writer, Joseph Mankiewicz. He directed your scripts for *The Ghost and Mrs. Muir*, *Escape*, and *The Late George Apley*. Were there conflicts? Was he apt to make changes?

This was during the Zanuck reign and the scripts were simply untouchable. On *The Ghost and Mrs. Muir* Joe contributed three or four excellent lines for the character that George Sanders played. We had recast it. Richard Ney was impossible in the part, so he was taken out and Sanders put in.

When you became a director, did you refrain from tampering with the writer's script?

This would have been my dream. I would have loved to say, "Yes, here is the script and I'll direct it word for word." But. . . .

With *Prince of Players*, Moss Hart's script was about half an hour too long. It had to be trimmed down somehow. So I went back to New York to get Moss working on it. And what happened was, Moss had me doing the writing and he was doing the producing. He'd say, "Those changes are fine; you'll work those out and I'll see you tomorrow at lunch." And he'd go off. But I guess Moss was just being kind of lazy about it. I did have a facility, always, of being able to write in somebody else's style, whether it was O'Hara's for *Ten North Frederick* or the Old Testament or whatever. And so I could pretty much keep up the style that Moss had in his script.

But I tried very hard *not* to write anything. I wanted very much to be the great producer-director who didn't soil his hands with writing. But I was forced.

The next time was Eddie Anhalt's script for *In Love and War*. We went into production with half a script. I was on location in the Pacific and I had to do it. I'd call the studio, saying, "Where are the scenes?" And Jerry Wald was dictating pages of proofs with Eddie Anhalt, scenes that we weren't going to shoot for six weeks. And I didn't have what I was supposed to shoot on *Thursday*. So again I was forced. But I would much rather have had an ironclad script. Jerry simply didn't work that way.

On *Wild in the Country*, the Presley picture, they fired Clifford Odets with the script only half finished. They fired him because they had paid him what they contracted to pay him and they weren't going to pay him any more. So they said, "Dunne's a writer, he can finish it." What could I do? I should have quit. My agent talked me out of it, telling me to protect my pension and a few other things. Having three children in private schools, I went along. That's the trouble with the world, you know.

You've said that you might have been happier as a director than a writer.

As I said, I'm not very inventive with stories. I really enjoyed directing. I thought I got on well with actors. I thought I handled them well. But I started directing too late and, no question, at the wrong time. Twentieth Century-Fox, the studio system, were falling apart. The boat had sailed.

But you have gone on record against the critical exaggerations of the director's influence.

Yes, well, the *auteur* theory led to such nonsense. The entire premise was based on ignorance, lack of information. If John Ford was the supreme creator of *How Green Was My Valley*, then who was Darryl Zanuck, me, Richard Llewellyn who wrote the novel, or William Wyler, the director who prepared the script for production with me?

Pinky is now called a film by Elia Kazan. But Kazan came in at the very last minute when John Ford had to drop out. Kazan was assigned on a Saturday and started shooting on Monday. And he didn't change one word that was in the script approved by Zanuck.

To give sole authorship to a non-writer director is just absurd.

And yet, in the '60s, the studios, who should have known better than the critics, bought the theory.

Yes. I saw it over and over again. The studio would hire directors and build them beautiful bungalows and all that stuff, and no pictures would come of it. They went to the wrong guy. It would be like hiring a conductor and saying, "Now, let's have some wonderful music that nobody's ever heard before."

You wrote a rather irate review of the Leonard Mosley biography of Zanuck. You found it inaccurate?

Oh, what a terrible book. I just couldn't understand how a book could be so inaccurate, in minor and major details. And Mosley had not consulted the people who really knew Zanuck. Never talked to Jules Buck, never talked to me, all sorts of people still around. He talked mostly to Milton Sperling. I like Milton very much, but he was simply not the only source. There were lots of others who were a lot closer.

You take credit—or perhaps I should say blame—for Ronald Reagan becoming president. Can you explain that?

Yes, my most *meaningful* contribution to American politics. There's two parts to the story. I was directing *Blindfold* at Universal, and I got word that Reagan wanted a part and could he play the villain? It was a not very dignified part of a communist spy, given a kind of comic comeuppance at the end. I thought Reagan was wrong for it, too much the middle-aged Boy Scout, and I turned him down. A couple of months later, while on location, I hear that Reagan has decided to run for governor of California. And, as we know, he went on from there.

Dore Schary heard this story and he said, "You may have that claim, but I have a greater one, the crucial influence." And he explained that years back he'd gone to Dr. Loyal Davis to cure his bad back. In gratitude he set Reagan up with the doctor's daughter, Nancy. Until then Reagan had been a sort of *meshuginah* liberal Democrat. And Nancy converted him to her father's conservative politics. So that was Dore's claim to fame.

And I said to Dore, "Do you remember how you got that bad back? The ball game?" There had been a cockeyed ballgame between 20th and Metro-Goldwyn-Mayer. Dore hit a weak ground ball down to me at first base. He wasn't going to bother running it, you know, this chief of production, and I yelled, "Well *run*, you bastard!" And he tried, and he caught his spikes in the dirt or something, and out went his back. So it was all really my doing, Reagan and Nancy and the rest. And Dore thought for a moment and said, "That was no weak ground ball, that was a vicious line drive!" Later, he put the story into his book, *Heyday*, and by then it had become a triple with the bases loaded.

But I have had to live with the theory that, on the first day of World War III, as we're gently vaporized, people will say, "It's all because Dunne made Schary run out that ground ball. . . ."

Overleaf: Mickey Rooney, Lana Turner, Judy Garland, and Ann Rutherford in *Love Finds Andy Hardy* (1938).

6 · WILLIAM LUDWIG

William Ludwig
in the 1950s.

Love Finds Andy Hardy was the surprise hit of 1938. Its cast featured a number of talented teenagers—Mickey Rooney, Judy Garland, Lana Turner—all on the eve of superstardom. The warm, very funny screenplay was by another fresh talent, a young New York lawyer named William Ludwig.

Ludwig did not invent the Hardys. They had been languishing through several previous installments. But he did make them a success, changing the focus of the series to Andy's *everyboy*, and bringing a youthful spirit to the comedy that would make the moments of sentiment all the more touching. He wrote four more in the series, movies of modest intentions and lasting achievement: Andy Hardy's Carvel became America's small-town dreamscape. Who would not wish for an adolescence as summery as Andy's, his innocence, unlike ours, never to be lost. Hard-headed Louis B. Mayer was said to have cried at every new Hardy picture. He wasn't the only one.

Bill Ludwig's long tenure at MGM took him from "junior writer" to Academy Award winner (*Interrupted Melody*, Best Screenplay 1955). In between he worked on a wide variety of assignments: screwball comedies, crime melodramas, dog stories and musical biographies. But the Hardy Family series indicated his real strengths—Americana, children, gentle humor, and sentiment. *An American Romance* was the epic account of an immigrant's rise to power in the Midwest steel industry; *Journey for Margaret*, a heart-tugging tale of homeless war orphans; and *The Human Comedy*, the William Saroyan story to which Ludwig made a large contribution, a sort of road-show version of the *Hardys*, including Mickey Rooney's Andy-like messenger boy. These were old-fashioned movies that gave their old-fashioned audiences a smile or a tear as they left the theatres of the world.

Ludwig, in 1985, resides in Santa Monica, on a u-shaped lane that boasts an expansive view of the Riviera Country Club's rambling golf course. He faces his interviewer from behind the desk in his living room. In his mid-seventies, Ludwig is a dapper, courtly gentleman with a trim white moustache and a gleaming cigarette holder tilting upright from the side of his mouth. He is articulate and precise in conversation, and a moving spokesman for a period in Hollywood's history that will, as he says, never be the same.

I was a practicing attorney in New York, and I took ill. After I spent a year in Arizona, the doctors told me not to go back to New York because of my condition. I came out here to California where I planned to study for the bar—of course, you must get admitted to the bar in each state where you practice. I was broke. I'd been in a hospital for nineteen weeks and been ill in Arizona for a year. I needed eating money. A fraternity brother of mine at Columbia—I'd gone to Columbia Law School—had written some stories for the *Saturday Evening Post* and was out here working for Goldwyn. Everett Freeman. He let me move in with him when I arrived from Arizona. He recommended me for an opening in the shorts department at Metro, and I got it. I was to report on Monday, but, the Friday before, I took ill again and had to fly back to New York for some more surgery. When I returned, my spot in the shorts departments had been filled.

Metro then opened a junior writers group, and I was recommended for that group. There were twelve of us altogether, and we got $35 a week. All twelve of us worked in one office. We discovered that, no matter how much we wrote, nobody was reading anything we wrote. It wasn't taken seriously. One day we all went to lunch, and when we came back we were all fired. They decided nothing was coming out of this project, and they just decided to give it up. Economically I don't think it was a smart idea to get rid of us. The same day they fired us, they bought a book through their Paris office—*A Cook's Tour of Europe* by Jacques Bestanami—for $35,000, an amount that would have carried our unit for a year and a half, and it wasn't until the book reached Culver City that they realized it was a collection of recipes. But, in any case, I was out.

What sort of writing had you done previous to that first job at MGM?

When they were hiring me, they wanted to see my bio and asked for my published materials. My writings included, *Insurance Trust and Considerations of the Rules against Perpetuities*, and another was *Life Insurance Forfeiture Clauses, with the Consideration of the Suicide Clause*. . . . Didn't have much box office possibility.

I did some varsity shows at Columbia and worked with amateur groups, mostly in staging and directing. And I'd done writing for the Columbia *Spectator.* And that was it.

So, now I was out of work. I had become friendly with a couple of producers at Metro. One in particular, Fritz Stephani, who's long dead, and his wife Lenore, God bless both their souls, knew me. And he came home one day hysterical with laughter. Metro was looking for the cheapest writer they could find for a picture they had to make right away.

They had made two films about the Hardy family, *A Family Affair* and *A Family Vacation.** They'd been bombs, and the original Judge Hardy, Lionel Barrymore, had flatly, rather violently, refused ever to appear in another one.

But this was in the days of block-booking, and the studio had already sold another Hardy picture. They didn't have anything, but they had to make it, and they wanted to make it as cheaply as they could, naturally, because they had no expectations for it.

Fritz came home and told his wife this, and she said, "Bill Ludwig needs work. Why don't you recommend him?" And he said, "I wouldn't recommend my worst enemy for this thing." And she said, "He needs the money." And he said, "Okay," and recommended me. I got called in, and they showed me the two previous pictures. They said, "Can you do a screenplay for this? We've got to go right into production. We're in a big hurry." And I said, "Certainly"—never having written a screenplay in my life. I stayed up all night reading a stack of screenplays. And the next morning I came in and began. The secretary they gave me *did* know how to write in screenplay form. I started dictating to her, and dictated off the top of my head for about two hours straight. When I stopped finally, I said to her, "Piercey, let's be honest with

*MGM had produced *three* Hardy films before *Love Finds Andy Hardy—A Family Affair, You're Only Young Once,* and *Judge Hardy's Children.*

each other. I don't know what the hell I'm doing." And she said, "I didn't want to interrupt you, because it was going so well. I just took the liberty when you said *this* of putting it like *this*, and then when you did this. . . . " And I said, "Look, I'll just keep dictating and you show me what you do with it." So through her I learned how to put a script together.

I wrote the picture—*Love Finds Andy Hardy*—in fifteen days. And I got paid $74. For the whole job. I was paid $35 a week for fifteen days, and there were some deductions. It was my "junior writers" salary. They weren't going to give me a raise—my God, they had just fired me. But they did sign me to a seven-year contract this time just in case I amounted to anything. A contract with options, so they could terminate it every six months or so.

So they had their script, and they wanted to make the picture as cheaply as possible. They had taken an old-timer, who'd once been a leading man, Lew Stone, and made him the judge. And then they had a little kid who'd been Andy Hardy in the first two, Mickey Rooney. Then there were a couple of girls they had under contract for $100 a week. The option had just come up on one, and they dropped her—that was Deanna Durbin. The other girl had a couple of months to go, and they figured she might as well earn her keep before they dropped her, too—that was Judy Garland. And then Mervyn LeRoy was at the studio, and he had a girl under personal contract, paying her $75 a week out of his own pocket. He came in crying to our producer and said, "Can't you put her in something so I can get off the hook?" So they put her in, and that was Lana Turner. And they had Sara Hayden, and Fay Holden, the mother and the aunt, and Cecilia Parker was the sister. And they had Ann Rutherford for the girlfriend. And they took one of the old-time directors, one of the sweetest men there ever was, George Seitz, to direct it.

They locked them up on the stage, and they shot the picture in eighteen days. It shipped for $165,000. It opened at Grauman's Chinese, on the bottom of the bill under *Yellowjack* (which was written by a friend of mine, Eddie Chodorov). And after the response from the first three or four days, they changed the billing. *Andy Hardy* moved to the top and *Yellowjack* to the bottom. And they immediately put me onto another Andy Hardy, because my first one was doing so well.

Did you get a raise?

They took me up to $50 a week. And I became the example in the Writers Guild's argument for minimum wage in our first contract. The Guild had reformed, and I had joined as soon as I got on the lot. There was still a lot of conflict and I heard the usual threats, but it didn't matter too much to me at the time because I didn't figure on being in the business for long. I was just trying to save a little money so I could study for the bar.

Then a column came out in *The Hollywood Reporter*. It said that after my first picture, Metro had torn up my contract and given me a new one for $750 a week. It was all made up, a false publicity story to destroy the Guild's argument when they were trying to negotiate a deal. I got a call from the Guild people, and they said, "Jeez, look what you've done to us! Made us look like. . . . " I said, "It isn't true. I'll give you an affidavit; I'll testify, don't worry."

I got a call as soon as I hung up. They must have had my phone tapped. Come up to L.B. Mayer's office. I went up and Mayer says, "Billy, my boy, you know you're part of the family. We want to take care of you. You know you don't want to get mixed up with those communists, those radicals, those crazy people. Now, if anybody asks you about that salary, you tell them *that's the way it is.*"

Now, even as he was saying this, Selznick had wanted to borrow me—at $1,500 a week. He didn't know what I was getting. Metro wouldn't loan me to him because they figured if I knew what I could get, I wouldn't be happy, I'd be discontented with my $50 a week. $1,450 from

Mickey Rooney and Lewis Stone in *Love Finds Andy Hardy* (1938).

Selznick would have gone to Metro, because the overage on a lendout always went to the studio. All you got was your contract salary.

So I said, "Mr. Mayer, you'll have no trouble with me. None at all." He said, "I knew you'd understand." I said, "But there are two conditions." He said, "What *conditions?*" I said, "Well, in the first place, you have to pay me what you told the paper you pay me. In the second place, you've got to make it retroactive to when you said you did it." So Mayer screamed and yelled and pounded the desk and threw me out of the office. He told me I was a stupid sonofabitch and I'd never amount to anything. Out!

Well, as a footnote to that, I was at Metro for twenty years under contract, the longest any writer was under contract to that one studio. But every time I went to Mayer's office he told me I was stupid, I would never amount to anything. At one time he wanted me to head the shorts department. I wouldn't do it. What was the advantage? I was writing features for the top studio. And then he wanted me to produce. I said no. He said, "It's a promotion." I said, "I like writing. What do I want to be a producer for?" He told me I was stupid, would never amount to anything. And yet when he was out at Metro—and Dore Schary was in—and he formed his own independent company, he wanted me to come with him as his writer, at double my salary and with a percentage of the profits.

So Mayer acceded to my conditions, and I did two more Hardys in a row. They became very close to L.B.'s heart, no question about that. They always got good reviews and made a lot of money, and they represented values Mayer wanted to see represented.

How would you develop the Hardy stories? They always had an underlying theme or lesson, didn't they?

Underlying was the relationship between the father and the son, and I would give them parallel problems in a story. You gave Mickey a problem, and he found his solution in the case that the Judge was working on. Or the Judge would have a case that had him baffled, and the way Mickey would work out his problem would give the Judge an idea for the case. The two were integrated in the end.

One of the advantages of my law degree was that I could base the stories on law cases I knew of, and this helped me to develop a plot.

I came up with a story for the next Hardy picture based on the case of Lawrence against Fox, which is third-party beneficiary rule in the state of New York. I went and checked it out with the Metro legal counsel, I.H. Prinzmetal. He's dead now, but Prinz and I were quite friendly. I told him my story, and he thought it was sound legally and it worked. I then went to tell it to the producer.

The original producer had been Lou Ostrow. He was one of the nicest guys that God ever made, much too nice for the business. He wasn't an infighter at all. And he left and the series was taken over by Carey Wilson. I went up and told Carey the story and then went back to my office.

About two days later a lady writer named Kay Van Riper came down the hall, and I waved to her and she waved to me and came in. My office door was open. She had been in with Carey Wilson, and she said, "Oh, he's come up with the most wonderful story." I said, "What's the story?" And she told me. It was my story.

I thanked her, she went on her way, and I went to Carey's office. His secretary, Doris, was typing away and I said, "What are you typing, Doris?" She said, "The story that Carey was just dictating to me." I said, "Oh," and I leaned over the typewriter. It was my story. I reached down and pulled the page out of the machine. She asked what I was doing, and I said, "That's not his story, that's *my* story." I went toward his office. She said, "He's busy!" I said, "He's going to be a lot busier." I walked in, said, "This is my story and you stole it from me. I will not work for you again, and I will not work on the Hardys again." I walked out, and, behind me, he said, "You're going to have a helluva time getting anything else here." I said, "Then I'll go into some other business. I can always practice law. I don't need this." And I walked out.

I got a call to go up to Mayer's office. He said, "What happened?" I said, "I'm not going to go into it, but I will not work for that man and that's it." He said, "Well, we can't have our writers telling us what producers they'll work for and what ones they won't." I said, "Then I'll have to leave, that's all. I won't work for him." He said, "Why?" I said, "I don't want to go into it." But he insisted, and I finally had to tell it. And Mayer said, "Sure he stole your story. He gets a $5,000 bonus for any original story he comes up with."

So that was that. But he agreed I didn't have to work for Carey again. Then, several years later, Mickey Rooney was going into the army, and they wanted one more Hardy before he went in. They asked me to do it. I asked who was going to produce. Carey Wilson. I said I wouldn't do it. I got a call from Joe Cohn, the production executive, calling me into his office. He said, "I've spoken to L.B. and he said if you'll do this script, you will have no meetings with Carey; he will not be permitted to touch anything you write. When you hand it in, that's what he'll have to shoot. You will not have to see him or talk to him. Will you do it?" I said, "Fair enough, Joe." And I did it. And I did one more, my last Hardy Family picture.*

And that ended the series. But I said to L.B. at the time, "You know, you can keep this series going forever. It's like the comic strip 'Gasoline Alley,' where the kids grew up and had kids and so on." I said, "What you want to do is shoot a second picture now, one about the kid leaving college and going into the army. He wants to be a lawyer, maybe a judge like his father, but he figures if we lose this war there aren't going to be any more lawyers or judges." And I told him that if Mickey gets out okay, then you throw the next one right into release and you continue the series. The boy becomes a lawyer, has a family, the whole thing. But no, no, no. So they stopped the Hardy series, which was their problem, not mine. I kept on, and did every kind of picture, westerns, Lassies, Powell and Loys, Garson and Pigeons, musicals, everything.

One of your biggest hits was *Journey for Margaret*. How did that project develop?

I wrote that with my partner, David Hertz. We found a small piece by W.H. White, a foreign correspondent in London. It was in a collection of his, just a few pages, but we saw it and thought, what a picture this could make, about the shell-shocked kids in London during the Blitz, and the work of the Anna Freud clinic.

Dore Schary was then head of the B unit, and we went to him and asked him to buy it. He read it and said, "Gee, I don't know." We talked to him about what we wanted to do with it for quite a while. I knew Dore from years back on the Borscht Circuit. I replaced him when he was fired by Jennie Grossinger. And our social director there was Don Hartman, who later became head of Paramount. And Dore said, "Well, it can't cost much. I'll buy it. You fellows are crazy about it; we'll try it." And that's how we made it, and that was one of the advantages of the big studios. They could take a chance if they thought you were worth it. You can't understimate the great movie executives of that era. They were the real robber barons, most

---

*Ludwig collaborated on *Andy Hardy's Blonde Trouble* in 1944, and in 1946 on *Love Laughs at Andy Hardy*, his last contribution to the series. Surviving members of the original cast were reunited twelve years later in *Andy Hardy Comes Home*, an independent production released by MGM. Judge Hardy was dead and Andy was in dour middle age. The film was not a success.

of them. Ethically, personally, morally, forget 'em. But they were great showmen. They weren't like the bankers or the MBAs from Harvard we have now. The great showmen realized that the movie business meant gambling on people. It's the only industry in the world where the capital assets go home at night. The only one where the capital assets get pregnant or drunk or killed in an automobile accident.

I asked Mayer once, "What's the secret of running this place?" He said, "I'll tell you the secret. I hire the best people I can, and I leave them alone. If they deliver, they stay; if they don't, they're out." He was a great showman and a great executive. He *knew* his business. And I'll give you an example of that.

We'd been shooting *Journey for Margaret* for a week. They had assigned a documentary director to it, and he was a very good documentary director.* But he had no feeling for people, really. And after we saw the first week's shooting, all the dailies, we realized it was nothing, nothing.

David and I went up to Mayer's office first thing in the morning and asked to see him. They asked what it was about. "Very personal, very important," we said. Well, they didn't know if we'd get to see him. But we waited from nine until five that afternoon. We didn't even go out for lunch. We finally got him in his office and he said, "What do you want? I'm very busy." We said, "There's a picture shooting on this lot. We've seen the first week's dailies. They're no good. You've got to shut it down." He said, "What's that got to do with you?" We said, "Well, we wrote the script. We've got our blood in it—and you've got the company's money in it. And it's no good."

He said, "All right. I'll go down and take a look at it. If you're right, I'll close it down. If you're wrong, I'll take care of you good!" We said, "fair enough." He buzzed Benny Thau and said, "Benny, meet me in the projection room." And we went down. They screened the dailies. Across the hall the producer of the picture and the head of the unit were hiding, afraid, because they knew what was happening.

The lights came on finally, and Mayer turned to Benny. He said, "Close it down." The others came in and they started saying this and that, and Mayer said, "Shut up all of you. You people don't know what you're doing." And he began to tell them everything that was wrong. "How could you let Laraine Day have that hairdo?" Everything! Every little detail, and nothing escaped him. And he was right on everything, things we hadn't even seen.

The director was taken off, and he put Woody Van Dyke on it. W. S. Van Dyke, a giant of a director at Metro. We went down to the projection room again, and Van Dyke took a look at the stuff. He said, "I can't use a fucking foot of it." Mr. Van Dyke was an old-line cultured gent.

The producers said, "Well, the boys are here to work on it. . . . " The writers were always referred to as "the boys." I got very tired of being referred to as a "boy," and I made it a rule in my twenty years at Metro never to go there without a tie and a suit or a jacket. Anyway, the producers told Van Dyke we would do whatever was needed. And Van Dyke said, "I don't want anything. I read the script. It's all there on the paper. My job is to put that on the screen." And he did. And he made a helluva picture, a real three-Kleenex crier.

What was your contribution to *The Human Comedy*?

That was a very unusual script that I worked on. It was written by William Saroyan. The screenplay was written first and the novel afterwards. I never got a credit on it and probably should not have. But some of my proudest moments were when the reviews came out and

*Herbert Kline

Robert Young and Margaret O'Brien in *Journey for Margaret* (1942).

Guinn "Big Boy" Williams, Ruth Hussey, and Edward G. Robinson in *Blackmail* (1939).

the reviewers referred to five or six scenes I had written as "typically Saroyan." That made me feel very good.

I got a call one day from Clarence Brown to come over and meet him in the projection room. He was working on dailies for something else, but he gave me a script to read. It was about 900 pages long—Saroyan's beautiful script, brilliant script. Clarence said, "I can't shoot this, you know. The picture would run sixteen hours." He had already given it to Howard Estabrook, a very good screenwriter, and Howard had cut it down to about a 400-page version. It was still too long. It was wartime and the theatres weren't going to take terribly long pictures in any case.

I had to take the script and cut sequences out and put some in and not lose the story. It was much more than bridging. I had to develop character scenes that would pull the script together and leave it at a reasonable length.

The film has a lot of the qualities of the *Hardy* series.

Yeah, small town stuff, family stuff.

What were some of your scenes?

The opening with the train going by, little Butch Jenkins down there—"Goin' home, boy, goin' home." That was my opening. The scene with the fellow in the drugstore, frightening the kids. The scene in the house, with the harp. The scene with Frank Morgan and Mickey Rooney delivering the telegram. These things.

Clarence was not an emotional director. But he was a great, great technician. We took the picture out for a preview. There was the scene in the troop train—they're on their way to the West Coast to ship out, kids going to war. Lionel Stander* was in the scene and he starts singing, "Leaning on the Everlasting Arms." And he says, "Now come on, sing everybody." And all the people on the train join in the singing. Well, they get paid for it. But nobody else, nobody in the theatre, is singing. After, we get out of the theatre and into the car and Clarence says, "Goddammit, that scene . . . I wanted everybody in the audience to start to sing. I really wanted them to get into it. But nothing."

We all went home, but Clarence went to the studio. He had quarters there, and he used to be able to sleep right on the lot. About 4:30 A.M. my phone rings. It's Clarence. He says, "Get over here as fast as you can. Meet me in my projection room." So I go over and meet him. He says, "We're going to take the picture out again tomorrow night, and this time we're going to have that audience singing." He had Dutch Shearer, head of the sound department, there with us, and he told him what he wanted. And, oh, he was a smart man.

We took it out that night and when Stander comes on and says, "Come on, sing everybody," the troops start to sing, and then you hear—from somewhere in the back—an untrained woman's voice starts to sing. And then another. And someone else. And the people in the audience are convinced that other people in the audience have started to sing, and pretty soon the whole goddamn house was singing. And Clarence had done it. He had dubbed those other voices on the track to sound as if they were coming from the theatre. The audience stopped being self-conscious when they believed others were singing, and they sang, too.

It was wonderful to see.

Did you think the preview system was a good thing?

Well, you'd get cards telling you what to cut, what not to cut. Somebody, I think it was Nun-

*The soldier was Frank Jenks.

nally Johnson, was asked about sneak previews. He said that it was the only time where grown men who have spent their adult lives learning a business, sit around getting heart attacks because some sixteen-year-old is telling them how to do it better. That's a sneak preview.

How often would the results of a preview cause reshooting on a film?

It was not often you did massive reshooting. You might change this or that. But I've been on some that not even massive reshooting would help.

David and I got called in one morning by Sam Katz. He handed us a script to read and said, "We have a meeting with Eddie Robinson at eleven o'clock, to go over the script." So we read it fast and got up to his office. We told Katz, "We read the script and it's no goddamned good. We don't want to do it." He said, "I didn't ask you if you want to do it. Nobody wants to do it. Everybody knows it's a piece of shit. But you're under contract, so you're gonna do it." He said, "We have to start shooting because we've borrowed Robinson from Warners and we have to get him back on a certain date or we pay the overage. The sets are built, it's cast. You're doing it!"

This was *Blackmail?*

Aha. A piece of crap. And I said to him, "You know, most of this is stolen from Warners' *I Am a Fugitive from a Chain Gang.*" He said, "What do we care! We've got enough on them; they won't say anything to us." It was, in fact, the only "original" I ever did where I refused to sign the release certifying that it was original. And they didn't make me.

Robinson comes in and we're introduced to him. He sneers at us and says, "This script is a piece of shit." Then I said, "I couldn't agree with you more, Mr. Robinson." He said, "What do you mean?" I said, "We were introduced to you, but you obviously didn't have the courtesy to hear our names. If you look at that script, you'll see that our names are not on it." He looked and said, "I'm sorry about that." I told him what we thought of the script and that we didn't want to do it, but we had to. Robinson said, "I understand. Take all the time you want, fellas." And Honest John Considine, the producer, jumped up and yelled at him, "They can't! We've got to have you back at Warners!"

Well, for six weeks we lived at the studio. They gave us two offices, secretaries on twelve-hour shifts. We took our showers in the gym. One of our offices had day beds you could open up. We'd be working while they filmed. We'd go down and look at the dailies at the end of the day and then go right back to work to write the next day's stuff. And we tried to keep up with them, and they tried to keep up with the story. We got to a sequence where Robinson is on a chain gang and he's discovered that the murder he's in prison for was done by his former partner, who has now taken his wife, his business, and his kid. They're filming this and one of the executives calls us in and asks what's next. We say, "The next sequence will be his escape." And the executive says, "The escape? What makes him decide to escape?" I said, "Bad food." Well, he threw us out of his office. But they had to finish the picture, so they wouldn't throw us off that. And the picture was awful, just *awful*. But that picture proves an important thing about the movies. There is no picture ever made that cannot win some kind of an award: About a year later I'm walking on the third floor and Johnny Considine calls out to me from his office, "Hey, Bill, I want to show you something. Come on in." I come in and he's got a plaque. For *Blackmail*. It had grossed the biggest second Thursday afternoon in August in Buenos Aires.

How often would you be on the set during a production?

I tried to be around as often as I could, whether they needed me or not. And I tried to be around the cutter on a picture. In fact, on my first film, *Love Finds Andy Hardy,* that was the

King Vidor, Ann Richards, and Brian Donlevy on location for *An American Romance* (1944).

way I really learned how a picture was made. Conrad Nervig, one of the great cutters of all time, was put on the picture, and I would go into his cutting room to see how he put the sequences together. I did that a lot, and I saw how the cutting became vital. When George Cukor first came to direct, from the stage, he knew nothing about angles and how the shots ran together. Basil Wrangell, who was a great cutter, was assigned to be on the set with him, and he would explain how the setups would come together. And that was how Cukor learned. The good cutters were worth millions.

When you'd write a script, how technical and how detailed would you be? Did you write in directions, close-ups, and so on?

I would put everything in. You write a master scene, but a close-up is an italic. You're writing a film, and if you want something emphasized, camera angles are the way you emphasize it. If a reaction shot is more important than the line being spoken, you make sure the script shows it.

I always tried to write *for* the screen. There were writers who didn't—or couldn't—do that. They wrote a script to be *read*. There was a writer who did a script that opened with a horse race. He had about two-and-a-half pages of description—the look of the track, the faces of the crowd, the horses thundering down the stretch. When he got it back from the production department, the two-and-a-half pages were out and the new opening said: "Fade in; stock shot: horse race." So there were things you didn't bother to try and write. But when there was something significant in the action or the characterization, a detail to be shown, a reaction, then you had better make sure it's in.

I remember one case we were all hysterical over. It was a Joan Crawford picture. She's in the bathroom, washing her stockings, getting ready to go out. Her mother says, "Why don't you wear the red dress?" And the script then reads: "(Joan pauses for a moment, remembers that the red dress is still at the cleaners) Joan: No."

Now I don't know how any performer can act out that she has *realized* a dress is at the cleaners! So that is the kind of description in a script that is sheer nonsense. But other description is not, obviously—when a certain angle must be used to tell the story, to tell the audience what to look at.

Do you remember any disagreements with directors over an approach to a scene?

I did *An American Romance* with King Vidor. We had one scene where Brian Donlevy, who was patterned after Walter B. Chrysler, is having a board meeting at this long, long table. There are dozens of board members, his son, and John Qualen who had started with him in the old days. It was a six- or seven-page scene, and King didn't like the scene in the script. He couldn't get a concept of what was significant in the scene. He had me write the scene fourteen times, and he never liked it, it never suited him. But he couldn't tell me what he wanted. He shot the sequence from the head of the table, from the foot of the table, from the left, from the right, a two shot, a close-up, everything. There was enough film shot to make another picture. I came down on the set and I see him talking to Hal—Hal Rossen, our cameraman, a great one—and I listen to him talking about the scene, about the characters. He's got the script pages in his hand, and I pulled them out. He said, "What are you doing?" I said, "I'll be back in ten minutes." I went into a trailer on the set and rewrote the scene in ten minutes. I brought it back and said, "There's the scene you want." He looked at it and said, "Sure it is. Why the hell didn't you give it to me three months ago?" I said, "Because, you sonofabitch, I didn't know what the hell you were talking about. But when you get your tools in your hands, the camera, the actors, the set, suddenly you are *literate*." The scene, the things he wanted between the father and the son—I didn't know what he was talking about until then. So that's what can happen when you *are* on the set.

Were you happy with the way *An American Romance* turned out?

It should have been a great picture. We shot for eighteen months on location all over the country. It was the history of American industry through one man. We started with raw metal and a raw man, the immigrant, and we moved them both up. It was a fabulous picture at about four and a half hours, and it was supposed to go out road show. The war came, with double daylight savings time, and the exhibitors wouldn't run anything that long. So it was cut in half, to two hours and seven minutes. One whole enormous sequence I had to take out and make it an announcement on the radio. It doesn't give you much left to work with. But King was a great director.

You had a couple of regular collaborators—David Hertz, and, later, Sonya Levien. How would you work with each?

Some sequences you sat and did together, some you didn't; some you felt better about, and some the other one felt better about. Then you'd swap and do little changes. David Hertz wrote, in my view, some of the most beautiful love scenes that could ever be written. And when we came to a love scene, I'd say, "that's yours." And when we came to, say, a comedy scene, he would say, "that's yours." Sometimes you sat in the same room and bounced dialogue and business back and forth.

Sonya Levien has been dead these many years. She started in the silent days. She wrote two-reel pictures with Frank Capra. They got $200 and had to do one every two weeks.

We were called in and asked to work on something together, *The Great Caruso*. And we hit it off very well. She was a very bright lady. She looked like a demure, short, chubby middle-class housewife. And that helped her get away with murder. She was a lady who never gambled, but one time she was at the Clover Club with Willie Wyler and a couple of others. They're losing and they ask her to throw the dice for them; she gets eight passes in a row and doesn't have a nickel on the table.

We were writing *The Merry Widow* and we're doing the Maxim's scene. Lana gets out of the coach, pulls down her bodice and goes upstairs to meet Fernando Lamas. Lamas pulls her into the *salon privé*. We're called into the censor's office and he says, "You can't have that scene like that, you know." We said, "Why not?" He says, "Everybody will know what's going on in that room." And Sonya says, demurely, "He's going to give her supper." And Jack, the censor, says, "Yes, thank you, Sonya." He turns to me and says, "You put that in like that, didn't you?" And Sonya says, "What are you talking about?" And the censor turned to me again and says, "You dirty-minded s.o.b., what are you doing to that nice old lady?" But we got the scene okayed. She knew what she was doing. She was terrific.

Would you know in advance the stars of the films you wrote? And did you ever have to rewrite something because of a cast change?

You might be told, but the problem was you might be told you were writing for William Powell and Myrna Loy, and by the time you got done they had it for Hedy Lamarr and James Craig.

But the stars of that day were no problem. They were true professionals. They did their job. Clark Gable was the perfect professional. He came in every morning ready to work. I was in the dentist's office with him one day. I was waiting to go in and he was coming out. The dental technician was walking him out, a cute young girl. They'd been capping his teeth,

Mario Lanza and Ann Blyth in *The Great Caruso* (1951).

Gene Nelson (center) and ensemble in *Oklahoma* (1955).

and she says, "Mr. Gable, it's terrible what the studio makes you go through." And he said, "Sister, for the dough they're paying me they can take my arms off."

The good ones were professionals, not "stars." You know what Spencer Tracy said when somebody asked him what was the secret of great acting?—"Don't bump into the furniture."

Tracy, I remember, used to do something very funny. They'd call him for a picture after he'd been off a while, and they'd say, "Spence, we'll start shooting October 15th, and you're going to have to take off twenty pounds." And he'd say, "Going on a diet, off the sauce, nothing to worry about." Well, he had three identical gray suits—one was too tight, one was just right, and one was baggy. He'd come to the studio in the tight one after the first meeting, then a couple weeks later he'd wear the one that fit, and they'd check how the diet was going. And when the picture started shooting, he'd wear the baggy suit, and they'd see him and say, "Perfect." But he'd stay the same, never lose a bloody ounce.

You mentioned *The Great Caruso*. Most of the musical bios of that period were not particularly accurate. How much concern did you have for the facts in writing that?

We certainly tried. *Caruso* was a construction problem, really. Traditionally, in that sort of story you have the singer rise to glory after everybody tells him he's rotten, he'll never get anywhere. But nobody in the world ever said Caruso was rotten. He wasn't rotten even as a little kid, singing in the choir. Well, if you were going to be true to the facts, what the hell was going to get the audience rooting for him? Where were you going to go if you started out and he was a success?

So I went over his life from the beginning to the end, and I finally came up with something. When he was a kid singing in a church procession, his mother is sick, and she's dying, and he can't leave the church procession. Later you meet his wife to-be, and the night he's supposed to ask her parents for her hand, he can't go, he has to replace somebody at the Met. When his daughter is being born, he can't be there because he's scheduled to sing somewhere. And then he dies, and he dies of a throat hemorrhage. And you realized that the thing that made him, that voice, was the thing that *destroyed* him. And once I had that idea, I could do the picture. There's a line I put in the script, he says towards the end: "A man thinks he has a voice. But the truth is, the voice has the man."

How did you approach adapting *Oklahoma* to the screen?

The problem was in convincing the Broadway people of the difference in the medium. You couldn't do things exactly the way you did it on a stage. Rodgers and Hammerstein. Book and lyrics by Oscar Hammerstein, music by Richard Rodgers. They'd reach a place in the script and say, "How come you only have that line once? On the stage we used that line three times." I said, "We're shooting in Todd-AO. When he says that line he's in a twenty-eight-foot close-up. *Nobody* is going to miss that line." I said, "On the stage you may have to do it three times to make sure they got it." But they had a book about three-inches thick—a record of every performance of the show—and they'd flip it open and say, "See, in Boston, the second time that line comes on it got a two-and-a-half-second laugh." And it went back in, all three times.

And that was our problem with Agnes De Mille. Freddie Zinnemann called me over one day. He's got a huge goddamn stage—all of Oklahoma you could see, farmhouses and silos and fields. And Freddie's got a thirty-eight-foot boom to use. He tells me, "Watch." And Agnes is rehearsing the dancers just the way she did it on the stage. She tells them, "That's your proscenium there, and that's your proscenium there." Freddie says to me, "I tried to tell her we have no proscenium in the movies. We can go all over. That is why we have the big boom.

But she doesn't believe me." And she did the numbers as if they were still on a Broadway stage.

Those are some of the reasons why the picture never really took off. But Freddie was a dream to work with. He'd work with you; he'd call you to go over a scene. He'd say, "Tell me what you have in mind with this scene." And sometimes he would say, "Right, I see," and sometimes, "No, what I think we could use here is this. . . . " We were both very disappointed with that film. I came out of the preview and went over to him in the lobby. He said, "It wasn't worth two years of our lives." And it wasn't.

You were the Writers Guild's shop steward. What were your responsibilities in that position?

I was the original shop steward. You had to police what went on between the studio and the writers, protecting the conditions in our first contract. Previously, the producers had a habit of putting four or five writers on a script, unknown to each other. You might find out at lunch that you were both doing the same thing. The producer would take a scene from one script and from another, and he'd put them all together, and put one name on it—possibly his own, or a friend's. So we had a rule in the contract that any writer assigned to a script had a right to ask if any other writer was working on the same material. He then had the option to either refuse the assignment or take it under those conditions. And if you were already on a script, you had the right to be told in writing if anyone else was assigned to it. There was a sheet sent around only to the producers, the executives, and the directors, listing every writer and his current assignment. I asked for a copy of it. Dwight Henderson, the head of Metro's legal department—who was unique in that he wasn't a lawyer—said, "No, why should we give it to you?" I said, "Because the contract says so. And every contract has an implied condition of cooperation. Where would it hurt you to just run off one more copy?" He said, "We're not required to." I said okay. At that time they had 135 writers on the lot. I said, "There are 135 writers here, most of them good Guild members. I'm going to instruct every one of them to come in tomorrow morning and ask the story department if anyone else is on their material. And you have to give it to them in writing. And I will instruct them not to write a word until they get their answer." I said, "You figure out how much time you're going to lose." We got the list from then on.

And then another thing I had to do was watch "Guild shop." Our first contract carried eighty percent Guild shop. This meant that eighty percent of the writers had to be members of the Guild. This was to protect the writers who'd been with the Screen Playwrights and wouldn't join the Guild—they'd been loyal to management. This shop quota went out not long after. Anyway, if the shop quota fell below eighty percent the studio had to get the one, two, or however many writers needed to join or had to pay their dues.

I got a call one day that Fox had fallen below the quota by one writer. So I called Zanuck and told him he was below the shop quota. He said, "What are we supposed to do?" I said, "You'll have to get another writer to join." He said, "Who? I don't have anyone." I said, "You have Fidel LaBarba." Fidel LaBarba had been flyweight boxing champion, and Zanuck put him on the payroll so he could work out with him in the gym. He didn't want to pay him himself, so he called him a writer. Before the Guild, that was the place to bury somebody. H.N. Swanson, the agent, said, "If Dillinger had had a pencil, he could have hid out in the Thalberg building for two years." And Frances Marion said to me, when I was just beginning, "I'll give you the rule for a writer's survival in this business: keep out of the halls."

So Zanuck said, "Oh, come on, he's not a writer." I said, "We don't make writers, Mr. Zanuck, the producers do. If you hire somebody as a writer, to us he's a writer. Either he's going to have to join the Guild, or you're going to have to pay his dues." He said, "That's ridiculous. This guy just works out in the gym with me. He can't write, I tell you." I said, "What *can* he do?" He said, "He can't do anything." And I said, "So why don't you put him on the payroll where he doesn't have to do anything?" He said, "What do you mean?" I said, "Make him a producer." Well, Zanuck slammed down the receiver. And a couple of days later Fidel LaBarba went on the Fox payroll as an associate producer.

And then there were occasions when I had to see that the writers themselves didn't violate the contract. There was a strike by the studio painters. They were out picketing. We had in our contract, as contracts do, a no-strike clause. Unless you were threatened with bodily harm, you were supposed to go to work. I'm in my office working, and I get a call from the assistant story editor. He said, "What the hell is happening with these goddamn writers? They've all walked out. They're having a mass meeting across the street." I looked out my window, and sure enough they were there. And the painters had cheered when they went out, thinking the writers were joining their strike—which would have voided our contract.

I rushed out and told them the meeting was illegal, a breach of contract. Several of the writers who had arranged this tried to shout me down. We had a real verbal brouhaha. But finally I was able to get the writers to walk back in. And this made the painters madder than ever at us. But we could not jeopardize the Guild's contract, and I couldn't permit it as the shop steward. I was caught in the middle, but those were the things that you had to do.

They were real messy times.

One morning I'm working at my typewriter and two fellows who shall remain nameless come in. They close the door and lock it. I say, "What's up?" "Well," they say, "we have been observing you, seeing the kind of person you are. And we'd like to invite you to join the Communist party." I said, "Fellas, it's not for me. I'm not the kind of person who likes to be told what to think and when to think it." I said, "You go your way and I'll go mine." And they left. I went back to work. When I came back from lunch a certain director, King Vidor, comes to visit. He said, "We've been watching you, and we think you're the kind of person we want to invite into the Alliance." He was very big in Sam Wood's right-wing Motion Picture Alliance for the Preservation of American Ideals. I said, "Well, that's interesting, King. What are you people for, anyway?" He said, "Well, we're against this, and we're against that. . . ." I said, "No, no, not what you're against. I want to know if you're for what I'm for. What are you for?" He said, "We're against so and so. I know *that*." I said, "King, not against. What are you *for*?" He thought for a minute, and then he said, "I'll have to ask Sam Wood." And he walked out.

Can you discuss the Guild's attitude at the time of the HUAC hearings and the Hollywood Ten?

I remember one big meeting we had at the time of the Unfriendly Ten. Our counsel was asked questions, and he said, "I'm sorry, I can't answer that." He explained that his firm represented—I forget how many of the Ten. I got up and said, "I think that is a conflict of interest. Either you represent them or you represent us." It wasn't that I was for the Ten or against them, but the Guild had the right to have proper legal counsel. I quoted a great judge to the effect that if the question of conflict arises, it exists. Well, I was shouted down, booed and hooted. The left was strong and vocal. They had the technique of holding off a vote till the very end of a meeting, when everybody but the most committed had gone, which helped them carry various things.

The following day the attorney called me. He said, "Bill, you're an honest man and I respect your views. If you feel there's a conflict, then there's a conflict. We're resigning as the Guild's counsel." It was a very decent thing to do.

I believed, and I said at the time, the whole thing was ineptly handled, largely to get headlines and to create martyrs. They were laying themselves open to a contempt charge, and that was what they were going to get. And contempt is a charge you cannot beat. Their answers could have been very simple. When they were asked, "Are you now, or have you ever been, a member of the Communist party," they knew damn well who had the registration card. And all they had to say was, "If you mean a member of the American Communist party, which is legal on the ballot in thirty-eight states . . . yes. If you mean the Russian Communist party, no." They could have done that, but they didn't. I think what they did was definitely in the hopes of arousing a furor in the nation. But that was not the sense of the nation at the time. They miscalculated. And the result was a lot of ruined careers and a lot of people destroyed.

It became both horrible and absurd. Some people suffered so much from it, while some of what happened afterward was absolutely ludicrous. Shirley Temple was listed in Red Channels—she was a kid then! I was at a casting meeting one time a few years later and somebody mentioned Adolph Menjou for a part. Menjou was an active rightist and testified as a member of the Alliance for the Preservation of American Ideals. And when his name was mentioned, one of the executives at the meeting said, "Oh, no, no, Menjou . . . he was one of those guys in front of the McCarthy committee." Well, he had testified, but he was on the *committee's side*. And already people didn't remember or didn't care.

It was quite a dramatic time. There are many books on the subject. But I've always wanted somebody to do a book on the eleventh man, the man waiting after they got done with the unfriendly ten. That was Robert Rossen. And Robert Rossen talked. And built his career from there. Which was a little . . . not nice.

You said that when Mayer was out at MGM he hired you for his independent productions?

Yes, doubled my salary and gave me a percentage. But he never made a picture as an independent. He was afraid to make a picture. He was the great man until he made a picture that wasn't any good. He could have gotten financed wherever he wanted. We had a couple of projects ready. Jack Cummings, for whom I wrote *Interrupted Melody* and got the Oscar, was his nephew, and he was there as line producer if anything was made. We had a couple of scripts all ready— one that John Wayne and Jimmy Cagney had agreed to co-star in. The financing was there. And he wouldn't go, kept finding reasons not to go. Well, he died a year into my two-year contract with him, and his estate paid out the full amount.

He had his faults, of course. But I was very fond of L.B. He was a short man with a barrel chest, but he had tremendous energy. In those last two years, when he was dying of leukemia, I had to trot to keep up with him. He got that barrel chest as a kid in St. John, New Brunswick— there's a synagogue there he endowed in the memory of his mother. He dived for salvage from the wrecks in the harbor. He had no scuba equipment or anything, just his lungs. He was supporting the family—the father was never much. And he was arrested. The other people in the salvage business called the police because he didn't have a business license. As a kid he couldn't get one. And he was hauled in before the judge. And when the judge heard about the boy supporting his family, he had his father set up a business so the boy could say he was working for him.

Later on he moved to Boston. He showed pictures. He rented a store. And he did everything— turned on the lights, sold the tickets, started the projector going, and he bicycled the prints back and forth from the movie company. That's how he started.

For twenty years I worked for him and he was like an irate father, always telling me I'd never amount to anything. He nearly fired me once. The commissary at Metro always had one thing permanently on the menu—L.B. Mayer's chicken soup. His mother's recipe. It was the greatest thing in the world. You got an enormous bowl like a birdbath, full of rich, delicious broth, with chunks of chicken and huge matzoh balls. It had to be on the menu at all times, whether he was in town or not. Well, we had had a bad year. We were at lunch and everyone was talking about how bad the pictures did. And I said, "We made a mistake. We should have shelved the pictures and released the chicken soup."

I got back to my office and there's a message to go up to Mayer's office. He said, "What are you doing? We're supporting you. We're letting you raise your family. We're paying your bills. And you're running down our product! You're tearing down our studio!"

That was one thing about L.B.—he had no sense of humor.

You were there as the studio system began to dissolve. Were there things the studios could have done to prevent it?

The studios destroyed the business themselves. There's no question about it. When television came in, they hoped it would get uninvented. Nick Schenck would not let you mention the word "television" in his presence. The advertising agencies begged the studios to make television programs. We had the technicians, the actors, the writers, the sets, everything. But the execs thought, why should we fatten the opposition?

One day at the studio, I heard that Lassie's contract had been dropped. L.B. said, "We don't want to make any more dog pictures." I had done some Lassie pictures, and I said, "Mr. Mayer, the dog gets $250 a week, and the trainer, Red Weatherwax, gets $500 a week. That's $750 a week. This dog is worth millions in television, if you ask me." He said, "You're stupid. We're not interested in television." Well, Jack Wrather was interested in that dog, and in television, and he made a nickel or two with Lassie.

Then one Friday Metro closed out eighty-nine of its contract players. It was like dumping the family silver out the window. But Mayer said, "They're not working fifty-two weeks a year, why do we have to pay them fifty-two weeks a year? When we need them, we'll get them." He didn't foresee that the studio would end up paying them more; they would have to give them percentages, approvals. The studio had lost its capital assets, and that's really when they went down. And the exhibitors themselves helped destroy it when they won the case against block booking. Metro's policy was that no theatre owner lost money on MGM pictures. When a theatre owner said, "Well, this year we lost $6,000," the salesman would take out a checkbook and write a check for $6,000. "You don't lose money on our pictures," he'd say, and the theatre owner would sign up with MGM for another year.

Five major studios, a couple of minor ones. Hundreds of actors, writers, directors under one roof. But the businessmen thought there was a better way. I remember, I was standing outside the commissary one day in December, and I heard a couple of grips talking. One of them was saying, "The trouble with this goddamned business is there's no *traditions*." And the other one said, "Oh yeah? What about *firing before Christmas?*"

But it was a wonderful business. It was great fun. And it will never, *never* be the same.

Opposite page: **"I've paid a month's rent on the battlefield." Groucho Marx in *Duck Soup*** (1933).

7 · NAT PERRIN

Nat Perrin on the set of *Abbott and Costello in Hollywood* (1945).

His name may be unfamiliar, but Nat Perrin has probably made as many people laugh as Groucho Marx, Buster Keaton, Lou Costello, Bob Hope, Gracie Allen, Eddie Cantor, and Red Skelton. These are, after all, only some of the celebrated comics for whom Perrin concocted the gags, punch lines, pratfalls, zany plots, and assorted funny stuff in dozens of screenplays since 1931.

To hear him tell it, his long career began in starry-eyed innocence and with a comical ease that must make any aspiring screenwriter faint with envy. An abrupt backstage encounter with Groucho and the brothers Marx took the young New York law student to Paramount Studios and collaboration with S.J. Perelman and a gaggle of gag writers on the script of *Monkey Business.* The following year (1932), he returned to the Marxes to co-write their last Paramount picture and their anarchic masterpiece, *Duck Soup.* Depression-era audiences may have found them a little too anarchic, but, if the box-office take was a disappointment, Perrin's stock was on the rise. He would go on to write for nearly every major comedian in Hollywood.

For much of the rest of the decade, Perrin worked in partnership with another Marx graduate, Arthur Sheekman, forming one of those legendary staples of '30s Hollywood, a rollicking writing team not unlike Benson and Law of *Boy Meets Girl,* simultaneously spinning plot twists and hoodwinking producers. In the '40s Perrin was himself elevated to producer status at MGM, and, later, with the studio crumbling from various setbacks, he joined the enemy camp of television, producing, directing, and writing several hit series, including *Death Valley Days* and *The Addams Family.*

Nat Perrin lives in the flats of Beverly Hills, his apartment house a few doors south of Wilshire Boulevard. He is small, trim, deeply suntanned. The day we meet he's dressed country-club casual in light slacks and a tan cashmere sweater. He speaks with an elegant New York rasp reminiscent of the late Nelson Rockefeller. He claims to be eighty years old, but looks two decades younger. Witty, insightful, he is an interviewer's dream.

My people were musicians and they played a lot of the Broadway shows, the Shubert shows, in the pit. As a kid, they'd take me and I'd sit with them. I fell in love with the theatre very early in my life, when I was nine years old. I played an instrument in the grammar school orchestra. I played drums. We had fifty violins and a drummer, no piano. New York City, Public School 40, Prospect Avenue in the Bronx. The teacher in charge of the orchestra—his name was John Stonewasher, later became John Stone; his son, Peter Stone, did *1776,* many well-known pictures—got a job as a social director and he took three of us to play with him in the orchestra. I was not quite twelve. He took a pianist and a violinist and a drummer, and he used to put on shows on Saturday nights. There were sketches, and every two weeks the cast would change and he would always have to get new characters to do the same few sketches with him. Sometimes it was hard to find someone to handle it, and I hung around him so much and got to know all the sketches, so when he couldn't find someone to do it, I volunteered. And I began to do these things on a regular basis, and that was my entry into show business. Later on when I got into college, I used to put on shows in the Borscht Circuit myself.

You were still in school when you first met the Marx Brothers?

I was studying for the bar, and I happened to write a sketch with Groucho and Chico Marx in mind, because I was wild about them at the time. This was 1931. Somebody in my class said he could get me an agent who could get it to the Marx Brothers. He thought it was good. The agent was a woman, Frieda Fishbein—she had handled Moss Hart for *Once in a Lifetime*, handled Elmer Rice's *Street Scene*. And so, with law books under my arms, I went to the city with this fellow who worked for her. It turned out he was no more than an office boy, and I couldn't get to see Frieda Fishbein.

But I took some of her stationery and typed out my own letter to the Marx Brothers, who were doing a personal appearance in New York with the picture *Animal Crackers*, their second movie. I went out to the theatre in Brooklyn with my sketch and law books, and went to the stage door. It was a very quiet, dreary place—it wasn't like the musical theatres in New York. I gave the sketch to the doorman, and about five minutes later he came out and said, "Mr. Marx will see you."

And Groucho came out and said, "We don't do sketches. We're going out to Hollywood to do feature pictures. But I think you could be useful. Would you like to come out to Hollywood?" And I must have said yes, because here we are. This was a Thursday or Friday, and they were leaving for California by train on Wednesday. In those days you went by train. Tuesday, I took the bar exam, and the next day I went to Hollywood.

Did you sign a contract before you left?

When I was with Groucho in his dressing room, he called the others in and told them about this kid and so forth. And he told me to meet Chico at the Paramount Building, where the Paramount offices were, 43rd and Broadway, to talk business.

About a year before, I'd gotten tired of law school and wanted to get into the picture business, and I had the opportunity, through a friend of mine, to be a publicist. So I went to see Charlie Reinfeld at Warner Bros., and he offered me the job of publicist. And that was fine, and we got to talk salary and he said it would be twenty-five dollars a week. Well, I used to play around with an orchestra in those days and make fifteen to twenty dollars a night, so the salary didn't seem like that much. I didn't tell him that it wasn't enough, but he read my expression and said, "You're not really happy with that," in a kind of hostile tone. I said, "No, that's fine." But he said he didn't want to have any unhappy people, and he literally shut the door in my face, and that was that.

Now, a year later I'm going to meet Chico. I'd already gone home and told my family and friends I'm going to Hollywood. It was kind of a crazy thing. And I went to meet Chico, and in the back of my mind was this previous experience. We hadn't talked about money. We hadn't talked about anything. And Chico said, "We'll have to set the salary." I didn't want to repeat what had happened before, and I said, "Anything you give me is fine." I didn't have a dime at the time. He said, "Well, how about a hundred dollars a week?" I said, I don't want a hundred dollars a week, I'll take *anything*. And Chico says, "Well, a hundred dollars is fine." I said, "Please, Mr. Marx, *don't* ask for a hundred dollars!" And I begged him, literally begged him, not to ask for it. And he started to get annoyed with me because I didn't want the hundred. It was too much.

And then we went out into the street and I met a man named Russell Holman, and he was filling out all the details, preparing all the tickets for the train. And he said, "This Perrin, how much on him?" And Chico said, "A hundred dollars," and the man never looked up from the piece of paper. Just wrote "$100." And I can tell you that created one of the most unhappy moments of my life when I got out to Hollywood and I met people like Sid Perelman and others, and nobody was making less than a thousand a week. Some were making $1,200, $1,250, $1,500 . . . and I was schlepping along at a hundred dollars a week.

You all took the same train to California? How was the journey?

Everybody was on the train. All the brothers, all their wives, all their children, everybody was on the train. It was westward ho.

I met Morrie Ryskind on the train. He was coming out to do a picture, and he was very friendly with the Marxes. And on the train they picked up Arthur Sheekman, who had been a newspaperman in Chicago, and he helped Groucho write one or two of his early books—I think *Beds* was one of them. And we became partners after the Marx Brothers picture.

The evening we arrived, about five o'clock in the evening, we had dinner, and then there was a meeting at the Roosevelt Hotel, in somebody's room—I think it was Groucho's—for a reading of the script. Sid Perelman has written about this. S.J. Perelman and a man named Will Johnstone, who was a cartoonist in New York, a very well-known cartoonist, were out here, oh, weeks ahead of us, writing the screenplay. We came out, ostensibly, to punch it up a little bit.

Well, the reading of the script's become a kind of famous affair. It was the most dismal reading in the history of all script readings. I was there. It wasn't exactly as Perelman wrote about it, but what the hell. . . . Perelman and Johnstone wrote the script, and Perelman read it. Johnstone was a much older man, a white-haired man then. And Perelman read it, and it was a dismal reading. First of all, professional comics very seldom laugh at material, certainly not material being prepared for them. And it's very difficult to read a script in which you're describing action by Harpo. It would be difficult to detect it from the reading even if it *was* funny. "He slips on the banana . . . "—hard to get it geographically. It's almost impossible.

Did Perelman try to act any of it out?

No, it wasn't his nature to do that. He . . . read the script. And after he finished, Perelman said, "What do you think?" And Groucho said: "I think we need a script." Didn't say a "new script." He said: "*We need a script.*"

Did you think the script was as bad as that?

I didn't know enough about scripts then . . . but it didn't strike me as very funny. And that was the beginning. We had to redo the whole script.

How was the writing done—in groups, separately?

Sheekman and Perelman were both quite a bit older than I was. I was literally the baby of the outfit. We had a suite at Paramount Studios. They worked in one room, I worked in another room. And I would try to put scenes in. I knew the characters were aboard ship—they were stowaways. I knew they were being chased. I had the general outline of the plot. And I thought up scenes and got scenes in. The story, the basic story, was pretty much the same as what Johnstone and Perelman had written. Everything was embellishment, scenes, jokes. And if I had known then what I know now, about credit and all that, most likely I'd have gotten a screenplay credit with Perelman and Sheekman. I didn't say anything, but I had enough material in so that Herman Mankiewicz recommended me for another picture.

Mankiewicz was the producer of *Monkey Business*?

They were called supervisors then, but he was the producer.

I liked Herman Mankiewicz quite a bit, but he didn't seem particularly interested in what he was doing with the Marx Brothers. It was just a romp for him. He thought—in a kind of an agreeable way—that he was far superior to that stuff, and it was all very easy to him. If you had enough jokes and the people laughed, that was it.

My introduction to Mankiewicz was when we walked into his office at Paramount for a meeting to decide what was going to be done about the picture. As all of us came tripping into Mankiewicz's office; he opened his desk drawer and he took out the clammiest looking deck of cards, and he said, "Anybody in the crowd—casino, ten dollars a deal!" That was my introduction to the big Hollywood producer.

And we had quite a crowd in there—all the Marx Brothers and the writers. There was a fellow brought along—I don't remember him on the train, but he'd come with his wife on a honeymoon. That was J. Carver Pusey. And he was a cartoonist, too. Had a strip called *Benny*. A real Ivy League guy—looked like F. Scott Fitzgerald and Zelda, he and his wife. A very handsome Princetonian type of guy—what the hell he was doing in this crowd, I don't know. And his wife was gorgeous. He was there, and Mankiewicz, and our agents. And we sat around the floor for this conference, and Mankiewicz couldn't have been less interested. "All right, let's get some jokes," that was his general tone. But he was a very bright guy, you know, and made pretty good jokes himself. He was a very witty man.

You said Mankiewicz got you your next job?

He got me my very next deal, when I was finished with *Monkey Business*. He called somebody at Metro on a Buster Keaton picture, and he recommended me. It was customary to ask, "What's his salary?" Now, the studios would cut your salary, but nobody would *increase* your salary unless you really had them, you know. And I was getting a hundred a week when they asked him "what's his salary?" And he said, "$300 a week." Then he asked me, "Can you get over to Metro tomorrow?" And I said, "Sure, of course."

What was the picture?

Sidewalks of New York.

Did you get to know Keaton? Was he involved in the writing?

He was around. I don't remember if I worked on it with him. He was a very strange, quiet, removed guy. I got to know him in later years, ten, twelve years later, at Metro. He was through by then, and he was flat broke. They brought him back, as kind of a gag man. It was a job.

There was a Red Skelton picture called *A Confederate Yankee*,* and they had a preview on it. I was working at the studio, and they felt the picture needed a lot of work on it, so they

A Southern Yankee (1948)

The four Marx Brothers in *Monkey Business* (1931).

asked me to stop what I was doing and come on this for retakes, added scenes. Keaton was also around to work on it. So I'd go to lunch with him and see him, and I liked him. He was a very, very nice guy . . . but he was *dull*. I can't say "dull" in the sense that he said dull things—he didn't say *anything* much, you know. He may have been very shy, so he couldn't open up much. It's hard to know. He must have been a pretty creative guy, because he had some great gags in a lot of his silent films.

Did he show any interest in the job they'd given him—or was it just a paycheck?

It's hard to tell. I don't think you could tell with a guy like that about anything, whether he felt enthusiastic or degraded to be doing it. Nothing. He was just a guy who came and sat around with the fellows and once in a while something would remind him of a routine he did for a certain picture. With that he was forthcoming. But it was hard to know if there was much more behind the facade of the man. I didn't detect it if there was anything more.

You went back to Paramount and the Marx Brothers to write *Duck Soup?*

Yeah. Leo McCarey was the director of the picture. Leo was a very attractive man, very attractive personality. He was the real-life Cary Grant of the movies. And he was fun to be around.

He had worked in the silent pictures, and apparently when you were sitting around a conference in the silent days, you were dealing with visual things, you know, so they would act everything out. And Leo never lost that habit of acting things out. He'd say to you, "How about we have a little . . . " [makes drinking motion]. Or he'd say, "Why don't we go play some . . . " [imitates swing of golf club]. Always the gesture, the silent gesture to indicate something. He was very funny, he was colorful.

But one of the problems that I found with McCarey was that . . . sometimes creativity in comedy can be a dangerous thing. If you've been around a comedy script for a long time, by the time you're filming—I don't care what's in there—it starts seeming very stale. And if you have someone on the set trying to be creative—and he is, to a degree—and his is the *newest* and *freshest* idea to come along, by comparison to what you've already got in the script, then you might say, "Yeah, let's do that instead." And it's altogether possible what you've suggested may be amusing, but it isn't one-tenth as good as what's in the script. But when you hear it for the first time, you're giggling. You're not giggling at the stuff you've already heard for three months. . . . So they were improvising, McCarey and Groucho, and they went so far overboard, they must have gone crazy. They must have been having a ball on the set.

I thought the picture could have been very much better if they stuck to the script. But I understand completely how you can be sort of hypnotized by a guy like McCarey and his humor. A very, very good comedy director, but he should have stuck more to the script and he would have had a much better picture.

How was the script of *Duck Soup* put together? Similar to *Monkey Business,* a thin story line with the gags and scenes worked in?

Oh, Jesus, I don't remember. There was a little story there that Kalmar and Ruby wrote. They were mostly songwriters. Harry Ruby was a very entertaining man, very cute. Groucho loved him.

It had a good satirical slant, but it got too crazy. See, the guys were already crazy, and in this thing *everything* was *meshuginah*. And when you have crazy on crazy, it's no good. Instinctively, Thalberg knew that, and that's why his Marx Brothers pictures are far and away the best ones. He was a man brought up on the stage; his relationship was to the audience, to tell them a story. And for the Marxes especially, that was a very sound theory.

Can you recall an example of when the Marxes altered a scene you had written?

I wrote a little scene for them, in *Monkey Business*, where they sneak into a barber shop on board ship. They're stowaways, hiding from the officers. Now what was supposed to happen there is they jump into the place of the barber and the shoeshine boy. An officer has got his face covered with a steam towel. He's wearing his white uniform and white shoes. The gag that I had was that Harpo was so preoccupied that he inadvertently reaches for the black shoe polish and polishes the black all over the white shoes. Well, that was the gag, and it was supposed to get laughs. Now what they had him do, instead of inadvertently reaching for the black polish, they had him *deliberately* take the wrong polish—and that's just being deliberately crazy, and it's implausible, you see? By just a little change. It got a laugh anyway, but it made me cringe. I only mentioned it because you asked . . . you never remember the positive things.

I've got a list that was made of the hundred best pictures ever, and *Duck Soup* is in there. But when I saw the picture, I probably was thinking what should have been there from the script.

Actually, *Duck Soup* didn't do too well on release, did it?

I don't think it was a hit. I don't think any of the Marx Brothers pictures were particular hits. It was always thought, well, if we get it done faster and cheaper, we'll make money. But they just stretched out, timewise, and they weren't making the kind of money expected. They were never flops in that sense, except maybe at the very end. I don't think the country was quite ready for them in their time. They are now, with a much more sophisticated audience.

You and Arthur Sheekman became writing partners for your next assignments, right?

Yes. It was a collaboration, 100 percent.

You'd work in the same room, toss dialogue back and forth?

Yeah. Unless we got into some bind about time and we had to show something to somebody. He would take a scene, or I would take a scene, and we'd go over it. Otherwise, it was a total collaboration.

Our agent, who was then with Famous Artists, Charlie Feldman's agency, said he could get each one of us the same amount of money he was getting for the team. And that seemed like a pretty good deal for us, so we decided to try it on our own. And that's what broke up the team. But we always remained friends, and our families remained friends. As a matter of fact, I was at Gloria Sheekman's house Sunday. The kid I had seen in the hospital crib was fifty years old yesterday. His daughter. After Sheekman, I worked on my own. I had one assignment where I was thrown in with somebody else, but just one.

It was a Machiavellian experience. I was called in because a script was in trouble. I came up with what they thought was the solution for the script, and the producer said, "Great, go ahead you guys." I don't want to mention the writer's name because he's still around. So we were put together, and I would sit with him and nothing would happen. I would come up with ideas—I didn't know if they were good or bad, but out of sheer embarrassment I would throw them in, because you can't just sit there like two dummies, you know. But nothing. I would be talking and in the middle of talking he'd lift the phone, start dialing. Nothing happened for about three weeks, and we were called in by the producer and the executive producer and they wanted to know why no pages were coming through. And the minute we got into the room with them, the dam burst. This other writer had all sorts of ideas. He didn't want to discuss them with me. He made it sound like he just thought of these. He was so prepared for that meeting, to be the winner of the day. And I realized that he was a total fraud. Harry was his first name. And I said, "Harry seems to really have a hold of this thing now. Why don't I get the hell off and go back to what I was doing?" And they were glad to see me go because it began to look like I might have been holding everything back.

Wasn't it frustrating for a writer to be shuffled to someone else's project or to be taken off one you might have initiated?

There were jokes about the number of writers they'd let work on a script; you know, when the script was dead, they'd beat it to death again. Well, that was unavoidable. It wasn't as crazy as it seems.

Certainly, if a writer writes a script, his own inspiration we'll call it, it's his baby; the chances are you'll get a more cohesive script, of course. However, you must remember that a script at a studio like Metro evolved for one of the stars under long-term contract. Metro had about forty to fifty top stars. That was a fact of life. And the studio couldn't wait for the right script to come along for Clark Gable or Marie Dressler or Judy Garland or the Marx Brothers. With their salaries, you had better have a script ready when they finished their previous picture. And so that's why they couldn't wait. You have a commitment to begin in February, and this writer turns out seventy-five pages the first month, and you're getting nothing for the next four, five weeks . . . you better get another writer on the picture. It's like a pitcher in a big ballgame when he's just not doing the job; you get a fresh man. It was natural. I don't care what writers were out here, and they had some of the world's greatest—Noel Coward, Lillian Hellman, Zoë Akins. They were all taken on and taken off scripts.

You and Sheekman worked on a couple of Eddie Cantor vehicles for Goldwyn—*Kid Millions* and *Roman Scandals*. Would Goldwyn be actively involved with these productions?

Goldwyn was of the same school as Thalberg and had very high aspirations. He didn't want to do cheap gags. He wanted stories with charm, with a little heart. Goldwyn had very good taste, but he was a kind of humorless man, a man born in Russia, talked with a thick accent— the idiom was not his, you know. Eddie Cantor and the other top comics were very far removed from him. I don't think he would have taken Cantor if Cantor hadn't worked for Ziegfeld—Goldwyn had very high respect for Ziegfeld.

I knew that Goldwyn was seeking the very best, and sometimes it just doesn't turn out the best. But at least Goldwyn strove for it, whereas the people who were involved when I was writing for the Marx Brothers, their attitude was, "Let's get all these gag men together and do it." It didn't matter to them. But it did matter to Goldwyn. I thought he was a terrific person, and I can understand why he had all these classic pictures. They were more to his taste. Comedy wasn't. He was going in against his basic instincts.

He was so unsure of comedy that whatever we brought in, even if he liked it, he would try to get someone else's opinion. You'd give him some comedy bits, and afterward he'd go to a party and he'd run into Charlie Chaplin or David Selznick or whoever the hell it would be, and he'd start to tell them with some enthusiasm what the boys had come up with.

Always referred to us as "the boys"—*"duh boys"* with his accent. And that provided complications because he had Dubose Heyward working for him at the same period. So, *duh boys* and *Duboys*, you know, it was a real problem for the secretary, who'd he want to talk to.

Anyway, he'd be at a party and tell somebody what we'd come up with, and I'd imagine Goldwyn telling a comedy line was like somebody reading a telephone book. And he'd go from the earlier enthusiasm he had down to the reaction he'd gotten telling our jokes at the party. And the next day it would be, "Fellas . . . it's no use what you got." And we'd have to start again.

Eddie Cantor in *Kid Millions* (1934).

But it worked both ways. Sheekman and I came up with an idea—I think it was the idea for *Kid Millions*. We had about an eight- or nine-page outline. Goldwyn and his wife were in New York, and Eddie Cantor was appearing at the Paramount Theatre, lines around the block—big, big star at the time. And we were sent for because Cantor was getting impatient. So we came to New York and went to Goldwyn at the Waldorf Astoria and told him our story idea. He didn't like it. And we had already tried about ten different ideas. Goldwyn was getting impatient, too, and he had already, before we got there, contacted the playwrights Lindsay and Crouse, to write the picture.

So Goldwyn said he didn't like it. And then Eddie Cantor came in. It was a bitter, windy afternoon, and he came in full of piss and ginger, wearing a racoon coat. And we told Cantor the story and he loved it. He was so enthusiastic that Goldwyn said, "Well, let me read it again." And he went in the other room, and I know what he did—he asked his wife, Frances, to read the thing. And he came back five minutes later and said, "You're right, Eddie. This is it, this is great." Now, five minutes before he'd said it was no good at all. And then somebody reminded him he's hired Lindsay and Crouse to come up with something. And he said, "Well, they'll work on this story with *duh boys*." And somebody said, "Suppose they don't like this story?" And Goldwyn said, "*Don't like it*? If they don't like it, *they're crazy!*"

With some producers it seems that for a writer to get something through he had to be as good verbally as he was on paper.

Yes, that was very common practice. A lot of what you did was never on paper. You'd go in and tell the story line, especially when you're starting from scratch. And some people were good at it and others weren't. Some writers were verbal spellbinders, and others might have a very good story to tell but fuck it up in the telling—stutter, or forget the point, or whatever. With a writing team, very often at a meeting one of the partners is telling the story and the other one keeps interrupting, "No, no, you left out so and so. . . . " Or maybe the writer's bluffing through a pitch, or he gets stuck, and he'll turn to the collaborator and say, "Now you take over, take it from there." And the other guy whispers: "Take it from there? Where? We haven't got any more." There were writers who were very well known for this. Baker and Towne were spellbinders.

At Metro they had this famous character, Robert Hopkins. Hoppie never had an office. He wandered the halls and the commissary having coffee with everybody. He was an "idea" man. He'd been up in the Klondike, the Yukon, this and that, a real character. He was an old man in his seventies when I got to know him. He worked on *Sidewalks of New York*. He'd come in and tell you a few ideas and then go his way and have coffee with somebody. The story is he was walking through the halls at Metro and passed the producers looking for something for Gable. And he says, "Two guys in San Francisco, one's a priest and the other guy runs a big saloon, and you end it with the San Francisco earthquake—bang!" And he gives them a shot in the ribs. "Do I have to tell you any more?" And that became the picture *San Francisco*.

You worked at just about all of the studios. Did you find one more congenial to writers, one more oppressive?

There were some studios that wanted you to check in in the morning and leave in the evening. But others never kept track. Metro didn't care if you showed up at the studio or were home or wherever you were. I found, generally speaking, very adult treatment for everybody, and you were pretty much on your own. They only cared about the end product.

What was the function of a "story editor" like Sam Marx?

When somebody needed a writer, he would tell Sam Marx what was needed and Sam would figure out who would be best-suited for that particular kind of script—from background readings. And he would recommend someone and sometimes make the deal if you were not already under contract. Producers very seldom talked money to anybody. If you were making deals with outside people, the casting department made the deal for actors; Sam Marx made the deal for writers. Nothing to do with writing the script.

While under contract, could you turn down an assignment?

You could turn it down. You could say, "I don't think I can handle this thing. I don't think I can deliver what you want because I don't like it," whatever. Well, they wouldn't want you on it. They would try somebody else on it. But if you consistently turned them down, sure, they would say, "Look, maybe you belong in another business. Why don't we terminate our agreement." Many people didn't work out. There was a big parade of writers in and out of offices.

I remember when Tennessee Williams was at Metro under contract. We saw the name on an office, but nobody had seen or heard of Tennessee Williams. Later, word seeped out that he was this young guy out of the South, and somebody who knew some top executives at Metro had recommended him very highly and they put him under contract.

And there came the time when they tried him on a script. There was a producer named Leon Gordon, a fussy, English gentleman, but he was from New York—I think, the Bronx. He had started out as a writer, wrote the play *White Cargo*, for which he was sued for plagiarism. He lost the suit. An elegant kind of guy. And he needed work done on a script, and they decided to try it on this new writer, Tennessee Williams. Williams read the script, and he came in for his meetings with the producers to say what he thinks about the story, how he would approach it. And right away, the producer says, "This guy's a *weirdo*." And dismisses him. A second producer has him do some work, with the same result—"he's a weirdo." And a third producer, the same. And the studio thought, "Christ, we've got a real turkey here."

Milton Beecher was authorized to discuss it with him and see if there was anything they could do with him. And Milton called him in and said, "Maybe we haven't been giving you the right things, 'patch-up' jobs. . . . Why don't you go away and write something of your own, what you think would be a good motion picture script for Metro." That was the phrase, "for Metro."

Anyway, Williams goes off and works on a script for two, three months, his own story, "for Metro." And he hands the script in and they read it. And now they're *sure* they've got a nut on their hands. They called him in again and said, "Look, this script, it just . . . *isn't Metro*." Williams had about four months left on his contract. And they said, "Suppose we make a deal. You can keep your script . . . " (the story and script would normally belong to Metro because he wrote it for them) " . . . and we tear up the contract." Now, most writers, knowing they had four months' salary coming, would say "The hell with you, keep the script, I'll take the money." But Tennessee Williams was obviously a young man who believed in his work, and he said, "Oh, that sounds fine." And they tore up his contract for, I think, $250 a week, and he took his script and left the studio. The script turned out to be *The Glass Menagerie*, and he later sold the movie rights for about $500,000.

You wrote a couple of scripts for Shirley Temple at the height of her popularity.

Yes. Nothing I particularly remember about it. Just an asssignment.

Robert Paige, Lou Costello, and Bud Abbott in *Pardon My Sarong* (1942).

That was at Fox. I remember Zanuck as a very good executive. I didn't think he was overly creative, but he was on the line for what he did have to say. He was the only executive I knew that after a story meeting with him, you would get a typewritten record of the meeting, the minutes. It was like a court record.

Zanuck liked to work at night—that's how he functioned—when there were no interruptions, no telephones ringing. A secretary would call you for the meeting with Zanuck and say, "Be available about midnight." Then you'd come and wait in your office, because Zanuck would have other meetings with other people. It was a very common thing to be there in the middle of the night with Zanuck. And you'd get this record of the meeting. And there was no question of—as with some executives—you go away and do something and he says, "This isn't what we agreed." With Zanuck it was on record, no nonsense, and, whether it was a good or bad decision, he had come to a final decision.

You worked on several films for Abbott and Costello. How would that compare with writing for the Marx Brothers?

Oh, they were a couple of mugs, you know. They were at heart burlesque comedians, burlesque mentalities. They were much better than they allowed themselves to be. The little guy was a very, very talented comic, I don't care what his background was, he had a real comic sense. But they never knew a line. They came in, got the general sense of the scene, and then winged it. And their ad-libbing wasn't . . . they were good comedians but they weren't that sharp.

They were very undisciplined, real slobs as far as the work was concerned. They owed themselves a lot better than they allowed themselves to become.

They'd stick those long burlesque routines in without the slightest motivation.

That I wouldn't mind so much, because at least it was something set in their minds and it was tried before an audience. But when they really had a scene that you wrote for them and they didn't take the trouble to memorize the lines and come in and give it a shot—that was something else. Even if they had said, "We don't like the scene, we've rewritten it." But they just came in and said, "What do we do?"

They were both sloppy about their work, and it was no fun writing for them. I rather liked them both, personally. They were nice guys, genial guys. In those days before TV, I used to run films at home, and Lou Costello had a fantastic library of 16mm films, and he was very generous and I would go out to the Valley and pick up fresh films every week. But there was no fun in trying to write out things that had a flow to them and a comic undercurrent to the thing, because their attitude was, "Throw it together. Let's get the hell out of here." They just wanted to get out of the studio.

In spite of it, their pictures were very profitable at that time.

I suppose so. But listen, the public's taste—you can't go by that.

You also worked on a picture for another, but less successful team, Olsen and Johnson. *Hellzapoppin'* was a hit on the stage, but it must have been a problem adapting the format for film.

They had it around, they couldn't get it on film, and they asked if I could lick it. I got a helluva deal on the thing, and I came in with the idea that I knew would do it, and they knew it too. The idea was to have the writer telling the story, and you cut to flashbacks, and you could go to any place you wanted. They needed a gimmick like that because otherwise it was just a crazy review.

But it was just wrecked. I wrote them physical things, and I could see the director didn't know what the hell was on the paper. And it was a mess.

That was H.C. Potter?

Yes. It was not his dish at all. He was a New Englander, New Yorker, traveled with a sophisticated crowd, Margaret Sullavan, Leland Hayward, that whole crowd. And this was not him. He just took the assignment. I just took the assignment, too. I didn't really want to do it. I didn't like the show. I didn't like the guys. They weren't funny guys to me.

Did you have a particular method for constructing your scripts?

Not particularly. You always started in a state of desperation, because it was blank. You sat there and said, "What can we do for Wallace Beery or Red Skelton or Eddie Cantor," whoever the hell it was. You rack your brain; where can I start? And you come up with something. Could be a character, could be a background.

I remember I had to get a picture for Wallace Beery. Nothing came in for Beery, and you had to do it from the ground floor. I ran across a guy I knew to be part of the mob that ran a very posh gambling club out here called the Clover Club. He was a very nice guy, looked like Vladek Zbysko, the wrestler, with a shaved, bullet-head. He married an interior decorator, and she had a lamp shop on Beverly. And I saw this guy sitting there, handling a lamp. And this was the basic idea for Wallace Beery's character, an ex-con getting involved with redecorating his apartment.

Another time they came to me and said, "We need a *Thin Man*." That's when I became a producer, for *Song of the Thin Man*. And I thought, what could we do with *The Thin Man* this time? And at that time jive talk, the beebop era, had just started. And I had an idea to use that background. And I consulted a man, Harry the Hipster, who played piano in a Vine Street joint. Keenan Wynn and Peter Lawford were going to be in the picture, and they were excited about the idea of doing something with that background—you know, crazy jazz musicians with their weird idiom. And I remember the evening they called and said, "We want to bring Harry the Hipster over." And they brought him over and he finished a whole bottle of brandy while playing some crazy songs on the piano. The point is, that was the first thing I thought of, the background, and then you develop the line of your story.

What was your relationship with the directors you worked with?

The directors of that era were afraid of writers, many of them. Many came from the editing department: they were ex-cutters, ex-production men. They were men who knew how to shoot film to make it go together. It's no use having the world's greatest script if a guy goes down there and you can't put the picture together. That's money, that's the millions. If you waste your money on the script, that's comparative small potatoes. If the picture's shot and it won't go together, you have a fiasco on your hands. Ninety-nine percent of the directors that I've watched—if I wasn't chased off the set—never gave a real direction. Not one real direction. If they wanted a scene done differently, they'd say, "Let's, um . . . " [snaps fingers] "*snap, snap, snap.*" That was the biggest direction in the world, snapping fingers. They felt the scene didn't look right, but they didn't know what was wrong with it. They couldn't articulate it. They couldn't communicate with the actors on that level. So they would just try it again and hope it would be better.

I remember a direction I heard on the sound track of *Song of the Thin Man*. Eddie Buzzell was the director, and I expected him to be better because he had been in the New York theatre as an actor, and I thought he was showwise—he wasn't an ex-cutter. Don Taylor was playing a character who played the clarinet, and he had gone whacky from drugs—he's in a sanitarium. It's a very dramatic moment, and I hear the director say on the sound track, "Do things with your face." Now what the heck kind of direction is that? "Do things with your face." As I say, they didn't know how to communicate, to express themselves.

Did a lot of writers feel a rivalry with the directors?

Every director thought that every writer thought the director stank. And they were right. You'd go to a party of writers anywhere in Hollywood and someone would start to say, "You know what that fucking director did? This is the scene and he. . . . " And then all the stories about stupid direction would come forth. There'd be a deluge.

The Epstein brothers—Julius and Philip—told a cute story about directors. They were casting a picture that was being done, and they were testing a boy and a girl. The scene was very, very brief. And the boy in the scene says, "Why don't we go up to my pad and have some fun?" And she's supposed to say, "I don't think I ought to do that." And he's supposed to say, "What's the matter . . . *scruples?*" And that was the little scene. And they're doing it, and there's the director, with nothing else to do but *listen* to them. And they film it and he says, "Come up to my pad"; she says, "I don't think so," and then he says to her, "What's the *matter*, Scruples?" And, you know, the Epsteins renamed her Scruples in the script, and every time they sent in a page the director would say, "Oh, cut it out, fellas!"

And that was a typical thing. They might misread lines by the ton on the set and the directors would never catch it. And I never heard a director correct a reading.

Were you often asked to rewrite scenes while the picture was being shot?

You could be, especially if you were working with difficult people . . . the *brooders*. Stars who would think about it, discuss it. And they come in and—something in the script that they'd known about for three months—but they'd come in and say, "I don't know, it doesn't feel right."

Was it always just appeasing the stars, or would you sometimes agree with them?

Oh, yes, maybe actually the chemistry is not there on the set between certain people, and it isn't playing. You know, on paper it's one thing, but, when they start to play it, maybe there's an artificiality about it that even the best acting can't overcome. So they'll say, "Jesus, the scene just doesn't play. What can you do with it?" And you would work on the scene, hopefully bringing in some fresh pages later in the day.

It was not uncommon to be writing or rewriting during the entire filming. Morrie Ryskind was always on the set for *Stage Door* because, somehow, they were never satisfied completely with the script and they were forced to start because of commitments. And he spent the entire shooting of the picture on the stage, scribbling, changing lines and bringing new scenes over.

Can we talk about your experiences in the so-called writers' wars following the formation of the Screen Writers Guild?

It was a very bitter fight, a very big political battle, and of course, as you must know, leading to the investigations, the Hollywood Ten, the destruction of many, many lives and careers—and the most horrendous thing that ever happened in any industry, I think. Families broke up, lifelong friendships were destroyed, and people went to jail.

In the '30s, did anyone try to recruit you for the Screen Playwrights, the company union?

They were set up to try and break the Guild. It was union busting, working directly for the producers. But it was political, too. A lot of these high-priced writers in the Screen Playwrights were rock-ribbed Republicans.

You ask me about their recruiting. Sheekman and I were working at 20th then, and we were called by Bess Meredyth, who was a very well-known writer in that day. And she said, "I just want you to know that Darryl says if you don't resign from the Writers Guild, you'll never work in this industry again." Now, if she were working for another kind of a union, she wouldn't have had to report what *Darryl says*. Whatever *Darryl* said, she would have come to us with arguments that went beyond Darryl and the producers. So there was no question about it—they were representing management. The stooges of management.

I was friendly with a few of them, and I just thought they were very foolish fellows. I was friendly with a guy named Richard MacCauley—he was a journeyman writer. I said, "Dick, you guys may 'get' us *communists*, but it's gonna be a doubled-edged sword. The other side will have some power, and they'll 'get' people like you. You're just a working guy. The top guys will get back in—even if they're Hitler." It was like Jack Warner said, "That guy will never work in this studio again—*unless I need him.*"

And it *was* a double-edged sword, and the minute it started to settle, MacCauley dropped out of the business. And there were quite a number like him. The producers decided to get rid of all the political troublemakers. They decided they had enough of this. The industry comes first, you know, peace and quiet. And so a lot of the Screen Playwrights fell by the wayside, too. MacCauley said, "Look, I'm a Vermont Yankee conservative. I can't help it, that's the kind of guy I am." I don't think he *knew* of the shenanigans of the leaders of the movement. I don't think he understood. It was all beyond him.

John Mahin, I think, regretted what he did the remainder of his life. I began to see John Mahin again years later. I liked John Mahin. I think that he regretted it all very much. It was a great tragedy. He lost the friendship of the people he really liked and respected.

But he wanted to stay close to Jim McGuinness and some of the guys who would keep his career going at that stage of his life. He didn't realize.

Jim McGuinness—a writer and producer at MGM—seems to have been one of the most malicious forces in all this. You knew him, didn't you?

He was a very sharp and very personable guy. I used to like to go off by myself for lunch, have a drink, sometimes meet a girl in those days. And I used to run into Jim McGuinness in a little bar, and we'd have very pleasant conversations, even political ones—you know, let your hair down kind of talk. And on the whole I liked him. But he was a very dangerous man. They're the most dangerous, the genial, likable, smiling ones. He was a pretty awful guy.

McGuinness said to me, "There are people who walk, and people who ride, and I intend to be part of the people who always ride."

Wasn't there a script of yours he tried to have rewritten as an anti-union story?

How'd you hear about that? Well that's absolutely true. He was my executive producer on a Red Skelton picture, *Whistling in Brooklyn*. And in the story there was this cab driver who was murdered, and Red was figuring it out and planted himself to catch the murderer. And we established in the story that the cab driver was murdered because he tried to form a union of cab drivers. So when we were talking the story line, McGuinness says, "No, he wasn't murdered because he tried to form a union; he was murdered because he *refused to join* the union." Well, I couldn't write that. I didn't want to write that for anything under the sun. And there comes a time when, even when you don't have guts, you have to *pretend* you have guts, you know, and I just wouldn't change it. And I was just a writer then, I wasn't even a producer yet, and I wouldn't do it!

Myrna Loy, Keenan Wynn, and William Powell in *Song of the Thin Man* (1947).

Ann Rutherford, Rags Ragland, Jean Rogers, and Red Skelton in *Whistling in Brooklyn* (1943).

And it was taken up to Mayer. McGuinness thought, my God, Mayer would throw me right out of the studio. And don't you know, Mayer says, "What was the original story line?" And he says, "I don't see any reason to change the original." And that's the decision that came through. "The original line stays there." And he was the supreme court. But that's the kind of confrontation you could have then.

Later, during the hearings, I was called in for raising money for what was called "The Committee for the First Amendment"—Humphrey Bogart, Huston, a gang of others, going to Washington because the hearings had started. And I went around the studio getting money. Some people gave cash. They were afraid to give a check.

I got a call to come to Eddie Mannix's office. I was turned in for raising money for political purposes on company time. And it was true, I did do that. I went to Mannix's office and every executive was there—Sam Katz, Benny Thau, and McGuinness. The witness chair was next to Mannix's desk. Mannix liked me very much, wanted me to become his assistant. But I didn't want to become anyone's assistant.

And I was given the witness chair, and they told me why I was there. Well, there was no point in denying it. But the discussion went on, and I said, "You don't understand that we're fighting for Hollywood, we're fighting for *your* good name. You have been accused of injecting communist propaganda in pictures. Is it true? You're the executives. Are you that dumb that you'd let that happen? But that's the rumor that's around. And who started it? The Screen Playwrights." And I got into this argument with McGuinness, and, I want to tell you, I felt that everybody else in that room agreed with me.

I even said to them, "You're invited to our meetings." And they were. It was Eddie Cantor, oddly enough, who signed the telegram inviting them to discuss this problem. And I said, "We didn't hear from any of you. Everybody is ignoring this thing, and the only people fighting for the reputation of the industry are people like us."

And I think it *was* true. The Screen Playwrights had put it all in motion, had started the rumors and accusations. And it wasn't true at all. Nobody who saw motion pictures and had a brain could say it was true. Unless you could say a fellow who believes in freedom of speech in a picture is spouting communist propaganda.

You were friends with some of the men who went to prison?

Dalton Trumbo, Lester Cole, Adrian Scott—these were people I knew very well and liked and respected. I wrote a letter asking for a parole for Dalton Trumbo. I just saw his widow, Cleo, about a week or so ago at an art exhibit. I saw Paul Jarrico quite a lot. We kind of lost track of each other because he went to Paris and was there for years. I even tried to sell material for one of them. I tried to sell something for Adrian Scott, but couldn't. It was under another name, but they just didn't buy it, and I tried very hard.

In the late '40s you began producing shows for television, right? What shows did you work on?

I did a big hit called *My Friend Irma,* and I did *Shower of Stars,* and one old series I was with for four years called *Death Valley Days,* which was a western anthology. And I rather enjoyed that because if you didn't like an actor, you know, in two more days you'd never have to see him again.

The only regular was the Old Ranger, a fellow named Stanley Andrews. This was before Reagan did the show. And all the stories for that series had to be true. You had to authenticate the story with history books. Then I would have to send the documentation and the premise to the agency, McCann Erickson, to get approval, just on the premise. They wanted an authenticated "true story of the Old West."

And it was funny, because the woman who started it—you'd think it would be some old western lady, still smoking a corncob pipe. Well, she was a highly sophisticated New Yorker, Ruth Witting, with many articles in the *New Yorker* magazine, a real Old New York family. But she took a trip out West and became fascinated with some of the old people she met. When she took the trip, there were still people alive from the Wild West. Some of the Earps were still alive, and so on. And she originally did some stories for the *New Yorker,* of all places. Later, she went into advertising, and she and Gwen Bristow did the first *Death Valley Days.*

Were you writing as well as producing these shows?

I did an enormous amount of writing. *Every* producer in television on a weekly basis had to. They don't need anybody on a series with a stet cast, stet sets, to produce. What's there to produce? You get the script and you give it to the production department and you say, "Rehearsal Saturday at eleven o'clock." They need somebody who's going to make sure they have a workable, viable script, week in, week out.

Certainly this was true on the comedy series, and it was almost equally true on *Death Valley Days.*

The writers for these weekly shows were paid by the script, and they would do as well as they could, but they'd want to move on to something else, you know—they're not going to give it six weeks if they can get a script done in two and a half. You ask for a rewrite and they give you a fast rewrite. And I understood that. Get it done, get your money, and get on to the next thing was the writer's attitude. And so I had to work on the scripts, and I worked every Saturday and Sunday. My kids remember me Sunday mornings—no matter what time they came down, I was there with my briefcase next to the easy chair and scribbling away. You had to, that was the job. So I did an enormous amount of writing. But I liked working on those series. And I directed about forty of them. And that was fun. Great for your God complex. You say, "Action," and everybody moves. You say, "Cut," they stand frozen. And you also got to control the final product.

I also had a very big hit, but a very difficult show, *The Addams Family.* We had a tough time there. They were in a house and they were mad people, and they didn't want to leave the house. And to bring in characters, and to play on their surprise at seeing this crazy house, became very repetitive. It was very difficult to keep your central people in any kind of plot because they were so mad. That was tough writing, to do it well, to keep something going and string all the madness on it. It was like Marx Brothers stuff. But I loved the cast of *Addams Family.* I just adored Carolyn Jones, who tragically died a while ago, and I loved John Astin, and I was crazy about Jackie Coogan. And it was all real, real fun.

What do you see as the major difference between filmmaking now and in the studio era?

The producer lost a good deal of control when it became a "director's medium." And with everybody telling the director, "You're a genius . . . you're the *auteur,*" these guys would go crazy, shoot a scene from under the floor and from the ceiling and through the ears and up the nostrils, and everybody went broke—the pictures got out of hand. I think the producer is coming back into power.

The good pictures today are better than the good pictures from years gone by. And they should be—the subject matter is not confined any more by a Hays Code; there are no restrictions. What they lack today, and I think it's a very important ingredient, are the great number of personalities, the stars. It was a personality business then. You tailored everything to them, and you made it fit them. But now it's a content medium, and, if the picture doesn't stand on its story, it's going to fall on its ass. Then or now, there will never be a *lot* of great pictures made. After all, how many great symphonies do you get in a century?

8 · ALLEN RIVKIN

Joan Crawford and Fred Astaire before the camera in *Dancing Lady* (1933).

Allen Rivkin (center) with
screenwriters Daniel Taradash
and Leonard Spigelgass, 1970.

The Writers Guild of America (West) is headquartered in a sleek new building in
Beverly Hills, a long way from the back rooms where the first members used to meet
in clandestine defiance of the studio bosses. In a small office on the second floor you
will find Allen Rivkin, the Guild's director of public relations and editor of its newsletter.
He is, as well, its resident link to the past, to Hecht and MacArthur and Herman
Mankiewicz and all the irreverent ex-newsmen turned screenwriters who made
Hollywood movies in the 1930s the fastest, funniest, wisecrackingest the world has
ever seen.

"I'm an old Hollywood hand," he says. "So old it shakes." He's eighty-three now,
moves with the elaborate slowness of the elderly, and his hearing's not so good. But
Rivkin, who wrote forty-some pictures in a long career, can still tell a story or two.

He was born in Wisconsin and grew up in Minnesota, studying journalism at the
University of Minnesota and graduating to reporting jobs on the *Minneapolis Journal*
and the *Chicago Tribune*. He left the Midwest for a public relations post in New York,
which eventually took him to the Hollywood publicity department of RKO. With
a foot in the studio door, Rivkin sold his first screen story. For the next twenty-seven
years, alone or teamed with various colorful partners (Gene Fowler, gun-toting
P. J. Wolfson, a young and ambitious John Huston) he turned out MGM musicals
(*Dancing Lady*), a snappy James Cagney vehicle (*Picture Snatcher*), political comedy
(*The Farmer's Daughter*), wartime propaganda (*Joe Smith, American*), postwar tragedy
(*Till the End of Time*), westerns, romances, mysteries. To Thalberg and Selznick and
Zanuck, faced with producing fifty-plus movies a year apiece, Rivkin was one of the
versatile, dependable pros they staked their schedules on.

With his strong interest in politics and social change, Rivkin became an activist for such liberal and Democratic party causes as the anti-Nazi Fight for Freedom and the Committee for the Arts. In 1960 he produced the Democratic National Convention in Los Angeles. And from the beginning, Rivkin worked with the Screen Writers Guild, formulating policies, implementing them, serving on the Guild's board of directors in the '30s, as its president in the '50s. His most satisfying screen work, not suprisingly, was with stories like *Till the End of Time* and *The Farmer's Daughter*, where he could express his social concerns in the guise of entertainment.

In the guise of remembrance, he conjures up a comic and romantic era of rakish, eccentric talents churning out moving pictures by day, roistering in night clubs and gambling joints (or sweating through pre-dawn story conferences) by night. There were those, as the Eastern literati always proclaimed, who were frustrated or degraded by Hollywood, but Rivkin wasn't one of them. He did good work when he could, and did what he could when it was just work.

If you want to know about writers in Hollywood, Rivkin's the man to ask. He knew them all, the legends and the names remembered now only in the jumble of faded credits on a Late Show screening somewhere. It was a long time ago, and most of them are long dead, but Rivkin is their witness. "He was a funny fella," Rivkin says affectionately, laughing at the memory of some old friends' misadventures, making you long to have known them, too.

Your first job in Hollywood was in a publicity department. That was 1931?

I came out here earlier than that, '23 or '24. A friend of mine, Milton Hock, was out here working as an assistant director at Universal. I got a job at his studio as a "juicer," an electrician. I worked at that for a while until a couple of incidents happened. One time I was standing underneath an arc, and in those days we used real arcs, not electric bulbs. The arc fell out of the lamp and went past my pocket and hit the floor—a thick oak plank floor—and burned all the way through. I got a little nervous about the job. And then something happened out on location at Malibu. In the generator there's a box where we'd plug all our lights in. The waves came up and blew the whole goddamned thing, and my lamp shattered. I quit.

I got a job as a press agent over at Ince Productions. Joe Kennedy, JFK's father, owned it, because Gloria Swanson was his mistress. So I was a press agent for a while. And then Milt's sister was getting married back in Minnesota, and he went home and I went with him. But Hollywood continued to fascinate me, and during the time I was a newpaperman in Minneapolis and Chicago, and later in New York, I was always trying to get back to Hollywood. In New York, for months every lunch hour, I would go and bug the head of the publicity department at RKO and sit in his office. He finally got sick of me and said, "All right, go to Hollywood." So I came out again and joined the RKO publicity department under an awfully nice guy named Hy Daab. My wife and I stayed in a room at the Hollywood Plaza hotel, and for four months I took a bus from the hotel to the studio, until I got a car—on time, of course. My first assignment was to put on the premiere of *Cimarron* in downtown Los Angeles at a theatre called the Hill Street. It would have been quite a premiere, too, except that, as the line of cars got to the theatre, a gas main broke and manholes and things exploded all over the place. All the top names in the movies were there and it could have killed them all. It was a disaster.

And on top of it, all the papers reported what happened but none of them mentioned the name of the picture.

My office mate at RKO was a fellow named Ben Markson. He and I decided to write a one-act play about a couple of New York columnists, Walter Winchell and Mark Hellinger. It was done by the Writer's Club, which, at the time, put on one-act plays every Saturday night. It was called *Is My Face Red*. And afterward we sat around in my little apartment in Hollywood and knocked out a three-act play from this.

I had a friend I met at the Hollywood Plaza, another New York emigré, named Leonard Spigelgass. He was assistant story editor at Fox. I gave him the play and asked him to see if he could do anything with it. And he called me a little later and said, "Jesus, I've sold it to the studio for $10,000." So I ran to find Ben Markson and tell him. I said, "We sold it to Fox for $10,000!" And Markson says, "That's tough shit, 'cause I just sold it to Selznick for $7,500." Selznick was the boss at RKO then. And they checked and had priority on the sale by an hour.

I was so naïve about the way things were done that when we didn't get paid on the spot I started to get nervous, and I got so worried that I went to find Selznick. I ran to the studio gate as he was leaving one day. I called out to him, "Mr. Selznick! I'm Allen Rivkin and you just bought a play of Ben Markson's and mine." And he shrugged, said, "Yes, yes, I liked it. Well?" And I said, "Well, *where's the money*?" He laughed and said, "I haven't got it on me." He said, "Come in tomorrow and there'll be a check for you."

We became very good friends later, David and I. We became neighbors after awhile, and I thought he was a wonderful fellow.

Is My Face Red **was filmed. . . .**

Yes, starring Ricardo Cortez.

And you began working as a screenwriter?

I got an agent, a crazy little agent, but he was good for me. He got me a job at Universal. Dick Schayer was the scenario director, and he put me on an assignment with "Pinky" Wolfson. P. J. Wolfson had been a pharmacist at Madison Square Garden: he wrote a book, and the studio brought him out. We became collaborators, and that lasted for several years, until we got to MGM. Then he thought that together we weren't making enough money and if we split up he'd get more and maybe I'd get more. He got more, but I didn't get more. He stayed at MGM and I went to Fox.

How would your collaboration with Wolfson work?

We would talk. And then he would write the scene. He wrote in longhand. Then I would type it, and as I typed it I'd make the changes I felt were necessary. And we would do it like that for the whole script.

Wolfson was quite a character, wasn't he? He liked to carry a gun.

Oh, he shot himself once. I don't know whether it was an accident or on purpose, to get his wife's sympathy. He was involved in an affair with an awfully nice lady. It wasn't going to work, though. He couldn't leave his wife and three kids. He was a very devious guy (laughs) and I always though he shot himself to get sympathy; but maybe not.

Ricardo Cortez and Jill Esmond in *Is My Face Red?* (1932).

ohn Huston and the cast of *The Maltese Falcon* (1941): Peter Lorre, Mary Astor, and Hum-

But he'd bring guns to the studio?

Oh, sure. And I did, too, for Christ's sake! To emulate him. We'd carry a little .25 calibre, loaded; put it right there in the waistband.

Did the studio bosses know about this? I can't imagine a producer feeling too safe with his writers packing loaded weapons.

Oh, Christ, at a studio picnic once we started shooting it up. MGM had a picnic every year. All the stars were there, everybody. And we got pretty loaded at this picnic, and we started shooting our guns in the air. Eddie Mannix, the number-two man under Mayer, came after us. He had been a teamster in New York—an awfully nice guy—but we were punk kids and didn't care what the hell quality was in a fella. He says, "Stop that shooting, you kids!" And we said, "Oh, fuck you, you old teamster." He could have fired us . . . but he didn't.

Another time we were at Universal, in the writers' building. It was a two-floor building, and John Huston and Pinky and I were on the second floor. For some reason, I don't know, we were celebrating *something*, and everybody was very drunk. Pinky shot at a liquor bottle, and the glass shattered all over the steps. Well, John got a call from the head of the studio, Carl Laemmle, Jr., and had to report there right away. He was drunk, and when he started down the steps he slipped and fell all the way down. The glass tore his pants and he stumbled out of the building with his ass all bloody and lacerated from the glass.

Later, John and I collaborated on *The Maltese Falcon*. And that was some collaboration. We were office mates, and we had a secretary between us. He came in one day and he says, "Jack . . . " meaning Jack Warner " . . . Jack wants us to take another shot at *The Maltese Falcon*." They had made it before and it was a bomb. He says, "Have you read the book?" And I said, "No." He says, "Read it." So I read it. And he says, "Let's give the book to the secretary to break it down into scenes and dialogue." Now, in every studio, whatever a secretary types goes into the pool for copies. How it got to Jack Warner, I don't know, but John came in one day all elated. He says, "What do you know! Jack says I can direct *Maltese Falcon*." I said, "Well, good. So we've got to write the script." And he said, "No. The *secretary* did the script, and that's what he wants me to shoot!" And he took the credit on it, naturally, because he was the director.

And that made John.

Huston had wanted to direct for some time?

He always wanted to. He had been bugging Jack Warner to let him. His father, Walter Huston, had been on the lot at the time, and Walter said, "This writing business will get you nowhere. You've got to be a director to be in control." And, of course, Walter was right.

Speaking of writing teams, you said the "wildest" was the team of Gene Baker and Graham Towne. What do you remember about them?

Well, Gene Towne was the greatest salesman of stories you ever heard. I was in a meeting with them once when he was selling something to Walter Wanger. I had nothing to do with it. I was just sitting there waiting for Walter to get to me. Gene pitched the goddamnest story, moving around, acting it out. Graham, knowing Gene so well, knowing he was pitching horseshit, is sitting there nodding off, half asleep.

Walter finally says, "That's a great story. I'll buy it! You guys go and write it." And the two of them went out, and that night they celebrated the sale. Next morning, Gene couldn't remember the story he had told, and neither could Graham.

They came back to Walter, sheepishly, and told him. Walter said, "Well, at least *I* remember." And he told them, and they went and wrote it.

What about writers like Robert Hopkins—who supposedly never actually wrote at all?

Oh, yeah, Bob Hopkins was the greatest *talking* writer of them all. He talked fifty pictures or so. He'd talk the story out, with every other word being obscene. And once he told the story, the producer had to get it right because it went straight out of Hoppie's head when he finished telling it. If the guy he was talking to didn't like the story, Hoppie just turned around and went back to the commissary to dream up another one. If a producer decided to go with something, Bob had to find a collaborator and ask him to be his "word man." And the writer would take Hoppie's story and try and make a script from it.

There were a lot of funny fellas out here. You remember Richard Connell?

The Most Dangerous Game?

He was a great guy, very creative, but he did some strange things. He loved to look at people's garbage. He'd roam through garbage cans, reading the mail, picking out things, roaming through the alleys of Beverly Hills. He'd find postcards and things and send them out again. One time he found an invitation to a bar mitzvah for one of the Warner brothers' kids, and he sent it to Frances and Albert Hackett. They got all dressed and showed up at the Warner's house to find out the party had been six months earlier.

Dick was a funny fella. Damned good short story writer. (Laughs.)

Your first big assignment was *Dancing Lady*, with Gable, Crawford, and Fred Astaire.

Dancing Lady we adapted from a book. I forget who wrote it.* We were usually assigned written material, something they had bought—although the script could end up as an original by the time it was done.

Pinky and I used to go out and shoot skeet with Clark Gable on Saturdays during that time. There was no shop talk. Just talk about guns and shooting and skeet. And a lot of talk about what shotgun was better than another one. Gable, of course, had some $1,500 Belgian handmade gun, and Pinky had a very good gun, too. I had one from Sears Roebuck, and I could still shoot as well as they did.

Joan Crawford was reluctant to be in *Dancing Lady* at first?

That was funny. We were all there in David Selznick's office to discuss the picture. And David knew that Crawford was thinking of turning the thing down. So he plays a game with her. He told her that the character was a bit of a hooker and maybe it would be better for Jean Harlow. And Crawford told him, "Listen, I could be a better hooker than Harlow any day of the year." Well, everybody wanted to laugh. But she stopped saying she wouldn't do the part after that.

Is it true you discovered Burton Lane for that picture?

Yeah. David had Rodgers and Hart working for him, but he didn't like what they did and

*The author of the novel was James Warner Bellah.

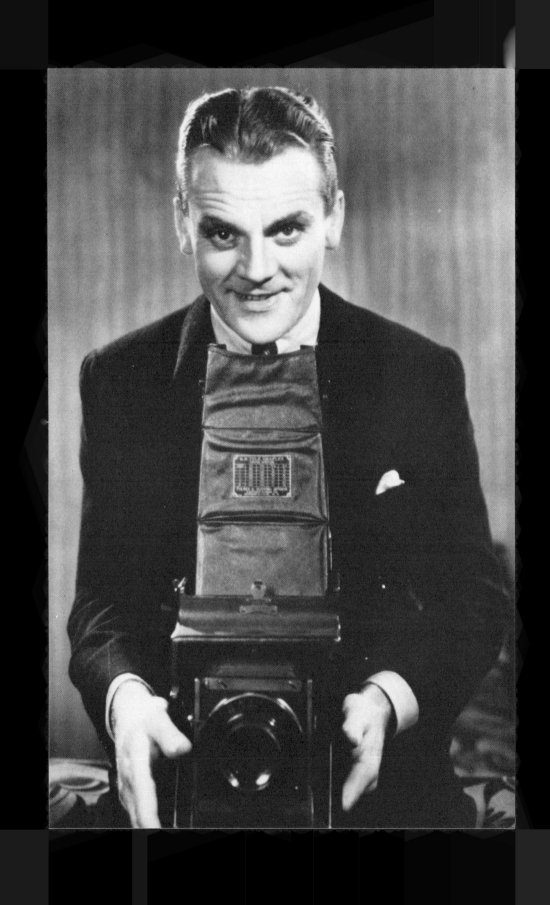

was looking for someone else. I heard the guy at a party and told David about him. He brought the guy and his partner in and they worked out fine. Did some good songs.*

You went to Warners and wrote *Picture Snatcher* for Cagney. Did your newspaper days help you on that one?

Sure. I had been up at Sing Sing to cover an execution when I was a reporter. For the picture we used the old Snyder case.

That was where a reporter snuck a camera in and got pictures of an execution.

Yeah.

The work was fast-paced at Warners in those days.

Let me tell you something about working at Warners back then. Zanuck called me in. Ned Griffith, one of his producers, was there, too. Zanuck said, "I understand you were at Sing Sing." I said, "Yes." He says, "There's the Snyder case." I said, "Yes." He says, "What if we do so and so and so and so?" I said, "Fine." He says, "We've got Jim Cagney." I said, "Great." He says, "The script will be ready in four weeks." I said, "All right." And then he called in his production manager, who used to run a burlesque house in Minneapolis. And Zanuck said, "Rivkin is going to do a script called *Picture Snatcher*, and he'll have it done in four weeks. I want the sets ready at the start of the fifth week. We will have a three-week shooting schedule. And we'll open at the Warners theatres on such and such a date. . . . " The picture opened nine weeks from the day he spoke. That's the way it worked back then.

I guess that's why those early Warner Bros. films move so fast. I read that the director, Lloyd Bacon, shot some of the rehearsals and used them in the final film to save time.

Oh yeah? That could be. I don't know. I was already on another assignment by then.

You wrote a play for Broadway, *Knock on Wood*, that was a satirical look at the way the studios operated. Did that cause you any problems back in Hollywood?

Knock on Wood was about two Hollywood agents. One was David Selznick's brother, Myron. And the mogul in the play was based on L.B. Mayer. I was working for David Selznick at that time—1933—and the play was about to open. The Shuberts were going to do it. David got wind of it, and he called me in. He says, "I hear you've written a play about the 'Old Man'?" I said, "Well, he's only a secondary character in it." Selznick said, "Is it vicious?" I said, "David, you know me." He says, "Well, then, it's vicious." Then he said, "Do you think it's wise to do it?" I said, "I want a play on. I've never had a play on Broadway. Is it going to bother you?" And he said, "No. Forget we had this conversation." He had been told by someone in Mayer's office, to do this.

Now, I had an agent named Frank Orsatti. Frank Orsatti was L.B. Mayer's pimp. He would get the girls for him. And Frank had a very successful agency. Why? Because MGM bought everything he owned. Including me. We used to have a thing here called The Clover Club,

*Burton Lane's partner was Harold Adamson.

a gambling joint run by Detroit mobsters. Everybody used to go there. I was at the bar one night with John O'Hara, and Frank Orsatti comes up to me. He says, "I'm glad I found you. I've been looking all over for you." I said, "You got a new assignment?" He says, "Worse than that . . . L.B. doesn't want this play of yours put on." I said, "Frank, you better talk to the Shuberts about this. It's out of my hands now. I can't pull it out; it's in rehearsal." Frank says, "You're making a terrible mistake. It may bar you from the business forever." I said, "Yes, that worries me." But the play went on. *I* got marvelous reviews, and it closed in two weeks. Seventeen performances. But . . . there were no repercussions from Mayer. If it had been a hit, God knows what would have happened.

Orsatti was a damn good agent. A little later he brought a partner in, a man named Milton Bren. A young man, and a real estate nut—he built all of Sunset Strip. His son today is one of the richest men in America. Now, I'd been on the track team in Minnesota, and Bren knew that, and one time he says, "I'll bet I can beat you at track." I said, "Well, maybe you can." And Pinky's there and says to him, "No, you can't. I got a hundred dollars says you can't." Bren says, "You got it." Nobody asked me what I thought of it.

It was one of the hottest days of the year. We took off our coats and started to run a block, about a hundred yards between the buildings. I beat him by that much. And he never got over it.

We had a real affinity with our agents in those days. They were pals. Later, when I went to Goldstone, and I was going with a lady who wanted a swimming pool, my agent lent me $3,000 just like that, to get the pool.

Not like that today.

The agents *or* the cost of a pool.

Yeah.

Producers often called you in as a script doctor, right? You'd rewrite scenes and add bits, things like that?

Yes. Any time anybody was in trouble they'd send for me. On *Mutiny on the Bounty*, Frank Lloyd wanted me to put some lightness in the thing. Well, he had a cook on board, and I dreamed up a three-time gag: the cook takes the slop on deck, wets his finger to test the wind, throws the slop overboard. The second time he does the same thing. But the third time he does it, the wind changes and the slop goes right in his face. It was a howl.

Frank remembered that I had done that gag when he was making *Under Two Flags*. It was a story about the Foreign Legion, where men joined to forget the past, okay? And there was a character in there played by a Russian comic who became a director, Gregory Ratoff. I was on the set a couple of days, and the set was so goddamned noisy that I gave Ratoff the line: "It's so noisy here I can't remember what I came here to forget!" It was a big laugh. And many years later I was on the Via Veneto in Rome, having some spaghetti, and suddenly I hear a Russian voice scream out, "Allen, my darling!" And I look up and there's Ratoff, with a bunch of people. He says, "See that man there." And they all look at me. "He gave me the greatest line I ever had in my life!"

I got called in on *Kid Glove Killer*, Freddy Zinnemann's first picture. Johnny Higgins had dreamed that one up. It was about laboratory forensics and he had all the technical material, but it was so goddamned technical nobody could understand it. So I was called in to fix it.

Is it true you wrote the Mae West picture, *Every Day's a Holiday*?

Yeah. I didn't get any credit on that. It was part of the deal. They needed a script, and a guy named Emanuel Cohen brought me in. Mae West had written a couple of pages of story, mostly about her character. I took her idea and made it into a feature script. It was something about a girl who masquerades as a French singer, and the various complications.

You met with West when you'd finished the writing?

Yeah. I went to see her at her apartment. One of her musclemen let me in, and she was waiting for me with the script in her bedroom. She was in bed, with the script on her lap. I asked her, "Did you like the script?" She said, "Yeah, what's this first scene all about?" And I told her what it was about. She just sort of mumbled. Then she asked about the second scene. And so on through the whole script. I was there for a couple of hours in her bedroom. And when we were done she said, "Thank you, Mr. Rivkin, you've done a good job. Now I'll make it better."

A little later, Cohen calls me in and he says, "You know, you can't get any credit on this picture. Mae West always gets a solo credit on the screenplay." But as compensation, he offered me a $10,000 bonus and a paid vacation.

So I took it.

When the picture came out, Mae said she had written the script by ESP.

In moving from studio to studio, did you find that one treated writers better than another?

Nah, all the same. The worst was Harry Cohn. Then Jack Warner. Writers used to drive Jack Warner crazy. He spent all his life checking time cards, when you came in, when you came out. At Metro it was relaxed. You could go home and write your script if you wanted to. The best shop to work in was when Dore Schary was the head of MGM. He protected you all the time. In a production conference Dore would say, "If it's in the script, that's the way I want it."

And Fox didn't give a shit what hours you worked because Zanuck always had his conferences late at night. You'd get a call at six o'clock in the evening, at dinner, and they'd say, "Stand by, you're on tonight." I'd say, "What time?" "Well, we don't know yet. Might be two o'clock." So . . . you read, listen to the radio. Get a call at one o'clock: "Looks like three now." "All right." Quarter to three: "Get over here." And you went. And then you didn't go in the next morning. But the next afternoon all the notes were on your desk.

When did Zanuck sleep?

God, I don't know.

Was it at MGM that David Selznick gave the writers money to decorate their own offices?

Oh, yeah. At MGM Thalberg had a building, so when Selznick came over he had to have a building. So they built a building for him. Now, he had a helluva stable of writers: Ben Hecht and Charles MacArthur, Gene Fowler, Oliver H. P. Garrett, Hugh Walpole, Herman Mankiewicz, and he had Pinky and me. He assigned us to offices in his brand-new building, and, to make us feel at home there, Selznick decides that, instead of us getting the services of the studio decorator, he'll give us each $1,200 to decorate our own offices ourselves.

So off we all went to decorate our own offices. Hugh Walpole bought a lot of English crap. And Pinky was nuts about Early American, so we went to Barker Brothers and bought all this maple shit and chintz draperies. And the other writers were all supposedly doing theirs. Fine.

Now Selznick was very proud of this idea, letting his writers have full reign. And when everyone was finished, an opening day was set and he brought his father-in-law, L.B. Mayer, with him to look at the offices. Well, Hecht and MacArthur and Fowler were sharing the first office as you came up the stairs, and when Selznick and L.B. came in there wasn't a stick of furniture in there, just a secretary in a bra and $3,600 worth of pornographic pictures on the walls. That was their big gag. Mayer damn near died. He stormed out, and Selznick just groaned and says, "I'll talk to you bastards later."

Must have been the last time Selznick gave a writer full reign.

They'd have a hard time figuring out the writers, you know. They'd try to discipline them, and sometimes it just backfired.

There's a funny thing happened to Samson Raphaelson. This was at Fox, where Winnie Sheehan, a former New York police commissioner, was production chief. Sheehan somehow got the idea that the way to punish writers when they did something wrong was to keep them from writing. So when Rafe made some trouble at Fox, Sheehan gave orders that he was to get no writing assignments until further notice—just report to the studio each day and do whatever he was told, but no more writing. And to further humiliate him, he was assigned to conduct the occasional visitor tours of the studio. And Rafe did it, because he wanted to protect the hefty salary he was getting under his contract.

So one day he's told to give the studio tour to some visitors—who turn out to be a group of Fox money men from a New York bank. And Rafe is so charming and erudite that they wonder why he's being wasted as a lowly tour guide, and, being bankers, one of them asks how much he's making. Seizing the moment, Rafe smiles and tells them, "Mr. Sheehan pays me $3,000 a week."

Did they question Sheehan about his generosity?

I think he was replaced by Zanuck or somebody a few weeks later.

What was the West Side Riding and Asthma Club?

That was a marvelous group. It started with a number of us out here in the '30s who had edited college humor magazines, and a bunch of New Yorkers joined up. There was Groucho Marx, Larry Hart, Harry Ruby, Claude Binyon, Preston Sturges, Dick Rodgers. About thirty of us would get together at a restaurant in Hollywood called Al Levy's. Upstairs was the big dining room, and once a week we all met for lunch. Everyone was working in the neighborhood, at RKO or Paramount. We met for lunch every Tuesday, and we'd eat, drink, crack jokes. Then Al Levy said we made too much noise and he threw us out of there.

After Al drove us out of his place, we decided to have our parties at our own houses, in the evenings. Everybody would pay a dollar to whoever hosted, so you'd collect around thirty bucks. But these were some parties, and with the drinking that went on with this bunch it would cost the host $500 to $600.

Well, I'll tell you when the thing ended. It got to be Preston Sturges' turn to be host. First we got engraved invitations. He was then running a restaurant, The Players, so he had the chef come to his home to cook for us. A beautiful dinner, with nine wines. And he had a six-piece mariachi band performing for us. And he hired one of the top photographers in town and the guy took each of our pictures, sent us a proof and after we okayed the proof, sent each of us a dozen mounted 12-by-18 portraits. There was a card enclosed, "Thanks for coming . . . Preston." Well, nobody could top that, so we dissolved the club.

During World War II you were a member of what was known as the Typewriter Brigade. What do you remember about that?

I had worked for a year with Inter-American Affairs, Nelson Rockefeller's outfit. I was the story executive there, and I'd hired a lot of friends. We got Disney to make our first picture, *Brazil*. That was a good experience. I had about ten writers working for us. Mike Blankfort was there, Winston Miller. Most of them went into the service then, when we had to reduce overhead. And Frank Capra said to me, "Come over with us. I need you over here."

Fox had turned over Fox Western Studio on Western Avenue to the government at the government's request, for a dollar a year. Colonel Frank Capra of the Signal Corps was put in charge, with Anatole Litvak as the number-two man. And they had Tony Veiller, the Hacketts, Claude Binyon, they had everybody. And I worked for him for a year and a half. That was the Typewriter Brigade. And we made documentaries and other things. I still don't think anybody's done a better job than Frank did with his *Why We Fight* series.

Across the street was a radio division, and working there were all the great radio writers, Panama and Frank, Hal Kanter, you name 'em. Bob Hope used to sneak around, meet them on the street corner and slip them a twenty or a fifty for some gags. There were some pretty funny things happening. I tried to write a play about it, but I couldn't make it work. Herb Baker and Iz Diamond also tried to write a play about the Brigade, and it didn't work. Now I hear Jack Rose and Mel Shavelson, who were both there, are working on a play about it.

***Till the End of Time* was about the veterans returning home after the war.**

Yeah. We did that for Dore. I was happy with that one.

It's a fine film. I imagine it would have gotten more attention if it hadn't come out about the same time as *The Best Years of Our Lives*.

Well, that script was based on a book. . . . It was called *They Dream of Home*, a very good book by Niven Busch.

There was a character in there, a prizefighter who lost his legs on Guadalcanal, and he came home and had to cope with it. I got a call one night from a soldier who had also lost both his legs. He just wanted to tell me that he had been planning to commit suicide and then he saw the picture, and on account of that he had changed his mind.

You must have felt pretty good.

Yeah.

Would you like to have done more films dealing with social issues? You were always interested in political causes, weren't you?

Oh, yeah. That was the sort of thing that got me really interested in a picture. I liked to do something with some substance to it.

During the war, did the government exert much influence on feature film scripts?

I encountered some government censorship. I was down in Palm Springs with Dore Schary,

Robert Mitchum and Jean Porter in *Till the End of Time* (1946).

and we dreamed up a story about three Germans landing in a raft on the shores of Virginia. They get into sabotage and terrorism. Dore had a good contact at the FBI, the number-three man. We sent the script to him, and he sent it to J. Edgar Hoover. Hoover said, "Burn it." It was too true.

This happened to me again and again. A screenwriter dreams up things out of his crazy imagination that have more reality to them than he ever suspected. I was at John Balderstone's house one night. Balderston was an American and had been a famous journalist in London. He was a good friend. The war was on, and the Allies were doing very badly. We were listening to reports on the radio, and we started talking and came up with the Normandy invasion, the whole goddamned thing.

I also had some censorship problems during the Korean War, with *Prisoner of War*. The Defense Department had at first okayed it. And then, when the picture was finished, they changed their minds and wanted us to pull the picture. And Dore wouldn't let them. He said, "We made it. I don't care if anyone sees it. We're going to release it." But it got the lowest possible advertising budget, ads the size of a postage stamp. And the picture went down the drain. It starred Ronald Reagan, and that, of course, didn't mean a goddamned thing at the box office. It was a good picture, too.

What happened on *Dead Reckoning*? You started but didn't finish the script.

I put that together from the beginning, but I had a fight with the director, John Cromwell. I didn't like him—too snooty for me. Cohn put me on that picture because I was on the lot, and from the beginning it didn't work out with Cromwell. But Bogie and I got along, friends for years and years. We used to play poker at Mary Baker's house every Saturday night. We went out on many toots together. But John and I never got along. Steve Fisher came on and finished *Dead Reckoning*.

You had a great success with *The Farmer's Daughter*. How did that film come about?

That was a beautiful thing. David Selznick had a contract to do one more picture with Ingrid Bergman. He was looking desperately for something. Over at Paramount they owned a property called *Hilda from Parliament*, written by a Finnish writer. But they could never lick the property. David brought the play to Dore Schary, and Dore gave it to my wife, Laura Kerr, who was story editor for him. She realized the potential and told me about it. I knew everything about Minnesota and I thought, why don't we put it in Minnesota? And I was also deeply involved in Democratic politics. I had worked on the Helen Gahagan Douglas campaign, and I put on Hollywood for Roosevelt, and I was chairman of the Committee for the Arts of the Democratic Party for years. So I knew a little about politics. I told this to Dore and said, "We'll do it with Bergman and David will be very happy."

At any rate, Laura and I went to work and wrote the script. And it came out good. But Bergman wanted to get rid of Selznick. She wasn't happy with him or her salary. So she turned it down. Loretta Young was free and wanted to do it, but she couldn't get the Swedish accent. Dore had a great idea. George Seaton's wife, Phyllis, was a dialogue coach, and he suggested David get her to work with Loretta on the accent. So the two women worked together like crazy. And then we got Joe Cotten to play opposite her, and Ethel Barrymore, and they put a very elite director on it, Hank Potter, an awfully nice guy. And it all worked like a dream, just like a dream.

Were there any problems in collaborating with your wife for a change?

It was easy. She's marvelous with dialogue, a great ear. We did three or four things together after that.

You've been publicist and editor of the newsletter here at the Writers Guild for some time. When did you start?

In '63, when I retired. I'd been doing P.R. work here for nothing, just as a Guild member. Mike Franklin, who was then executive director, said, "Will you come on permanent?" I said, "If the money's all right." And he offered me a nice fee and I came on. Two years later he says, "I think we ought to have a house organ." And in 1965 I put together the first edition. It comes out ten times a year, September through June.

Overleaf: Richard Arlen, Zita Johann, and Edward G. Robinson in *Tiger Shark* (1932).

9 · WELLS ROOT

Wells Root in 1950.

Wells Root arrived in Hollywood in 1928, at the very dawn of the golden age of screenwriting. The movies, having found their voice with *The Jazz Singer*, were in dire need of something to say. To the studios, putting the "talk" into talkies must have seemed as specialized an operation as brain surgery, and literary talent scouts were dispatched in a frenzied hunt for "word men" of any stripe—dollar-a-page pulpsters and celebrated playwrights. Root, a New York journalist for the *World* and a fledgling weekly called *Time*, was among that first lively crew of dapper Broadwayites and hard-boiled newshawks press-ganged from the speakeasies of Manhattan to the dream factories of Los Angeles.

A good all-rounder, Root was adept at adaptations, originals, construction, and problem-solving. David Selznick, for whom Root scripted *Bird of Paradise* and *The Prisoner of Zenda*, considered him a most reliable "fixer," pulling other writers' troubled scripts into shape at the thirteenth hour. As an early activist in the Writers Guild, however, Root found his career derailed by the union-hating studios, most of the plum assignments going to the mercenaries and conservatives in the Screen Playwrights.

In the late '30s and into the '40s, he spent a term at MGM, writing numerous programmers, including several vehicles for Metro vet Wallace Beery. As the big studio era ended in the 1950s, Root, like many of the contract writers with solid if unspectacular credits, moved into television, writing over seventy scripts for shows like *G.E. Theatre* and *Maverick*. At the same time he began to teach a class in screenwriting at UCLA, continuing this assignment through the next twenty years and 1,200 students. The course resulted in a concise and practical book on the subject, *Writing the Script*, published in 1980.

Wells Root is a kindly, modest man of quiet dignity, eighty-five years old on the summer afternoon when we meet at his house in Pacific Palisades.

I'd been writing since I was a child and worked on the school paper at Yale. After school a friend of mine who was working, and doing very well, on the *New York World*, recommended me for a job. The *World* was a Pulitzer paper, and one of the leading papers in the city. I was very lucky to get in there, and for five or six years I worked there in various capacities.

Laurence Stallings, the man who co-wrote *What Price Glory?*, had had the assistant critics's job on the paper, and he was leaving. He had lost a leg from being wounded in World War I and couldn't really keep up with all of the running around Broadway that he had to do. He was a friend of mine and let me know ahead of time he was quitting, so I applied for the job and got it. I became assistant critic and general legman for the dramatic department. Pretty soon I had a column of theatrical news called "Cast and Forecast." I'd done some moonlighting, writing film and theatre criticism for *Time* magazine which was just getting going. They became prosperous enough to offer me a job and a significant raise over what I was getting at the *World*.

People don't realize what that enormous *Time* empire started on. In those days *I* was four departments! Theatre, cinema, sports and aviation. All four. And there were a couple of men, one doing foreign news and one doing national. There was a man doing literature, and a couple of others, and that was it. But the magazine did very well and became more and more prosperous, and the staff got bigger and bigger.

Luce was there, of course, but the real manager of the operation was Britton Hadden. He was really responsible for the whole "Timestyle" and all that. Magazines in those days were usually literary and long-winded, and the idea at *Time* was to tighten the writing and give it a certain identifiable characteristic. And that style became so distinct that we were burlesqued for a while. But it was effective, and it said things so neatly and tightly that it became accepted. Now it's part of the language, and nobody remembers what the fuss was.

Anyway, there I was, writing for *Time*. It was a thriving period for the theatre. There were three or four times as many theatres operating as there are now. A lot of activity, and many newspapers and magazines to cover it. After a show you usually went to a speakeasy and had a drink or two with some of your colleagues and people from the theatre. One evening I was standing at the bar of a speak called the 21 Club when a man named Herman Mankiewicz walked in.

Herman had been on the *Times* when I was on the *World*, and doing the same things, reporting and reviewing and legwork. We had become friends. And then, a year or two before, Herman had gone out to Hollywood. Well, we greeted each other, and I said, "Have a drink with me." He said, "Fine." And we had a drink. I asked him what he'd been doing, and he suddenly grabbed hold of me and looked at me sideways.

He said, "Wells, how would you like to go to Hollywood?" I said, "What? What are you talking about?" He had some more to drink, and he said, "I've been sent back here by Paramount to get some New York writers." This was just after the talkies had come in, silent pictures were gone, and the studios thought they needed theatre people to write the dialogue. The executives didn't have any faith in their own writers that they had nurtured up from being grips or whatever. They had done a pretty good job for them all those years of silent pictures, but now the studios wanted new people.

And Herman explained all this and said, "I've got to find five writers to bring back. The deal is you get a three-month contract with an option for a year." The salary was rather good, much more money than you'd make writing for any newspaper or magazine. And so I told him I would definitely consider it.

It occurred to me that if I was going to continue as a film critic, and with *Time* becoming more important, it would be a good experience for me to learn how movies were made, from the inside. I went to Hadden and Luce and told them an offer had come my way. I said, and I believed quite sincerely, that I would be worth a lot more to them if I went and had this experience and could come back and speak with more authority on the subject of the cinema. I said, "Why don't you give me three months' leave of absence, and I'll take this contract and find out all I can. Obviously, in three months they won't take up the option and I'll come right back to work." And they said, "That sounds like a pretty good idea." It made sense. I called Herman and said, "I'll take that offer you made me." He said, "Fine." And I went out to Hollywood for three months. The studio took up my option. That was 1928, and I've been here ever since.

You arrived on the train in Los Angeles; you got yourself a taxi and found a hotel. Nobody was there to help me at all. The first day I reported to Paramount I was assigned to a director called Frank Tuttle. He was quite a well-established director in those days, and he was something of a writer, as well. He took me under his wing. He was an easterner and a very nice man. He helped me over the first bumps and gave me time to find out the obvious things I had to know. And David Selznick was working for Paramount in those days, and he was very friendly and helpful. He introduced me to people and made suggestions, things like that. It was a very useful and agreeable experience right at the beginning.

Were you assigned a project right away?

I was told to get an idea. A college story. And we talked it back and forth, with Tuttle and Selznick, who was producer on the thing. That's how things often began in those days, and still do. You had an idea, then discussions, changes. Then a producer says, "Yeah, I think that'll work, go ahead and do a treatment." The treatment was twenty or thirty pages, outlining the story, giving the structure. If that worked you went ahead with the screenplay. And that was how we did that first film, a college picture. It was something called *Varsity* and it was a horrible piece of junk.

As I said, Paramount took up my option and I stayed on, working on several more pictures. Selznick moved on to RKO, but he and I remained friends. We met socially, tennis and so on. When he married Irene Mayer, I went to the wedding. When he was head of RKO, he was making *Bird of Paradise*, and I was hired to write the script. It was a romantic story of the islands and had been a play. Dolores Del Rio was going to play the girl, and Joel McCrea was playing the boy. King Vidor was the director. Someone had already done a version of the play, and no one especially liked it, so I started again, using at least the basic framework of the play.

Selznick was quoted as saying, in effect, "Write whatever you want as long as there's a love scene and the girl jumps in the volcano at the end."

Yes. Well, I worked with Vidor on the script. We worked very closely for a month or two. The script was not finished when filming had to begin. Dolores Del Rio had to begin filming no later than a certain date. And David and Vidor had decided to make the film on location in Hawaii, so we all sailed off for the islands with the script still unfinished. The other reason I went along was because there were some scenes that we felt would probably have to be rewritten, as they would depend to a large degree on the kind of location that was found in Hawaii.

The production did not go very smoothly on location, did it?

We had trouble, even in Hawaii, finding just the right look for the picture. We found a lagoon that we could use for the main scenes, but there were no palm trees. Trees had to be taken out from the interior of the island and propped up. Then a storm came and blew all the palm trees off the beach. It turned out to be a very expensive trip for the studio, and I think David and King ended up shooting back in the studio and out on Catalina Island here in California.

The film is very sensual. It's a good example of how erotic Hollywood films could be before the Hays Code changed things a couple of years later.

Yes. There was a scene in there that caused a great many conferences. The script called for the woman to swim and come ashore in the nude just ahead of Joel McCrea. And Vidor thought it was very important for the reality of her character and the feeling of the scene that the girl not have any clothes on. Now Dolores Del Rio was playing the part and she was a wonderfully refined woman. She was awfully well brought up in Mexico City. A lovely, lovely woman. But, bless her heart, Dolores agreed that it was important for the scene and her character, and she agreed to wear absolutely nothing. She swims and then she reaches the beach and runs out through the waves. Vidor shot it from such an angle and cut it in a way that it wasn't vulgar or obvious. There weren't any closeups, of course, as there would be nowadays.

How long did you stay in Hawaii?

We were there over a month, and it was basically an enjoyable time. And that was how I got my next job, working with Howard Hawks on a thing called *Tiger Shark*. Howard had come to Hawaii for a vacation. Warners had bought a story, about tuna fishermen in San Diego, for Howard's next picture, but he hadn't started working on it yet.

Myron Selznick, David's brother, was my agent, and he was also out there, enjoying himself in Hawaii. He was a friend of Howard's, and he asked him what he'd been doing. Howard said he had a story, but no writer. I was getting through with my assignment on *Bird of Paradise* and getting ready to come back to Hollywood. And Myron told Howard, "You've got a writer right here. He's available and you two can get right on the thing without having to go back to California."

And Howard bought what Myron said, and I switched from *Bird of Paradise* to *Tiger Shark*. Howard Hawks and I wrote most of *Tiger Shark* there in Hawaii.

Sounds like a pleasant assignment. How did you get any work done?

We worked, but the circumstances were pleasant. The *Bird of Paradise* crew was off on whatever their locations were, and Howard and I were staying at the same hotel in Honolulu. We usually met each day after breakfast, down on the beach. We would sit on the beach, in the sun, and talk over the story, and break now and then to take a swim.

What did you think of Howard Hawks?

He was a very able man, very able. Very sharp and intelligent about story development . . . construction, motivation of characters. His pictures were tightly woven. They didn't unravel the way many did.

Would he articulate any personal theme he wanted to work into the story?

Bird of Paradise (1932), starring Joel McCrea and Dolores Del Rio.

It seemed that he was just telling a story and wanted to tell it in the clearest and most exciting way.

Did he ever write parts of the script on his own?

No. He would never sit down with a paper and pencil. It was all talk, and then I would go and write it.

He had a distant quality to some extent. He did keep a lot of things away from me. Usually the writer knew what the director was going to do on the set. Many directors would come to you ahead of time and discuss their ideas, if something new might happen. But in *Tiger Shark* there were scenes that I hadn't known about at all, that Hawks had figured out the night before, he'd say. It was something new he thought would work, and usually it did. He was a very skillful man.

You were still working on the film when you came back to California and he began shooting?

Yes. The script wasn't finished. And there was another rush to start filming. Eddie Robinson was the star, and they had to get it done because he had only four or five weeks before he was committed to another film. So I stayed with it to finish the script and do any writing on the set that had to be done. In fact, they were so jammed up to get going because of the starting commitment, that when we got back to the studio I had to dictate much of it. I had two secretaries—one I talked to in the morning and she'd go away in the afternoon and type it, and another secretary I dictated to after lunch who'd have it ready in the morning. We had to keep the flow of material coming as fast as possible. But I never particularly liked dictating a script.

Why?

Well, I'd been a newspaperman, you see. You came into the city room and sat at your typewriter and typed your story. You didn't have to be an expert typist, which I never was. But I just thought that when you're sitting alone in front of a piece of paper, writing with a pencil or on a machine, you had a better chance of turning out more effective work. But to my actual amazement, I found that it was possible to work by dictating if I had to.

With all the rush, you still seem to have gotten a lot of colorful detail into the script, the speech patterns of the Portuguese-Americans.

I realized from the start that it was a very special dialogue needed. And I wanted to know what it really sounded like, so I told Hawks, "Why don't I go down there for a day and talk to some of these people so we don't write a Hollywood version of these Portuguese-American fishermen." And he thought that was fine. I went down there for a day, and after sitting around and talking with them for a whole day, I realized that we'd never get it right. There was a lot of script to write and I didn't have time to gather all these odd phrases and words. So we got Warners to hire a Portuguese fishing captain to come up when the shooting started. He stayed with me and helped with the dialogue. We couldn't use all the dialect, of course, because it wouldn't be understandable. But just enough so the film had that authentic flavor. The fishing captain helped Hawks and Robinson all through the shooting. It's the kind of thing people never realized happened back of the camera.

Were there things you learned from working with Hawks?

Yes. Ways of doing scenes to make them better. I never forgot something he told me in one story conference. Let's say it was a scene at a dinner table, and I faded in and the people were talking. Howard said, "Let's fix that. I find that when you open on a group of people sitting down and talking, the scene sits down with them." He said, "The best antidote for that is an entrance. Begin the scene with someone entering, and somehow it's more interesting."

Things like that he showed me.

You mentioned Herman Mankiewicz's role in your coming out here. You were friends with quite a few of the legendary New York writers who worked in Hollywood in the '30s, weren't you?

Herman and I were pretty good friends for a time. Being on rival papers we didn't trade any secrets, but we often had lunch and drinks. Out here I didn't know anything about the self-destructiveness that may have been said about him, other than the fact he drank a great deal. But a lot of people drank a good deal. And he liked to gamble, but a lot of other people also liked to gamble. Herman and I always got along very well, until the Writers Guild started. Herman was on the producers' side, so we split and never saw much of each other after that.

Nathanael West was a close personal friend of mine. As a matter of fact, I was just filmed by a French TV crew for something they're doing on West. I don't think they found many people who knew him. He was killed in 1940 and didn't have too many friends.

Did West regret having to work in Hollywood? He tended to be at the smaller studios, and his assignments weren't exactly the more intelligent ones.

It weighed on his mind that his books didn't sell well. They didn't sell at all. He once told me that, outside of small advances, he never made a penny on any of his books. And he was happy to be out here and making money so he could write more novels. He was quite the reverse of some of the writers who came out here and thought they were slumming. West didn't think he was slumming. He was having a fine time and drawing a check every week. It wasn't his kind of writing the studios gave him to do, but he was quite competent and ready to do it. It didn't cause him any neurosis. In fact, if he hadn't gotten these jobs, he would have been much more unhappy because he had no other way to make money. Before he came to Hollywood he had been a hotel clerk. And when he did break away from that and holed up in a small house in rural Pennsylvania, to write, he'd been so lonely that in the wintertime—I remember him telling me this—he turned on the radio and danced with his two hunting dogs.

Many of the writers who came out here worked hard or played hard and didn't have any vitality left to write things on the side, to write their "serious" stuff. Many writers talked about the books and plays they were going to write while they collected their movie salary. Very few of them ever did anything. West had determination. While he worked for the studios, he wrote his novel *Day of the Locust*. And that's quite a novel

There were some who made light of Hollywood, and you might have a first-rate talent working on material that was third or fourth rate. I remember Dorothy Parker cracking about the difference between a writer and a Hollywood writer: in Hollywood, the writer comes into his office, takes off his coat, sits at his typewriter, puts the paper in, puts his fingers on the keys, and waits for the phone to ring.

The Muse was the call from the studio.

Yes. But really, you seldom heard anyone saying, "How awful all this money pouring in on us. What it's doing to us!" And certainly not from Nathanael West. He enjoyed many things out here. He loved to hunt and fish, and I did, too, and that's largely how we became close friends.

Did you know his wife, Eileen?

She was, as you probably know, the person the book and play *My Sister Eileen* was based on. And she was a marvelous human being. A great character, great sense of humor, expansive, and she loved martinis the way he did. They fell in love and married, and nobody could have been happier than they were. She died with him, of course, in the car accident.

You seem to have had good relations with directors you've mentioned—Hawks, Vidor. How typical was that?

I felt that the majority of those I was fortunate to work with did know their business quite well. Beginning with Frank Tuttle and going on to Vidor and Hawks, obviously. Once in a while on a cheap picture you'd get a director who was a dodo, with just the ordinary intelligence, and who knew where to put the camera as the horses rode by. But not very often. A man I worked with on two or three pictures—he's no longer remembered—J. Walter Ruben, Jack Ruben, was as smart as could be, as a writer and a director and a producer.

You wrote a script, *Sergeant Madden*, that Josef von Sternberg directed. Did you work with him on that?

No, I did not work with him. It was just an assignment he took and did. I rather suspect he was no longer getting many assignments, and in those circumstances your judgment takes you in different directions. I remember *Sergeant Madden* as one of the less triumphant I have written. It wasn't much good. I certainly wouldn't suggest that it was von Sternberg's fault.

That was a Wallace Beery vehicle, and at MGM I was stuck doing two or three of his pictures. He was contracted to do four pictures a year, at, I think, $75,000 a picture. When he got through with one, they had to have another script ready for him. And they didn't take time lingering over his scripts, wanting to get them perfect. They just wanted to get them made, because they would have to pay him the same amount if he made the pictures or not.

The studios seem to have been schizophrenic in regard to script writing. On the one hand they might nurture a property for years, revising and rewriting the screenplay, but then suddenly rush into production without a final script.

For one reason or another, delays or changes in schedules, there were always deadlines. When there was a deadline looming and pressure to finish a picture, I often went out of town. Staying at the studio, with whatever social life was around, you couldn't always concentrate. A number of times I went up to Lake Arrowhead. For a couple of weeks I'd go there, with no one at all around to bother me, and I'd work till I damn well finished the script on time. That was my solution to a deadline. But, yes, you often had to work much faster at the end of a script. Of course, I did tell them where I was going off to finish the thing. . . . Not like Faulkner who asked if he could work at home and then left town for Mississippi!

Normally, what would your working hours be?

At most studios, you got to work at ten, you took an hour for lunch at the studio commissary, and then worked till six. Writers usually all were housed in one area, a writers building. There would be a story editor there, and secretaries, who'd have the ear of the executives. They'd know who was dogging it. A lot of writers would spend all morning playing tennis or something and not come in till after lunch. But as long as the script pages were coming in, they didn't bother them. It wasn't too severe.

I Cover the Waterfront **had a lot of unusual elements to the story. That was an independent production?**

Yes. An independent producer was doing that, and my agent got there at the proper time and sold him a bill of goods. *I Cover the Waterfront* was a book written by a waterfront reporter for a San Diego paper.* It was a collection of his experiences on that beat. It was an interesting and popular book at the time. But not much from the book was usable for a film. There was no continued story, only separate incidents. One incident I did use in the picture concerned a drunken captain who'd come back to port and get drunk and go to a whorehouse, where the girls would steal all his money. His daughter got so upset by this that one night she barges into the whorehouse and knocks the girls aside and gets her father out of there with his money intact. I took that episode and used those characters, the drunken captain played by Ernest Torrance and the girl played by Claudette Colbert. And Ben Lyon played the waterfront reporter who falls in love with the girl while investigating her father and finding out he's a smuggler— smuggling Chinese in from Mexico.

That was directed by James Cruze.

Yes, James Cruze. He had been one of the famous early directors. His film, *The Covered Wagon*, was one of the first "million dollar" pictures in the silent days. Cruze and I worked closely together. I went over to his house every morning at ten o'clock, and we worked hard for two months knocking out the script.

He never regained the stature he had in silent pictures. Do you know why?

He had no respect for most of the Hollywood executives. He was terribly outspoken. And by that time he had a good deal of money, a lovely house in Pasadena and, I believe, big investments in Palm Springs. So he didn't have to work, and he didn't like working with most of the producers. When I was assigned to him, he immediately got hold of me and said, "You're coming to my house in Pasadena tomorrow, and you're not going to talk to anybody until we get the script written. The hell with the producers." And that's exactly how we did it. Every two or three weeks we'd turn in some script.

How creative was Cruze?

Decidedly creative. In a fascinating way. He was a roughneck, not much education. Had come to Hollywood by way of the circus, if I remember right. His English was never too good. He was a *really* tough guy. God, he was a tough guy—looked tough, talked tough. But he had the sensitivity of a young girl. He was a very interesting, special, capable man.

*The producer was Edward Small; the book's author, Max Miller.

You were one of the first members of the Writers Guild and served on the first board of directors.

Right.

Did you feel pressure right from the start to quit the Guild?

Yes. You were in considerable jeopardy. At one point, early in the negotiations before we were established, I couldn't get a job. I had a number of pretty good credits and should have been able to get a job, but I couldn't. So I went to Europe for a while.

The producers had set up their own union at the time, the Screen Playwrights, and if you didn't belong to that it was pretty darn hard to get work.

What did you see as the most important goals for that first guild?

One thing was credit. Before that your contract did not guarantee you credit. A producer might put his name on, or his nephew so they could justify his being on the payroll, or a big-name writer for the same reason or for added prestige, and none of them would have worked on the script at all. When writers got the right to decide what writer's name should be on the screen, that was one of the major accomplishments.

But, for a time, the Guild people weren't doing very well. The Screen Playwrights had a lot of very competent members, and the studios were very decided that those writers would work and we wouldn't, in order to bust our union. In those days there was no Directors Guild and no Actors Guild. The writers were the first creative union in Hollywood, and the studios fought it like tigers. They'd be on the phone with each other, spreading the word, "This guy's a radical, don't hire him."

Then the government passed the National Labor Relations Act, which gave us what we needed. The Act specified that the people working in any industry *had* to be allowed to get together and vote themselves a union if they wanted to. And if they voted to form a union, the managements had to negotiate with them on the various questions. In other words, the government forced the situation, guaranteeing us a union if we had the majority in favor. The vote was taken, the Guild was formed, and very soon after the actors and directors did the same.

You said you went to Europe in the mid-30s when you couldn't get a job. Did you do any film writing in Europe?

Yes. Through a connection I had here I got hooked up with a film job in Europe. It was a picture to be called *Beloved Vagabond* and starring the French actor . . . Chevalier. We worked in England and Florence, Italy. The producer was Italian, with an office in London and a house in Italy. And that was the most glorious location. I met with the producer in London and gave him my story ideas, and then I was assigned to work with an Englishman. It was a European story, and they thought it would be better if a European was also on the script.

And then we all moved on to Florence. The producer had a great, big, wonderful castle of a house. And then he had a house on the coast, a beautiful place, and we moved down there till we finished the script.

The picture was shot in Italy and at an English studio. The director was a German*, and

*Curt Bernhardt.

James Cruze (center) with screenwriters Maxwell Anderson and Jo Swerling, 1932.

the producer was Italian. And so, whenever Hugh Mills, my collaborator, or I said anything in English at a story conference, it had to be translated by interpreters into German, and his responses back to us into English. The producer didn't really know what he was doing, and I don't think the director did, either. It was a colorful experience. Hugh and I had a marvelous time.

We became good friends, Hugh Mills and I, and we later collaborated on a play, a comedy, that was done in London during the war. Unfortunately, while it was running, the Germans bombed London and destroyed the theatre. That closed that.

More dramatic than getting a bad review, anyway.

I should say so.

You went back to work for David Selznick on *The Prisoner of Zenda*?

He and I had continued to be friends as we moved along to different studios. He now had his own shop, his own studio. Ronald Colman was under contract to him, and he felt that *Prisoner of Zenda* was perfect for Colman.

Wasn't Colman reluctant to get involved in the part, having to play twins, the trick photography and so on?

I think he considered it too gimmicky. But David convinced him that it would work.

Selznick worked closely with you on the script?

He hired me and a Russian whose name I don't remember. The Russian hadn't written anything very conspicuous, but he was supposed to give the script some Old-World flavor. Then John Cromwell was hired to direct. So David and Cromwell and the Russian and I would get together every morning at eleven o'clock at the studio, and we worked on the story. After a week or so they discovered that the Russian wasn't adding anything and didn't speak very good English, either, so he was dropped. And I continued on with Selznick and Cromwell, they working as much as writers as I was.

They were long sessions. When we got to the afternoon, Selznick would send for lunch and we'd eat a big lunch and continue. And sometimes we'd eat dinner together there, too, if the going was tough.

Were you writing actual script, or what?

I would be making very careful notes of what was discussed between the three of us. In the evening I would go back to my office and write out what we'd discussed and decided on that day. The next morning we'd have all that ready and go over it, make sure it held up, before going on to the next scene. That was the way the picture was written.

Selznick was head of his own studio then. How could he give so much time to the writing of the script?

He didn't make that many films at a time, for one thing. On this one he had made the commitment, and he had to get going with it. The way David worked, it would have taken much more time if one man worked on the script right through and then we had the conferences and went back and forth. This way we had the story conferences as the script was being written, piece by piece.

Although it was a book, and there had been a previous silent film version, so there was a lot of background material, we still had to change a good deal of it. The ending, especially, we made a number of changes in. But the wife of the author of the book, Mrs. Anthony Hope—he had died—wrote a wonderfully congratulatory letter saying how close to the spirit of the book we stayed. I'll show you the letter she sent; I've got it here. . . .

Her letter refers to a sequel Selznick was planning, *Rupert of Hentzau*.

That never came to be. I think it may have been a little salesmanship on David's part, keeping the woman happy.

You're co-credited with John Balderston on the *Prisoner* script. Did you work with him at all?

No. He wrote a separate version to ours. They were incorporated.

You had high regard for Selznick as a filmmaker.

David had an absolutely magical talent for putting the right elements together. One has only to see *Gone with the Wind*. But his other successes were practically constant. I really don't remember David making any picture that was really bad. He had extremely good taste, as well as talent. He could have been a writer or a director or anything, but he chose to sit in the producer's chair and direct other people doing the film, and he was damned good at it. He was that single boss who knew exactly what he wanted to do. But he was never unpleasant or mean as a boss. He could lose his temper, but not very often. He was just sharp and sensitive and intelligent.

Did you know him later in life when he had been more or less forced into inactivity?

After he stopped making many pictures, I didn't see much of him, no. But, towards the end, I saw him at a New Year's Eve party, and I was very glad to see him. I asked him why the hell he wasn't making any pictures, that we needed people like him. He just looked at me and said, "It's different now. It's not a possibility."

In the 1950s you began teaching screenwriting at UCLA.

Yes. And it was not like it is now, with film schools everywhere. At UCLA I think there were three courses in film writing. Now there are something like forty just at UCLA, and combined with the other Los Angeles area universities there's well over 100.

That got started because a man who had been teaching there had to give it up when he was elected president of the Writers Guild, and he asked me if I wanted to do it. I hadn't taught anything in my life. But it was a challenge, and I said I was willing to try it. So I went and saw the UCLA people, and since the term was beginning in a couple of weeks they needed somebody pretty quickly. Now I didn't know what I was going to do with this course, but by instinct, seat of my pants, I went ahead. And the UCLA people asked me back the next year. I found that I enjoyed the job, meeting people and so on, and I found that *I* was learning things myself. I began to find out for myself why certain things had worked and other things hadn't. And I went on teaching for twenty years or more. Towards the end of that, I realized I had extensive notes for the classes, and I decided that this might make a book. I got the book together and submitted it through a friend of mine; Holt, Rinehart bought it, and it was published in 1980.

As I say, I enjoyed teaching, but it was a lot of work. I assigned a lot of writing and had to read and correct all of that. But that is the only way to teach writing—to make the students write and write.

Were most of your students writers first, who wanted to learn about writing for the screen, or were they people who just wanted to sell a script to a studio?

I suspect most of them were not intent on being professional writers, whatever the medium, but were primarily interested in selling something to the movies.

Was there any one essential fact you wanted potential screenwriters to know?

Well, I believe in the classical story form, not disjointed and unstructured. But generally speaking, the most successful stories are those of human character. The most important thing in a script is to have strong leading characters. Plot and structure and the rest are really secondary. It's how your characters behave and what they say that really makes a film live. *The African Queen* was a wonderful adventure story, set in Africa, lots of action, but it was the characters as played by Bogart and Hepburn, that made it outstanding. *Casablanca*, again, many interesting, colorful elements, but what really made it special? It was the character of Bogart's Rick, so clearly and *interestingly* defined.

Therefore, in general, the most effective screenplays and films are those solidly based in human characters.

How do you feel the films of today compare with those of the studio period, as regards the writing?

In the old days, because of restrictions in some cases, the writing had to "rise to the occasion." To take *Casablanca* as an example again, since I've seen it again recently, here was a war story, but there were no battle scenes, very little shooting and that sort of thing. It was almost entirely characters, dialogue, and people scenes. There were no sex scenes, no bedroom scenes, but you certainly felt that the Bogart and Bergman characters had been madly in love. You couldn't use four-letter words in those days as you can now, but there was no question that the Bogart character was *tough*.

So, there are differences. We no longer seem to have the same value for really great dialogue in films. Action, sensation, shootings, these are more common ingredients in films today. . . . A lot of car crashes.

Overleaf: Walter Connolly and Ginger Rogers in *Fifth Avenue Girl* (1939).

Allan Scott (with pipe),
Mark Sandrich, and
Claudette Colbert
on the set of
So Proudly We Hail (1943).

Allan Scott, born in Arlington, New Jersey, educated at Amherst and Oxford, wrote his first Broadway hit while still in his early twenties. In 1934, Mark Sandrich and Pandro Berman brought him west to work on a movie musical, the third for the team of Fred Astaire and Ginger Rogers.

To mention Astaire and Rogers together is to invoke a high-style world of exultant song and dance, tuxedoes and shimmering evening gowns, painted moons, white gondolas and gleaming black dance floors. Understandably, in this swirl of glamour the hole-punched pages of a screenplay do not come instantly to mind. But screenplays there were, and a screenwriter, weaving songs and dancers and gondolas into an irresistable whole. Of the nine films in the RKO series, Scott worked on seven of them. Critics who dismiss what went on between the musical numbers as formula farce should compare Scott's and his co-writers' efforts with the average musical "book" of the period, all those leaden backstagers into which comedy relief would be thrust by the Ritz Brothers or worse. The Astaire-Rogers scripts, full of wordplay and wisecracks and romantic jousting, gleefully winking at their own artificial plot twists, are worthy of comparison with the best of the '30s screwball comedies. There is froth and there is froth: Scott's work was cool and intoxicating champagne.

Fred and Ginger went their separate ways, but Scott continued to write for them—three for her, three for him. On *Fifth Avenue Girl* and *Primrose Path* (both Rogers vehicles), he worked with the legendary Gregory La Cava. (It's interesting that La Cava, known for his improvisational techniques, worked best in the company of "well-made" playwrights like Morrie Ryskind and Allan Scott). With Mark Sandrich again he went to Paramount, writing sophisticated comedy (*Skylark*) and wartime melodrama (*So Proudly We Hail*), both starring Claudette Colbert. He became a producer for David Selznick, and later an executive in Stanley Kramer's production company at Columbia. He returned full-time to writing in the late '50s. His last major screenplay credit, *Don't Look Now,* he refuses to discuss, due apparently to a particular dislike for the finished film.

Fifty-three years after his first Broadway success, he has a new play in the works. Producers in London and New York are talking to him about it. When I track him down at his home in Los Angeles, he has been working day and night. "I'm exhausted," he says. "I can't see anybody for a few days. But call me next time you're out here." Next time I call, he is just on his way to the airport, a business trip to England. We go over our respective datebooks, and Scott promises to see me when he stops in New York in a few weeks. He keeps the promise. On a cool October afternoon, we meet at his daughter's town house on Manhattan's East Side. The circumstances are unfortunate. Workmen seem to be tearing the house down from the inside out, and Scott has caught a cold. But we press on, shouting over the hammers and drills and barking dog. Allan Scott is a good-natured, white-haired, moustachioed man with a tweedy, professorial air. Not unlike so many of his films, he is very pleasant company.

I was a Rhodes Scholar, and my first play was done in England while I was up at Oxford. And after that I was hooked on the theatre. I came back and began working for the Theatre Guild. I did lecture tours for them, talking about certain plays, for example O'Neill's *Mourning Becomes Electra.* I prepared, oh, very serious lectures on the Greek background, etcetera. But I found that the audiences weren't a damned bit interested in that, so it dwindled down to a kind of intellectual vaudeville—I made a lot of jokes.

I did that for about seven or eight months. And as a result I had enough experiences for a play. This was during the Depression, and everywhere you went there were authors, some very big ones, doing this literary lecturing, because they had lost their shirts. So that was what my first successful play, *Goodbye Again,* was about. A lecturer on tour who meets a woman with whom he had had a forgotten, long-ago affair.

My wife, Laura, was a Theatre Guild actress, and starred in a number of plays. We lived entirely on her salary, and I banked everything else. Well, my bank never opened during the bank holiday. And my wife was then pregnant. So that's why we went to Hollywood about then.

I had been working for Jed Harris, revising two or three of his productions. One of these was a play that Freddie—Fred Astaire—had been in in New York, *The Gay Divorce.* It was the first time he hadn't appeared with his sister, and it was not enormously successful in New York. Dwight Taylor wrote it, based on something of his father's, and Cole Porter added the music. And the producer thought it could be made better for the London production. So we fixed it up, and in London it went better.

Word of my contribution somehow got around, and Mark Sandrich, who was making the Astaire-Rogers pictures, found out and asked for me. My agent, Leland Hayward, said, "Kid, you're getting $250 a week from Jed Harris, your wife's going to have a baby, they want you in Hollywood for a lot more. For Christ's sake, don't be silly." So I didn't be silly and I signed a contract with RKO, and from then on I was in the movies.

So Sandrich brought you out to work on the Astaire-Rogers pictures?

Yes. But I did something else for RKO in the meantime. It was a bad experience, a film called

A Village Tale, from a novel by Phil Stong. It opened with a train passing a small village, the people sitting at the back of the train looking out and saying, "There's a place where nothing ever happens." And then we zoom in, and it turns out that *everything* happens there. And what I really wrote about was Arlington and Kearny where I was born, just across the Hudson there. It was very depressing, a tragedy, and from the audience's point of view it was disastrous. I got one piece of fan mail, a wire from Eugene O'Neill, and it said, "That's the stuff to feed the troops." But I think he was the only one who ever saw it. And so, in self-defense, it was a good thing I started doing musicals.

How did the *Top Hat* script develop?

Dwight Taylor, who had written *The Gay Divorce*, broke the story down. I took it and rewrote it the way I wanted it. By that time Irving Berlin was here, and I worked very closely with him. I worked closely with all of the songwriters. They had to be part of it so everything would fit together.

With Irving it was very odd, because he was used to writing thirty songs for one of his musicals, and in this there was only going to be time for five at most. One big number and the rest all intimate numbers. And so he would be knocking out a song a day, but we would have to figure out what we could really use, what we needed where. I would show him the script, and I remember, for example, a scene where Fred and Ginger are alone in the park and the dialogue went, "Isn't it a lovely day?" And she says, "Yes . . . to get caught in the rain." Well, it gave him the idea for a song, and he wrote it.

It wasn't just mechanical. There were points where we knew we had to have it. You came to an intimate scene of some kind, whether it was flirting or what not, and that was the time for music.

But Irving was so fecund, and there were wonderful things he wrote that we just couldn't use. I remember him during *Top Hat* singing something called "White Christmas." We knew it was a wonderful song, but we had no way we could use it. He, quote, "demonstrated" the songs so well. He played that terrible piano of his, just banging with the left hand, and sang with great effect and passion. I'll never forget him "demonstrating," with that little wizened face of his, the things he did. It was marvelous.

I've read that Fred Astaire was unhappy with the way you had written his character in the first version of the script.

In the beginning he worried a little bit about the way I wrote. I was ironic, but without making jokes. You know, I never gave him a joke. I'd been used to stage dialogue.

But also—let's face it—he's a helluva snob. He could be perturbed very easily by the wrong reference. I had a line about "the nobility marrying American millionairesses." That went out. And later I used to deliberately put in "wrong" references like that so he wouldn't bother with any other lines. We'd feed it to him, and then we'd say, "All right, we'll take it out," and then he didn't pay attention to anything else.

Freddie, as a man he's not romantic. His love scenes were all dances. Irving called him the best damned *plugger* of songs, but he didn't have much of a voice. Neither of them did—I mean, Ginger had about four notes and you were lucky to get all four at once. But they were a marvelous pair.

What Hepburn said about them—Ginger gave him sex appeal and he gave her class—was absolutely true, in my opinion. After all, he was in his forties and bald. I remember one night—in those days we used to work Saturday nights . . . golden, golden time—and there was one particular dance they were trying to get. That was one of the things both Freddie and Mark Sandrich insisted, that he would do most of the dances in one shot, the camera following him. They finally got the whole dance done very well, and he and Ginger came down to the finish in front of the camera and his wig fell off. . . . They had to start over, do it again. Very often there was blood in Ginger's shoes. They had to change them a lot.

Freddie was the essential choreographer on the films. Hermes Pan was in charge of the big productions, but he and Freddie worked the other numbers out together. Hermes played Ginger in the rehearsal room, and, when it was all worked out, they showed Ginger what to do.

It's been said that the two of them got along, that they didn't get along. What's your recollection?

He didn't like being part of another team. He had been a team with his sister, Adele. They were wonderful. She was quite a cheerful character. She had married a British peer, and that was one reason he didn't like my cracks about nobility. But he didn't want to be tied to anybody again. So any chance he got, he was ready to get another partner. But he never got another partner like Ginger. He did that one, *Damsel in Distress*, and pushed Joan Fontaine around. And he really pushed her because she couldn't dance at all. Nice girl, too.

Ginger was one of the hardest working actresses. She was determined to become *an actress*. And she was. The musicals swung her into stardom, and she began doing pictures on her own, some of which I wrote myself. But for the musicals, we were writing for what they could do. They were required to act, but it required them to be themselves as much as anything. The same for the supporting players. We had our own company, in effect, and they were all marvelous comedians. We used one group in one picture and another group in the next picture, and so on.

It was artificial escape stuff, absolute entertainment—that was the whole idea of them. It was a dreary time for the country, and the public just flocked to these pictures. There was nothing quite like it at the time.

Mark Sandrich directed a number of the Astaire-Rogers films, and many other musicals, but he seems largely ignored by film critics. How strong was his contribution to the series?

He revolutionized the musical. Before that, musicals were like *42nd Street*. The music was not part of the story line. Mark Sandrich is one of the most underrated men. He was a first-class producer and director, and he was an innovator. That kind of musical was his idea; he had that angle. Even before he made *The Gay Divorcee*, he had made a small musical in verse, three of four reels, along the same lines. He always had the concept in mind. If you look at the directors of musicals, his contribution to the form is very underestimated.

Later, we both went to Paramount. We had our own company there, and after we finished *Blue Skies*, with Freddie and Bing, we were going to go to Selznick together. Then he had a heart attack. He had had a bad heart for a long time. I had just finished the shooting script, and Irving Berlin had gone off to somewhere in the South Pacific. We lived in Beverly Hills; I lived on Linden, and Mark lived two blocks away. I went out to get the morning paper, and it said Mark Sandrich had died. I rushed over to the house at once.

Somebody else directed *Blue Skies*—Stuart Heisler, a run-of-the-mill fellow—and I took my

name off it and joined Selznick as a producer. Mark was a friend of mine. His death was a grievous loss, and the dumb front office did what they did to the picture, so I said the hell with it.

You adapted *Roberta*. How close did your script stick to the Broadway version?

It had been successful, and the studio bought it. But there was nothing in it for the two of them, particularly Ginger. And so we had to change it. We devised a way of letting her play a kind of part she loved, with an accent, and that became a major part, with Irene Dunne's. That was Irene's last picture for the studio. They didn't think she would continue to be a star, and they let her go after that.

It was very curious writing that one. I had to leave for New York to put on a play, and I told Pan Berman, the producer, that, and he came with me on the train. You didn't often take the plane back then. So I was writing the script on the train, and Pan would get off at each station and wire the new dialogue back. I was typing in a compartment and he'd be standing by, saying, "That's great," and then rip it out of the typewriter. When the train came to a stop, he would get out and go to a wireless office and send it on back to the studio, four or five pages at a time.

Whose idea was it to take Astaire out of a tuxedo and put him into a sailor's suit for *Follow the Fleet*?

Everybody says the pictures were all the same. But for each one we broke our asses trying to get a different story line—so the music could be different, so Freddie could do different kinds of dances. For this one RKO wanted to do something, oh, semipatriotic. They owned a play called *Shorty*, which I never read, and they'd had a huge success with it years before. I think it was Pan's idea. It certainly wasn't mine. Berlin did the score, and the songs were all part of the story, as much as possible. But some of it—*I Want to Lead a Band*, for example— I'm sure he had in the trunk for years.

I thought *Follow the Fleet* was kind of silly, because Fred looked about as much like a sailor as I did. And then we couldn't get any help from the Navy. We'd gone down to the naval yard in San Diego, but the ships were too dirty to photograph, certainly for a musical. So we had to build our own battleship. We literally built an entire battleship on Stage Twelve.

Between the writing and conferring with the composers and so on, how long would one of these scripts take you to finish?

I never took any notice. And I hadn't looked at the things in all these years, but the people at Harvard have a new library there for drama and movies and things like that, and they asked me for my scripts. Unfortunately, I guess, there's no more of this stuff of giving it to colleges and deducting it off the income tax. So I got out these scripts, and I was horrified to realize that I might be writing five major pictures in a year. It took me a long time to get to where I could do just one picture in a year. But that's the way it was, you know. You did one and then started the next one.

You've spoken of Mark Sandrich's importance to the series. What about Pandro Berman, who was head of RKO then? How much did he contribute to their success?

Berman was a very genial fellow. A good snifter—he could smell what would work well. I never knew a man who was so good at getting the right group together. And he was a very young man, thirty-two or thirty-three when he was the head of the studio. He surrounded himself with new, young talent. We were all quite young at the time—I was twenty-five when I went out to do *Top Hat*.

But I remember—and this will give you an idea of how they looked at scripts back then—the first time I was called to the front office after I'd done *Top Hat*. I was sent up, alone, to meet with Pandro. I didn't have any particular trepidation because we all loved what we had done, but still, I thought, "Oh shit, who did I fall over? What did I do?" And Pandro said, "Allan, I like this, but there are fourteen more speeches in this than in the last picture." They used to number the speeches. And that was the extent of that conversation.

Swing Time is often called the masterpiece of the series.

Wonderful score by Jerome Kern and Dorothy Fields. Freddie liked that one. He liked playing a gambler and all that.

The problem with *Swing Time* was we never had a finish. Originally, the character is known to be dextrous with cards. We know how clever he is with cards, and he's supposed to do this card trick near the end of the story and get everyone out of trouble. George Stevens was directing that one, and, to my horror, on the first day of shooting, for lack of a good joke or something, George just took the card scene and used it at the beginning.

And so, later, we had to whack our heads for a finish. And George said, "Well, we'll just let him lose his pants, and they all start laughing." Everybody in the nightclub starts laughing. Everybody in the film thinks it's so funny when he loses his pants. We shot people laughing for days. The only people who didn't laugh were the audience at the sneak preview. They didn't think it was so funny. So we had to cut. There was five times as much laughing as you see in the picture now. Either way, I still don't think someone losing his pants is very funny.

How did Stevens differ from Sandrich in his approach to the material?

They were different types. I think George was an infinitely more important serious director. He had a good sense of humor, a funny look in his eye. He liked to sit and think, and he would go into this sort of reverie all on his own. Like a trance. Carole Lombard was working with him on a picture, and she just looked at him in this state one day and said, "I don't think he's thinking at all. He's sleeping with his eyes open. George, wake up!"

I worked with him again on *Quality Street*. It wasn't successful. It was from the play by J.M. Barrie. I thought Barrie was a master, a master craftsman, but dated. One didn't study him any longer. And there was absolutely no motion picture activity in that play. And there was no way to get any. But Katie Hepburn wanted to play it, and there was a marvelous cast. And George directed to the best of his ability. But it was the kind of picture that probably shouldn't have been made. It was dated as it was written. His kind of humor was absolutely un-American, and to rewrite it was absolutely beside the point. You could punch up the characters a bit, but it was just. . . . I was against the project, even though I admired Barrie as a writer. It just wasn't a movie.

On *Swing Time* did you work closely with Jerome Kern?

Kern just never stopped. I mean, he could write a song every five minutes. I lived about half a block away from him, and so we worked very closely. I remember one day he was just playing some songs for me, and Dorothy Fields hadn't arrived yet. His wife told us lunch was ready, and then a telegram was delivered at the house. He read it and said to me, "You go ahead and have lunch. I want to answer this telegram." And by the time lunch was over and I went back to him, he said, "How does this sound?" And he played "The Last Time I Saw Paris." Oscar Hammerstein had sent him a telegram with the words, the lyrics, and by the time lunch was over he had composed the song. A marvelous musician.

The old man and Ira Gershwin and I were doing a musical for New York when the old man died. He was going to New York and he dropped dead, and we never finished.

You worked with the Gershwins on the next one, _Shall We Dance_.

George you couldn't work with very much. Always had a headache, and of course nobody knew there was a tumor and he'd die so young. But he was always very pleasant. Ira worked very closely with me on the lyrics, and then George would put them to music. George kept a book of themes that had occurred to him. When Ira came up with a lyric, George would sort of look through his book and select one and develop it.

Shall We Dance was where Freddie impersonated a Russian. It was supposed to be funny. It didn't quite come off, but it gave him something to do. These were farces, let's face it. People running back and forth, mistaking each other and so on. There was a kind of innocence about them—even though underneath they were fairly sophisticated. There were so many naughty things in those pictures, actually, and never once would the Breen Office catch it or say "you can't do that." It never occurred to them to ask what Ginger was doing with these men on the Riviera, who was paying her way, paying the hotel bill and so on. Some of the reviewers pointed these things out. But as long as you stayed fairly subtle about these things, the office didn't catch it.

I was always worried that someone would question the relationship between Edward Everett Horton and Eric Blore. I worried that someone would ask me what was going on, if the characters were gay or something. I mean, when you have two characters of that _sort_, what are they? Well, I just said they were "good friends." But, you know, a master and a manservant just don't ordinarily argue that way. (Laughs.) You'd have thought that someone at the front office would have brought it up. But it was never questioned.

I've heard other screenwriters of the period speak of the legendary team of Graham Baker and Gene Towne. You actually colloboated with them, didn't you, on _Joy of Living_?

Yes. They were working on the script and Irene Dunne didn't like it and young Doug—Doug Fairbanks—didn't like it, so I was told to help the boys out. Well, it was a difficult thing, because Baker and Towne were sort of far from my realm. You had to ingratiate yourself.

In the script they had a character who used to squawk like Donald Duck. And I commented that Donald Duck squawked when he was mad and told them, "You've got the character squawking when he's on the make." Well, they looked at each other and then looked back at me and said, "Yeah, that's right." And somehow that happened to be the right thing to say, and from then on we hit it off and they didn't mind my making changes.

I kind of liked them. They weren't really writers, they were good gagmen. Always doing things for publicity, having their pictures taken in disguises, things like that. They thought it was very important for everyone to know who they were. They were kind of foolish, but I liked them.

With _Carefree_ did you have a sense that the series was running out of steam? It's very

Fred Astaire loses his pants in *Swing Time* (1936).

Ralph Bellamy, Mark Sandrich, Fred Astaire, Ginger Rogers, and Irving Berlin on the set of

funny, but the running time is much shorter, the music less memorable. It's on a much smaller scale than the earlier films.

Oh, possibly. It was a screwball comedy. That was the era of screwball comedy. Again we tried to do something different, a new setting. Freddie was a psychiatrist, and that gave us things to play with—hypnosis, dreams, tricks with photography. We did some really old gags in that one. One, with the truck, was probably the oldest gag in Hollywood. But it worked effectively in a more or less sophisticated story.

Who was Hagar Wilde?

She wrote the original story. She was quite a good magazine writer. I didn't know her very well, and she didn't really work on the picture. Died about ten years ago, of cancer.

The last of the Astaire-Rogers series was *The Story of Vernon and Irene Castle*. You started to work on this and then quit. What happened?

Irene Castle was still alive and she wanted to supervise this, wanted everything done exactly to her specifications. Very imperious. She was a pain in the ass, to be honest with you. And when she began to tell me how to write it, I went off and left for New York, to do a play.

I always had that in my contract, that I could leave every eighteen months to put a play on, however long it took, and then report back.

You next did two films with Gregory La Cava—*Fifth Avenue Girl* and *Primrose Path*. What was he like to work with? He was known to be a believer in lots of improvisation.

La Cava was great fun. You know, he would never show the studio a script. They would buy something, a play or a story, to be on the safe side, but that was the last they saw of it. For example, he did the Kaufman play, *Stage Door*, and he didn't use one word of the play. And he never showed a word of a script to the front office.

He admired my dialogue, but I learned from him something very important. He told me how to *stalk* a scene. He said, "You don't write it. You're a very good writer, and I've read your plays and seen your stuff in New York. But in movies you don't say the line, you stalk the scene." We would do six or seven versions of each scene. If the front office had seen the script they would have fainted—it was about 190 pages, whereas most scripts were about 130.

Then, with all these versions, we would get to the studio about 8:30 in the morning. There was no script for the actors yet, nothing for them to study. And La Cava would take all the papers scattered around, and he would say, "Okay, fade in." And he'd start dictating different things from the material. And I would be there reminding him of this line and that. He had a girl he called Winnie—her real name was Kay, but he called her Winnie—and she would take it down and then make four or five copies.

The people on the set knew what the scene was in general, and he would give them the pages and a half-hour later he would start shooting. And it worked. The actors were so full of trepidation that they played it off the top of their heads, and it was wonderful. It worked for La Cava and it could have worked for a lot of people. If you ever get a copy of a La Cava script, they'll say "as shot."

Did you have any trouble working this way?

Well, it was new to me, but I saw it work in front of me. The performers had a sprightliness about them, because they weren't all set and comfortable in what they were doing. They didn't know *what* the hell they were doing, in fact. As a result, it gave the films the kind of spontaneity that La Cava was noted for.

Fifth Avenue Girl was an original script, and it was interesting for me because we got to pull a reverse on the sort of story that might normally be made. Here was this kid in the Depression, didn't know where her next meal is coming from, and by chance she sits next to this millionaire. He admires her spunkiness and says, "Tell you what, you have dinner with me at my house." It isn't a come-on, and she doesn't take it as a come-on, but everybody in the house, the wife, daughter, the son, thinks the worst. Now, instead of the old story of "Bunky Pulls the String," where the character sort of takes on everyone's problems and solves them, this girl doesn't do anything. She's just there. And they solve their own problems around her. That was the way Greg could think, reversing what you were used to.

Putting the script together so close to the deadline, were there any mistakes? Anything that had to be done over?

Yes. On *Fifth Avenue Girl,* when everything was over and settled, Greg had Ginger just walking off by herself down Park Avenue. At the preview, a man in the audience got up and shouted, "No! No!" It was plainly an unsatisfactory ending. They wanted her to get together with the boy at the end. So we had to go back and reshoot the ending. The boy appears in the doorway this time and says—whatever her name was—"Come on back!" And then everyone was happy with that.

***Primrose Path* dealt with prostitution. Were there any problems with the censors?**

No. There was only the problem of a mistake I made in using the same number of the house as in the book. I think it was 49 or something, and it never occurred to me to change the number. We changed everything, and that was all that was left from the book. The people who lived at 49 sued the studio, for God's sake.

The censors may have worried a bit, but since Greg didn't have a script they couldn't read it. It was a tastefully done movie, though. We made it in Monterey. You know, I told him that kind of strand doesn't exist there, and he said, "Oh, the hell with it." And, in the middle of that picture, he just disappeared. And we found him, finally, selling hot dogs.

La Cava? What do you mean, selling hot dogs?

Yes! At a hot dog stand! For four days he disappeared and nobody knew where he was. We were living up there. It was a lot of fun up there.

You were on location and the director just disappeared to go sell hot dogs?

Yeah. And two days later the whole front office was up, *searching* for him. And they found him, wearing a white hat and an apron.

What was his explanation?

He didn't explain it.

With his way of working, I guess it would have been impossible to fire him.

He was a guy they had to have. But they didn't have to like him.

La Cava is probably the most important forgotten director of the bunch. Although, well, funny thing, most of his pictures never got abroad because of the war. And a couple of years ago they had just discovered him in Paris, and there was a La Cava festival. A couple of French critics interviewed me then because I had worked with him. He was a helluva director, and great fun to work with.

His only problem was he drank too much. By the end of the day we'd go back to his office and he would pour literally three-quarters of a glass of liquor. And he was drunk before he left the studio. Too bad.

I don't think he committed suicide. I think it was pure accident because he drank too much. I was living in Malibu at the time, and he was living in Malibu. I didn't see it, but I knew the policeman who had found him—there were only three or four there—and he said that La Cava had the phone off the hook in his hand, obviously trying for help. But that was a big scandal.*

Is it true that Mrs. Roosevelt asked you to write what became *So Proudly We Hail*?

That was a very curious story. About forty or fifty stars went on a bond-selling tour by train. All the great stars, Cagney, Colbert, all the stars who were available, all on the same train. I remember we'd arrive somewhere, like Cleveland, and they just couldn't believe all these stars were in town together. In Boston, for example, there were over a million people on the streets just watching the parade. There'd be four or five stars in each open automobile. And they would perform, in armories. I was the chief writer for these, and Mark Sandrich was the chief producer. I had two or three people helping me with the sketches and so on. We would have to revise things because the stars might change from place to place, as some became available and others became unavailable and had to start a picture back in Hollywood.

We ended up in Washington, D.C., at the White House. It was there that I met Mrs. Roosevelt. We had tea with her, and I happened to be sitting at her table. Now, in those days there was no Army Nurse Corps. The nurses were Red Cross nurses, and they were just beginning to make the Nurse Corps for the Army. Mrs. Roosevelt said, "What are you planning to do next, Mr. Scott?" And I said, "Oh, I don't know. I'll go back with Frank Capra and write some more two-reelers." We had been doing these propaganda films at the time. She said, "I think it would be a very good idea to make *big* pictures about the war." I said I thought it would, too, but no one had asked us. She said, "You know, it would be very interesting if you would go over to the hospital, because some of the girls from Bataan are over there." Well, I pricked up my ears. It was the first I'd heard of it. I didn't know any of them had been rescued. All I heard was that "Dugout Doug" got out and left the rest of them there.

So, with a note from her, I went over. Some of the girls were crazed. Some of them had babies, which we did not exploit in the movie. Illegitimate babies. The girls and the guys in the last days said, "Oh, what the hell." They never expected to be rescued. So they made love and got pregnant. But I met two or three very pleasant girls, one of whom I took back with me.

I told Mark Sandrich what Mrs. Roosevelt had said to me, and I wired him, "Think I have found a subject. Telephone me at hotel." He phoned me in the morning, and I told him about the story of these girls. They talked to me and I made notes. The script was a fairly true story, but I did have to keep away from some of the awfulness that did happen. The War Department sent a general to keep an eye on things. So we didn't want to make it too awful and bloody.

---

*Newspapers reported La Cava's death in 1952 as the result of natural causes, a heart attack. He was fifty-nine.

Claudette Colbert, Paulette Goddard, and Veronica Lake in *So Proudly We Hail* (1943).

Hans Conried and Mary Heal

And the film did have the desired effect: a whole lot of kids went out and joined the Army Nurse Corps.

That was one of four or five times I got nominated for the Oscar. I never won one. The other nominees that year, 1943, were Noël Coward, Lillian Hellman, and the one that got it was Norman Krasna for a little picture with a dog in the White House.*

You mentioned earlier your going to work for David Selznick in the mid-'40s as a producer. How much writing would you be doing in that period?

I would usually hire writers and then do a final script myself. But we weren't permitted, as producer, to take credit in those circumstances. So that's why it seems like I stopped writing suddenly. I didn't.

What was your assessment of David Selznick as a filmmaker?

Selznick was the absolute master. Everything was motion pictures in his mind. The best moviemaker of them all. He knew it all. I remember walking through the studio, looking very disconsolate, and he said, "What's the matter?" I told him some complicated problem I had with a scene. He said, "It's just a glass shot, Alan," and he passed me by. He could solve a problem like that. He *knew.*

But nobody realized that for the last decade and more of his life, with the exception of the remake of *A Farewell to Arms,* he never made a picture. He couldn't get the money. I remember we were going to do *Tess of the D'Urbervilles.* Probably the best script I ever wrote. I was so frustrated—the script was ready, we had Jennifer, we had the whole cast under contract. It took me two years to find out that he couldn't get the money. This was the tragedy of Selznick in later years.

But when I was with him he was very, very proud and secure with Selznick International Pictures. His own releases had to have a certain quality. Those pictures that weren't Selznick International quality went out as RKO, although they were made at Selznick in Culver City. They went to Dore Schary at RKO. I replaced Dore Schary at Selznick International when he became head of RKO.

Did you work on Hitchcock's *Notorious?*

That was just a rewrite. Hitch was also under contract to Selznick. I didn't have my name on that one; I took it off.

What about *Since You Went Away?*

I worked on that, rewrote it, but it was really written by David O. Selznick himself. He and a secretary went on a train, took trains everywhere, and they copied the conversation of people talking about their beloved ones who had gone away to war.

You had one last reunion with Fred Astaire on a musical called *Let's Dance.*

That was a Paramount picture, with Betty, Betty Hutton. Betty had become a big star. Buddy DeSylva had found her in New York. She had enormous fire and spirit, but this didn't really sit well with Freddie, who was a gentleman. She wasn't classy enough for Freddie. And I don't think she was a very good dancer. She could yell and scream and sing. But I think he had to

*Princess O'Rourke.

push her around. I don't think he was very happy with that picture. I wrote it, but, you know, I can't even remember what it was about.

You worked with Stanley Kramer's unit in the early '50s?

I was a partner. I made a lot of the Kramer pictures, as a producer, and wrote some, but couldn't put my name on them.

You did get credited with a wonderful film called *The 5,000 Fingers of Dr. T.*, co-written with Dr. Seuss.

Dr. Seuss, yes. It was his story. Stanley Kramer gave me Dr. Seuss's manuscript, which was about six inches thick, and he said, "I want you to take $3 million out of this." It had elaborate, impossible things in it. So I met with Dr. Seuss and he would say to everything, "Oh, you're not going to take out that . . . or that." I said, "We have to do something." We were under contract—the Kramer Company—with Columbia Pictures. Every time we had to make a picture that cost over $750,000, we had to go to Harry Cohn and beg him for the money.

I would never work for Harry. I liked Harry Cohn, but I just wouldn't work for him. People had told me not to. He was always trying to get me to work for him and I wouldn't. And I would have to go down to him, and he was so fed up with Stanley asking for more money, he'd say, "You son-of-a-bitch, you don't want to work for me, but you want another million dollars!"

Dr. Seuss was a lovely guy. A very *serious* man, not funny at all. He's funny when he's got his pen, but he's a very serious man. He lived in La Jolla and worked in a sort of tower, all this stuff strewn all around him—but he knew exactly where everything was. A very good conversationalist. I enjoyed him, liked him. To direct the picture, Stanley got somebody from Metro, who did a very bad job of directing.*

Stanley at that time was under attack for being a "red"—in fact, all of us were, but Stanley in particular. We had our first preview on the picture, and if I ever saw a set-up job it was that. When his name hit the screen—"Stanley Kramer Presents"—a group of people got up and began to hiss, and, as the picture started, they flocked out of the theatre. Someone had organized it. But those who stayed enjoyed it, I think. I kind of like it. Kids love it, even today.

A screenwriter's work is interpreted by actors as well as a director. Can you recall ways you might adapt your work to fit a particular star?

There were people I liked to write for. Colbert, for instance, was a complete professional. When Claudette Colbert said, "There's something bothering me in this script," she had a real reason, and I'd listen to her. She studied her part. Claudette . . . Greer Garson—these were stage actresses who took their art seriously, knew how to go about learning lines, working hard, and so a writer did pay attention to them.

There was a time with Ginger, on the other hand, where it got to be a joke. She would say, "There's something *radically wrong.*" And you had to go down and see what you could do. If she couldn't say the line, she couldn't say the line. But, then, what I found out was she hadn't studied, didn't *know* the lines. She'd been out the night before, dancing and whatnot. And in the morning everything was "radically wrong." So we used that term for Ginger for some time.

*Roy Rowland was the director.

For Ginger alone I wrote four pictures. For Claudette I wrote three: *Skylark, Remember the Day* and *So Proudly We Hail,* and when she took part in a story conference it was always very productive. If there was a flaw in the script she knew just where it was. On *Skylark* we were both agreed that the play was no good and we would have to start almost from scratch, and she was very helpful. There was a scene in the picture where she has to fix a big meal in the galley of a yacht in the middle of a storm. It involved some wonderful physical clowning and improvising, and she did it all in one take. She was quite proud of that.

She was a good friend, and I remember, after my wife died—we'd been married over thirty years—I wrote a play, and when some producers bought it they sent it to Colbert, hoping she would star in it. She had already written to me after my wife's death, and now she called and asked me to come see her in Barbados so we could talk. For the first few days she refused to talk about the play. Finally, one night, over brandy, she took my hand and said, "Allan, I'm not going to do the play. And I don't think you should do it, either. It's written out of bitterness and grief and if it's produced you will regret it." Well, I didn't know what to say, and we just sat there for a time. But when I left Barbados finally, I came back home and called off the play. And then I threw it away. She was right.

Looking back, do you have a particular favorite of the films made from your scripts?

No. When we were making the Astaire-Rogers films, it never occurred to me that they would be classics of any kind. And then again, some of what I thought were the more important pictures I worked on no one ever sees anymore.

Funny, isn't it, the way these things turn out.

Overleaf: **Lon Chaney, Jr., and Evelyn Ankers in** *The Wolf Man* **(1942).**

11 · CURT SIODMAK

The author and Curt Siodmak
at "the ranch," Three Rivers,
California, 1985.

The voice on the phone is heavily Germanic, lightly sardonic: "Drive past the general store—'we got it all,' the sign says—over the bridge, down Old Three Rivers Road two miles, and you turn right at the south fork. Don't turn right and you'll find yourself in a *real* dead end . . . *the cemetery.*" It is the voice of Curt Siodmak, author of *The Wolf Man* and *I Walked with a Zombie,* giving directions to his home in rural central California, near the big trees of Sequoia National Park. Three hours' drive out of Los Angeles, several miles in from the highway, Siodmak's ranch house is built on a lonely and rugged hillside. The view is minimal, the isolation complete. His few neighbors are working ranchers in pickup trucks and cowboy hats; it's a safe bet that Siodmak is the only eighty-four-year-old Dresden-born *emigré* author of classic horror movies for miles around.

This time his exile is self-imposed. The first one, from Nazi Germany, was not. Siodmak was a popular novelist and screenwriter living in Berlin when Hitler's "Jewish policy" began to take effect. With his wife, Henrietta (a gentle and gracious woman he has lived with now for over sixty years), he fled to England and France, leading the refugee's tightrope existence for several years before finding his way to Hollywood in 1937. He turned out journeyman work for Paramount and Monogram, including two sarong sagas for Dorothy Lamour (*Her Jungle Love* and *Aloma of the South Seas*), then linked up with another German, Joe May, to write the first *Invisible Man* sequel for Universal, putting Siodmak in his most successful niche as that studio's horror *meister,* revitalizing Universal's various resident monsters and creating a few new ones as well. His screen story, *Son of Dracula,* became Siodmak's talented director-brother

Robert's first American hit, and led to his subsequent series of *film noir* classics, including *Phantom Lady, The Killers,* and *The Spiral Staircase.*

Away from Universal, under the aegis of Val Lewton, Curt effected subtler shudders in *I Walked with a Zombie,* a quietly eerie little masterpiece in which the horror elements are allowed to develop piece by disturbing piece. For Warner Bros., on the other hand, he delivered an all-stops-out melodrama of severed hands and madness, *The Beast with Five Fingers.* Later in the '40s Siodmak went back to novel-writing, and with *Donovan's Brain* (published in 1943), he had his biggest hit, over a million copies sold and still in print more than four decades later. A film version made by Republic, *The Lady and the Monster,* starring Vera Hruba Ralston, is notable primarily for the fruity playing of Erich ("Get me the Gigli saw!") von Stroheim as a mad doctor.

In the post-atomic age, horror waned and science fiction took its place, and Siodmak turned out tales of more cosmic concerns in *The Magnetic Monster, Riders to the Stars,* and *Earth vs. Flying Saucers.* With *Bride of the Gorilla,* in part a rewrite of *The Wolf Man,* Siodmak made a half-hearted turn to directing as well as writing. He would direct several more films over the years, but, clearly, storytelling, not *mise en scène,* was his forte.

In recent years he has devoted himself to writing novels. He sells film rights to his fiction, but tends to avoid the fray of screenwriting in the "new" Hollywood. He has lectured at sci-fi conventions and universities and has been a special guest at a number of film festivals around the world. It's not surprising. Few men living have had such colorful experiences in the film worlds of several continents—from extra work in Berlin in Fritz Lang's *Metropolis* to directing in Brazilian jungle locations for *Curucu, Beast of the Amazon.* Of course, Siodmak considers most of his film work to be "silly stuff," jobs taken to keep the rent paid. But one must credit even the most lurid of his '40s work with an attention to structure and believable motivation, and a real feel for the Gothic. *The Wolf Man, I Walked with a Zombie,* and *The Beast with Five Fingers* and other of his credits need no apologies—they are well-crafted, thoroughly entertaining modern fairy tales.

Three Rivers, California, lacks the amenities of Beverly Hills or Berlin, but Siodmak seems comfortably self-sufficient in his ranch house. His spouse, it appears, is a dazzlingly complete homemaker and Siodmak's workroom has a state-of-the-art word processor and a photocopy machine vying for space with the musty volumes of research and author's copies lining the walls. In this room he writes his stories, scripts, novels, as he has written them in other rooms, in other parts of the world, for over six decades.

Siodmak seems to have forgotten he is in his mid-eighties now. At least he shows not the slightest indication of it in his appearance, memory, energy level. He speaks with clarity and precision. About the past he is drily sarcastic. But some memories— the nightmarish events in Germany before the war—leave him frustrated with disbelief even after so many years. The Gothic bogeymen he brought to life at Universal could not compare with the real-life monsters he had escaped. "I try to tell my grandchildren about those years," he says ruefully. "You've had it so good, you kids. You don't understand the things that can happen . . . the terrible things."

I was very unhappy as a child. I came from one of those matchmaker families, Jewish families, before the First World War. My mother didn't want to marry that guy. He knocked her up all the time, gave her four children. And she always wanted to run away. But what could she do? Women couldn't work in those days, except as washerwomen or prostitutes. My father was affluent—until the war cut off his business—and we had a big house, French governess. But I was unhappy. So I wrote, to express my feelings. I got A's in composition at school, but the teacher never read my stories aloud because they were too personal. She didn't want to expose me. I was published when I was seven years old. I wrote a story called "The Key," the story of a young prince who lives in a castle with a thousand rooms. I wrote it on parchment, put sequins on it, made it a little book. And my mother read it to a man who had a magazine for children, *Kinderwelt, Children's World*. And he liked it and printed it. And from that moment on I was hooked, never stopped writing. I did my studies, got my degrees, mathematics, engineering. But I wrote always. And it saved my life. When the Nazis forced me to leave Germany, who wanted an engineer? But a writer can work anywhere.

Let me show you something . . . *Amazing Stories*, volume one, the first edition, 1926. I was given this copy by Forrest Ackerman. You know him? *Famous Monsters* magazine? He is a collector of horror and science fiction. At his house he has 300,000 magazines. So, here is a story I wrote for a German magazine. I got twenty-five dollars for it, which was enough to buy food, sausage for a month, you know? I knew nothing of America at that time. I didn't speak English at all. But they sold my story to America, to Hugo Gernsbach and his *Amazing Stories*. And here it is, look: "We consider this short story an extraordinary classic, the best short story of 1926." And how could I know this story would become a classic. It was a whole new approach to this kind of fantastic writing because I went into great scientific detail. And fifty years later they republished the thing in a book of the best short stories of '26.

Do you know what is science fiction? I had a summer semester in Stanford a while ago. In the evening all those Nobel Prize scientists came to visit our apartment—why not, we had good liquor. And I said to them, "You are all doing science fiction. You have an idea that is not proven. You take ten years to research it. If it proves to be right, it is science. If not, you have spent ten years on science fiction." For me it is easier—I don't have to prove anything.

But I have written books I can show, with radar in 1931, lasers in '32. I wrote a book thirty years ago, *I Gabriel*, with microchips and things that didn't exist then. I sent it to my publisher in New York at that time, and he sent it back with the most vicious letter. "This is the most idiotic idea in a science fiction story since the miniature circus." Today these things in the book are reality. A producer optioned a book of mine, *City in the Sky*. He wanted to make the film. He took me with him to Lockheed and introduced me to the scientists. One of them laughed. He said, "We've read your stuff. We get all our ideas from you." You wouldn't believe it, but most of the ideas the scientists do primitively now come from ideas in science fiction.

You worked as a reporter in Berlin in the '20s?

I was a reporter in Berlin. And in Berlin they made movies, the big UFA pictures. I went to get a story for *Berlin Life* on the film *Metropolis*. They wouldn't let me in, so I became an extra in the film. And I got ten times more as an extra than I would get for the story. And you can see me — I was always in front. Fritz Lang was directing, and he was very tough, very Prussian. And there was an actress, Brigitte Helm, a rather hysterical actress, and she caught fire. So the fire department was there, knowing about this terrible director, things he would do. And Lang found out I was a reporter, and he had me thrown out. I told him about it years later, and he denied it, said it wasn't true.

You didn't like Lang?

No. A very powerful director, but he always took all the credit, you know. His wife wrote all his great films. Thea von Harbou. But he never mentioned her. It's like Capra, with Robert Riskin. Riskin wrote all his hits. After Riskin died, Capra never made another good picture. But he takes all the credit in the world for himself. Silly.

Lang was very hard on people. I saw him shooting *M* with Peter Lorre. I watched them shoot the kangaroo court scene, where all the criminals question him. Lang shot it from eight o'clock in the morning until after midnight. He shot till Lorre fainted. Did it on purpose. Once they tried to kill him, a couple of guys on his crew. They tried to drop a lamp on him. And I understand—I don't know if it's true—some crew guys dragged him into a room once and beat him up. But, you know, you can't treat people so badly and create such a bad atmosphere.

So I worked as a reporter. And then I had some success. I sold my first book. But I had a brother, Robert, Robert Siodmak. And Robert wanted to make a film. He was a cutter then. They gave him old Harry Piel films to recut. Of ten old films, he would make six new ones. The same actors were in all of them, silent pictures, so you could recut them and put new titles and have a new film. And now Robert wanted to do his own picture.

So he came to me. And I thought of an idea. And from this we made the film, and it became one of the most famous pictures in the world, *Menschen am Sonntag . . . People on Sunday.* You have the story, a simple story, a guy meets a girl on a Saturday afternoon. He tells her, "What about tomorrow? Let's go to the beach? And bring a girlfriend." And the girlfriend is prettier than she is, so the first guy goes after the other guy's date. This kind of thing. And you cut back to the city, the city on Sunday. Not a soul. The day ends, the boys say goodbye to the girls, tell them "Next week, next week," but when they are alone they say, "Forget about it." And Monday morning comes, vooom, the subways roar again, another week begins.

The film was a tremendous critical success. The story was stolen. It was done later as *Bank Holiday*, directed by Carol Reed, in England, without telling us, and done in Italy under the title, in English, *Sunday in August,* stolen. It was a *nouvelle vague* film thirty years before the *nouvelle vague.* It used real people, not actors, guys from the street, and it was filled with innovations, stop motion and all sorts of things. And on the crew, Fred Zinnemann was the focus puller. Edgar Ulmer was on the camera. And Billy Wilder was on it. He was a dancer, and he was only with the film for one day. But he got the credit, the screenplay credit, even though there was no screenplay, only the story, the idea. And on the screen it says, "Robert Siodmak, direction," and "Screenplay, Billy Wilder," and under, if you look very close, "after an idea by Curt Siodmak."

How did Wilder manage to get the credit if he didn't do anything on the script?

Robert and me, we had a sibling rivalry. He loved me and when I needed something he was there, and we were best of friends. But there only should be one Siodmak, not two Siodmaks. Like when you have two dogs, one bites the other dog. Robert was two years and two days older than me, and the story goes that father took Robert to the crib and said, "Here's your new brother." And Robert said, "I don't want your new brother." And that lasted till he died seventy-one years later.

Aboard the floating airport in *F.P. 1 Does Not Reply* (1933).

But Robert was a very complex character. He always had guys around who admired him, and he fell in love with certain men—he would only work with this man or that man. And so Billy Wilder became his favorite for a time, and so he gave Wilder the screenplay credit, not me. And then he got a contract with UFA, on account of his success with his first film, and he took Billy Wilder along, not me. Well, UFA was a big corporation, and they could afford to bring in some young guys who had a hit. But nothing happened. They didn't need Robert, and they didn't want Billy Wilder, either.

And I didn't need them either, actually. I was writing, for the newspapers, serializations, and whatever. I made lots of money. I lived in the outskirts of the city with Henrietta. We were not married yet, and you would not believe what a scandal that was, living together—the vice squad could come in on you! But we both came from broken marriages, and it didn't have any appeal for us at that time. So we lived together. But in those days it really was a crime!

And I wrote a story called *Der Kampf mit dem Drachen—The Fight with the Dragon*. And this story became Robert's second film.

The film had a man named Felix Bressart—his first job—and Hedwig Wangel, an actress who played Queen Victoria and many roles, and later became a Nazi. And here is the story:

The guy, a little clerk, lives in the rooming house of a terrible landlady. The furniture is all covered, to protect it from the dirt. And over everything, over every door, over the toilet, are Chinese wind chimes, so she will know from the noise what room you are in every minute. He must sneak around, and, when he takes his pipe out from where he hides it, he must blow the smoke out the window. But she knows this, and she gives him a bill for what the smoke did to her curtains, and so on. And it is too much. He kills her. He's arrested for murder, goes to court. And he is found not guilty. "Not guilty," says the Judge. "We have all lived in that dragon's house."

This was Robert Siodmak's second film.

Robert was a marvelous PR man for himself. He showed the picture, and he invited all his crew and the secretaries. And Erich Pommer came to see the film, Pommer of UFA, a great producer. I never saw a man like this in my life. And he took Robert into his unit. They took my script, *Der Mann, der seinen Morder sucht—A Man Looking for his Murderer*—which wasn't finished yet, and Robert took Wilder again. And I never worked with him again in Germany. But UFA bought one of my books, *F.P. 1 Does Not Reply*. Flying Platform Number One. The story dealt with platforms built in the middle of the ocean so the airplanes flying to America could refuel. The book was published in America in '33. UFA made the film, with Conrad Veidt, and it was a great success. And I wrote another picture, *Le Bal*.

This was the film that discovered Danielle Darrieux. We were looking for a French girl. And a little girl came for the job, a pretty, innocent little girl, a waif. It was Danielle Darrieux. She had just the innocence we were looking for. She crossed herself all the time. So we took her. Two weeks later I see her in a Bugatti with a short skirt, fingernails red. The innocence was all a fake. Her mother had gotten her to dress like a little girl to get the part. But she got her first part. And Robert used her later, and Billy Wilder, too. This was 1931. Much later, in 1950, I was working at Fox and she was there. She sat at the writers' table, and I said, "Danielle, you remember? I did the first picture for you . . . in '31." She snapped back, "'38." She had taken seven years off her life. I just said, "Oh yes, '38." What can you do?

How did the writer work at UFA? Was it similar to Hollywood, where you were expected to come to an office every day?

Pommer, Erich Pommer, used to have meetings in his house. He'd have many people waiting to see him. And he'd bring you in to talk about some film story. And Pommer would lay out one mark in *pfennig*, in pennies, a hundred of them he'd put on his desk. And if you had a good idea you got two pennies, or five pennies. And the writers might fight about it—not for the money, for the recognition. You might have an idea and Pommer would say, "That's worth ten pennies." And Billy Wilder would say, "No, that's only a five-penny idea!" Pommer was a powerful man. Eyes like blades.

You and Wilder were rivals?

I tell you, with Billy, I don't see him, he doesn't see me. We like each other. It's like if you go on a cruise: you make friends for life who you never see again. It's the same thing with motion pictures. We never worked together since Germany. I was at Paramount and made pictures there, and he was there, very successful. And then he became so rich, it's out of proportion. But, in the last fifteen years Wilder hasn't done a good picture, because he didn't keep up with the times. He tried to repeat his great successes, which you cannot. *The Lost Weekend*, the drunk, it was something new. Startling. Or *The Apartment*, a man giving up his apartment so people can screw. Shocking. But today it is a nothing idea. To shock you must be ahead of your audience. It's like when the book *Lolita* was published in Paris and forbidden in America. And the American goes to the Left Bank to try and find this "dirty" book. And he asks a Frenchman about this *Lolita* by Nabokov. And the Frenchman says, "What is it about?" The American says, "A man has an affair with a twelve-year-old girl!" And the Frenchman says, "Yes? But what happens?"

But Billy is very cynical, bitter. All his life. Even then, in Germany. He had his lousy times, I guess. These things you don't forget. I remember when he came to America. He lived in a small room at the Chateau Marmont. He had no money. And Pommer lived there also, and Pommer told him, in front of people, "I'll give you ten bucks to jump in the pool with your clothes on." And he did it. Pommer could be very cruel, too. But many were. Except me. I'm the nicest guy in the world because I'm a writer. I sit here in my library, lonely, like a man in a lighthouse.

What is your image of Berlin from that period, late '20s, early '30s?

They always talk of the decadence. Decadence! You have the same decadence in New York. There was a great feeling for literature, many great writers there. Many of them came out of my school, The Three Kings, in Dresden. There was a whole group of the most important German writers came out of that school within three or four years. But Berlin was in a renaissance. Lot of things going on, different kinds of people. After the Russian revolution, the White Russians came over with these beautiful girls, and more refugees came in. For me, a culture is like a flower—it starts to bloom, it wilts, something new grows up. Berlin then, there was a real spirit.

When did you know you had to get out of Germany?

My wife knew. I'm married to a Swiss wife, Henrietta de Perrot, from the old Swiss nobility. We are together almost all our lives. She saw it coming. She got out, went back to Switzerland and took a house while I worked in Berlin. I didn't believe it would happen. Maybe I didn't want to. How can you? It's not easy to think you must leave your country or else. If somebody says to you, "Lee, you have to get out of America permanently," what will you think? Where will you go?

Who knew what atrocities would come? No one knew. But Henrietta felt it.

And she was pregnant. We were married by then. And she ran away from me and went to England, wanted to have a British child. And I went. We lived in a whorehouse for six months, at Oxford Terrace. You know, one of those places where they rented rooms for an hour. And I went back to Germany to get some money that I'd left. I was so stupid—they could have kept me by then. And I got a letter from my publisher in Leipzig. . . . Here is the letter. I translate it for you: "Dear Mr. Siodmak. I herewith inform you that all copies of your books have been confiscated by the *Polizei*." They sent the letter to me. I met this publisher after the war. He had been eight years in a Russian prison during the war. He said, "Yes, yes, I sent these letters to all my writers."

I got to England and had no job. Little money. I didn't speak English. We went to the cinema at night, and I sat through one film about fifteen times to learn English. In '33.

Where was your brother at this time?

In France. And I had an idea, and I sent it to Robert in Paris. And he sold the picture. *La Crise est finie*. Also with Danielle Darrieux.

But in England I worked on my English. And I didn't write one German word after that. I walked to Elstree every day, hoping for a job. Two weeks waiting for the boss to talk to me, sitting in a room with his secretary. This was Mycroft, of British International Pictures, B.I.P. He was a hunchback. And finally Mycroft talked to me. He got me a job. And he became the godfather of my son later on. My wife had the child in England and I took him to the first *goyische* church. I said, "Enough with the Jews." And I made him a Gentile. (Laughs.)

I worked for B.I.P., 100 pounds per script. And I was already on the third picture when a man came to me. He said, "You're leaving from Dover tomorrow, for France." I said, "What about my labor permit?" "You have no labor permit. You have to leave the country in twenty-four hours." I said, "What about my child?" He says, "Well? Take it or leave it here. That's not our business." So I went to Percy Stapleton, of B.I.P. I said, "Stapleton, where's my labor permit?" He says, "I can't get it." "Well, you owe me seventy-five pounds." "Yes," he says, "but we can't pay you, because the contract says you have to stay here and finish. We'll have to take another writer, maybe, and pay him." I realized they were getting me out to save the seventy-five pounds.

So I went to France—with no money in my pocket. It was a bad time. My younger brother committed suicide in the park at Versailles. It was a mess. Robert was making *La Crise est finie*, and the tension between us was great and we fought. My child spent months in an orphanage in England.

Then I wrote a story. It is my best story. A historical story of a woman who slept only with kings. *For Kings Only* it was called. I wrote an outline. And there was a charming actress called Frances Day, and she liked this story. And she took my treatment to Maurice Ostrow at Gaumont-British and forced them to buy this story. And Ostrow thought, "My God, we'll have to pay Siodmak 750 pounds." And my agent went up there and he took 200 pounds. But it got me back into England with my last penny.

I had a little office. And I was trying to sell them on stories. It was tough. I was still working on my English. I would write English words on a piece of paper, very big, and paste them to the wall. Or I'd walk around with pieces of paper in my pocket, English and German words. Tough. You go to *Germany*, why don't you, and make your living as a writer. But it was life or death.

I tried to sell them *A Man Looking for his Murderer*. The story, actually, was stolen from a book by Jules Verne, *The Trials of a Chinaman in China* or something.

The man who wants to kill himself but can't, so he hires someone to do it?

Yes, that's right. And there was a producer working there at the studio named Felner. He was a German, and he didn't like any other Germans working at Gaumont-British. He hated the Germans. And I showed him my story. He said, "How can we do a picture about a man who commits suicide?" But he came back and asked me how people hanged themselves. I told him about that. And a day later he hanged himself. He had been waiting for his labor permit, to stay in England, and it was late—it didn't come through. And some of them there played a practical joke. They told him he'd been rejected for his permit, that he'd be deported. It wasn't true. A joke. But they didn't tell him. He hanged himself.

Who did it?

That Hitchcock crowd. One of those cold people.

So that *Murderer* story was never done. But then Michael Balcon, the head of the studio, was in New York, and Angus MacPhail, the story editor, had a story, *The Tunnel*, from a book. He asked me, "Can you write a script in three days?" Three days! But anything to stay with this company. And I wrote an outline and they cabled it to Balcon in New York. And he cabled back, "Give Siodmak a contract." I asked for eighty pounds a week. And I got it. I had been getting fifteen a week. And I wrote *The Tunnel*. And it was a good picture. Richard Dix, Helen Vinson, Madge Evans. Maurice Elvey directed.

Then an actor named George Arliss wanted to make a film about Cagliostro. Arliss was in his seventies and Cagliostro died in his forties, but he wanted to play this character. And there was a competition among the writers to write the Cagliostro script. So I wrote a story in which Cagliostro is traveling through Europe, claiming he can make people young. An old queen hears of this, and she sends for him to make her young again. He admits to her it's a fake. He can't really do it. She doesn't believe him. She insists. She threatens him. So Cagliostro says, "All right. I will do it. But there is one condition. A mirror will always show your real age." And the queen says, "Yes, all right, do it. And I'll remove all the mirrors!" And he manipulates her in such a way that she believes it has happened. And everyone around her is afraid to disagree. "Yes, how beautiful you are, Queen! More beautiful every day!" And then she falls in love with a handsome young prince. But he is repelled. He can't kiss an eighty-two-year-old woman like that. The queen goes to find a mirror and show that she is young. And then she finds out, she is tricked. She wants to kill Cagliostro. And Cagliostro gives his last speech, that beauty can be in your soul, things like that.

Anyway, I wrote that story and George Arliss liked it. And we were to go see him for a conference. And a servant opens the door, brings us in. There were etchings of nude girls on the wall. And everyone was nervous, wanting to please Arliss. He was a most powerful man in those days. He made the company. And he came in. He's wearing a big robe. Very stingy—he gave us a small glass of sherry. And he says to us. "Yes, I like the story. But I don't like all this with the mirror. Take the mirror out." And I spoke up, in my halfway English, "If you take out the mirror you destroy the story." He looked at me. Then he got up and he said,

"Gentlemen, you may finish your sherry. And nothing can detain you any longer." And he left. And that was the end of the George Arliss movie. I still have that script. The Shepherd's Bush studio burned down, but I still have the script.

You stayed under contract with Gaumont-British?

Yes, under contract. I worked on many stories. They would have us work on all the stories, get ideas from us. I worked for Hitchcock.

What did you do with Hitchcock?

I did work on the picture with Sylvia Sidney, *Sabotage.* I didn't get a credit on it. I did some scenes. There was a big scene in *Sabotage* where Sylvia Sidney goes in and gets a big knife and kills her husband. I remember Hitchcock didn't like Sylvia Sidney. And she was waiting for this, her one big dramatic scene. So what did Hitchcock do? He put the camera on the knife, only photographed the knife, and you never saw her.

Hitchcock was a great practical joker. He once sent me fifty pounds of herring for some reason. But you couldn't make a joke against him. I showed him a picture, a painting, 1798, looked exactly like Hitchcock in drag. I showed it to him, said it looked like him in drag. He just stared, didn't say anything. But, you know, in many ways Hitchcock was the most frustrated man you ever saw in your life. In his personal life was great frustration. He couldn't use a telephone. He would get tongue-tied.

At Gaumont you also worked on the script for von Sternberg's *I, Claudius*?

It was Korda, Alex Korda's picture, not Sternberg. Von Sternberg came in much later. It would have been a fabulous picture. But Laughton was unhappy. Everyone was unhappy. Von Sternberg walked out. And it was never finished. Von Sternberg came to work on a very high horse. A very big ego. I saw him in Germany, on the set of *The Blue Angel.* He was behind the camera, wearing this long Russian sable coat. He was watching Marlene Dietrich through the camera. I can still see her sitting there in front of him.

When did you decide you wanted to come to America?

In '37. I wanted to go to America. I wanted to get my child an American passport. They all said, "But you can get a British passport!" I said, "I go. I want it American."

I came over here with a British friend called Leslie Arliss. And Leslie came with me to run away from his wife, I think. We bought a six-cylinder Cadillac, second-hand, for $400. Four miles to the gallon, every 110 miles no gas any more. We drove all the way through America, headed for California. We didn't know anyone. We didn't know anything about Hollywood. We knew only the Beverly Wilshire Hotel. And Leslie sent a telegram from Phoenix, Arizona, "Reserve rooms," and signed it, "Arliss." And they thought George Arliss was coming. We got there and found they had reserved nearly a whole floor.

But we got there, Hollywood. And Arliss did know one person, a girl, and he called her up. Arliss was a writer. He never got a job out here. But this was our first day in Hollywood and we called the girl, and she said, "Yes, why don't you pick me up?"

So we picked her up in this big bus of a car, and she had us drive to a party in Beverly Hills. It was the house of a man named Cliff Henderson, a pilot, a kind of Howard Hughes character. And he has in his library a wall of live fish, a huge aquarium. And outside there are beautiful girls playing tennis and swimming in the pool. And Arliss met a princess, and I met this beautiful dark-haired girl. And they ask us, "Why don't you come have a drink with us?" And we go to their house, Tower Road, Filipino servants cooking shrimp. It was April, hot like blazes. And the girls went to swim, and they looked like orchids in the water. And I watched them, my first day, and I thought, "My God, *this is Hollywood.*"

But I never again had a day like that. Never again. In forty years I never saw anything like it again.

After the first few days in Los Angeles, I was taken to Paramount. They had a story there that they showed me. I didn't like it much. I was pretty cocky in those days. Today I am a quiet old man. But they were so surprised that they gave me the job. It was made as Dorothy Lamour's first picture, *Her Jungle Love.**

And I worked on that. And I did another picture for Dorothy Lamour, *Aloma of the South Seas.* Silly things. Dorothy Lamour got to wear her sarong. They put me on it with an old actress who they kept on the payroll out of kindness. Seena Owen. She had been a big star in the '20s. All doped up now. But maybe the old producers had had affairs with these old ladies when they were all young, you know, so they gave them jobs as writers so they could get some money. They put a young guy with them to write the story, and they got a credit.

She didn't do any work at all?

Oh, yes, yes. She worked. I put her out of feeling in the dumps, I think. I made her optimistic again. I think so. Looked terrible.

At Paramount I was getting $350 a week, and I sent all the money to England, to Henrietta and the child. This was '37. And she got a nice house, a car, a Chinese servant. And then I lost my job right away and didn't work again for eleven months.

Then, through my friend Joe May, I got a job to write *The Invisible Man Returns*, with Vincent Price, for Universal. And that was a success and I got into the groove. Began to get a lot of work.

Joe May had been a big name in Germany before he left?

Yes, big. But he had to leave. All the Jews had to leave. He came to Hollywood and did very well. And he got me on the inside at Universal. I became connected with George Waggner and others.

Your brother, Robert, came over after you?

Robert came over in '39. He went to see Preston Sturges at Paramount, talked to him, got him to call Sol Siegel, a producer. Sturges said, "I've got someone for you, a very famous German director. . . ." Then he turned to Robert. "Say, what's your name again?"

Robert got a job at Paramount, with the B unit. And he wasn't happy. He couldn't do his own stuff. He'd have his little assistant and he'd say, "You take the shot." The producers got mad. They'd say, "You're such a big director, why don't you do your own shots?" Robert says, "This is not a Siodmak picture, this is Paramount shit."

They fired him.

He couldn't get a job. And I had written one of my undying masterpieces, *Son of Dracula*, and I got Robert the job to direct. They gave him $125 a week. He came to me crying, "Look

*Jungle Princess (1936) was her sarong debut.

what they're paying me! It doesn't matter what the writer gets, but the director is so important." I said, "This is bullshit. Do it or not. I cannot get you any more money."

And then as soon as he began, I was off the job right away. He got another writer, Eric Taylor. He couldn't work with me. Who would be the boss? He couldn't push me around, I couldn't push him around. He only liked to work with new people.

But this, *Son of Dracula*, became a kind of classic through Robert's handling of light and shadow. He was wonderful on mood, characterization, atmosphere, the psychology of it. He could make marvelous scenes. But he couldn't write. He had no construction. He would come and tell me his new ideas and describe how he would do some scene—beautifully! But it didn't fit at all the story he was doing. It was just a scene. And Robert would try, psychologically, to destroy the writer and his work. He was best when he got a script he had to shoot in the next three days. Deadline. They'd call him, "You start in a week!" Then he didn't have a chance of fooling around with the script and destroying it.

But after *Son of Dracula*, he did a picture with Joan Harrison, *Phantom Lady*, a great success, and then the Laughton picture, *The Suspect*, and then *The Killers* . . . and he was through the roof. He made more in one day than I made in a year. And Robert was a star-maker. He gave the first big job to many people, Ava Gardner, Burt Lancaster. And Lancaster wasn't very nice to him later. When they were shooting *The Crimson Pirate*, he wanted to take the picture away from Robert and sign for the direction. But actors are like that. As Hitchcock said, "I didn't say actors are cattle . . . I said they should be treated like cattle."

It was funny, this sibling rivalry between Robert and me. When he was going to do *The Killers*, Mark Hellinger came to me and he said, "Curt, your brother gave me your latest book. He told me, 'Mark, you have to read Curt's last book. If you ever put it down, you can't pick it up!'" (Laughs.) Robert meant a compliment: you pick it up, you can't put it down. It was a slip. You see? He meant well, but it wasn't in him. He'd say to producers, "Why don't you take Curt? He's a marvelous constructionist. For the dialogue you can get someone else." And I wouldn't get the job. A left-handed compliment. He really wanted to do things, but he just couldn't get it out of himself.

But, anyhow, we always helped each other. He helped me. And I think I helped him. He was a genius. He pissed it away. . . .

How would the horror films at Universal develop? *The Wolf Man*, for instance.

George Waggner was usually in charge. He called me in. He said, "Curt, I have a title called *The Wolf Man*. It's Boris Karloff's title, but he has no time, so we can use the title. We have Lon Chaney, Jr., instead. We have Claude Rains, Ralph Bellamy, Ouspenskaya, and Evelyn Ankers. . . ." She was an Australian girl who had a terrific scream. "We have $180,000 and we shoot in eight weeks. Goodbye."

And I went and wrote the damn thing. We were really on our own at Universal in those days because they didn't have enough time or money to fool around with the scripts and "improve" them, the way producers love to do. You know the story of the two producers, lost in the desert, crawling through the sand, dying of thirst. And by chance they stumble upon a can of orange juice. They shout, "We are saved, we are saved!" And they are about to drink it when the first producer says, "Wait, first let's pee in it."

At Universal they were always broke. And horror kept them alive. I did sometimes five pictures in one year. I was pretty prolific.

In *The Wolf Man* I had trouble believing Lon Chaney, Jr., was Claude Rains's son.

Yes, originally it was different. I had an American mechanic come from Bausch and Lomb in America to install a telescope. And the first shot was lovely as he looks through this big telescope and directs it to the village and there's the girl in the antique store. The whole thing was very well constructed. But they did want to change that. They wanted him to have gone to school in America. In my original he was an American mechanic. This had more impact. An American mechanic comes to England and becomes a wolf man—it's even worse than an Englishman becoming a wolf man.

I invented a ditty: "Even a man who is kind at heart, and says his prayers at night, may become a wolf when the wolfsbane blooms, and the autumn moon shines bright." And the film historians tried to look it up—it must be some old German folklore. No! It came from right here, my typewriter.

I got a letter a few years ago from a professor at a university in Georgia. He had written of "A Parallel between Aristotle's *Poetics* and *The Wolf Man.*" I thought the guy is nuts. But, no, he showed me. The gods tell a man his fate and he cannot escape it. The parallel of the wolf man and a Greek play is perfect. And I didn't know it. By chance. I wrote it in seven weeks. Four hundred dollars a week.

I did the next one, too, and that's a funny story. It was wartime. I needed an automobile, and a friend of mine was drafted and he had a Buick. I wanted to buy it, but I didn't have the money. I didn't have a job, an assignment. So I went to the commissary at Universal, and I said to George Waggner, who did the first wolf picture, "George, why don't you make a picture called *Frankenstein Meets the Wolf Man?* I have to buy a car." He said, "Buy the car. You'll get a job." And for days I'd come in and he'd say, "Did you buy the car?" I'd say, "No. What's the assignment first?" Finally, the friend was leaving, so I bought the car. So I told George, "Okay, I bought it." And George shrugged. "Okay. *Frankenstein Meets the Wolf Man.*" That's how it was done.

So I was stuck with my title. And then I had an idea, which carried the story. The wolf man wants to die. He's a decent guy—he doesn't want to be a murderer. Who knows the secret of life and death? Baron Frankenstein. And he meets the monster. And the monster comes back to life and also wants to find Baron Frankenstein. So the two come together. And I built my script from that.

You know, I used to play a game on the producers, to see when they really read the script. They never read them until just before they broke it down for shooting. And I would write some funny scene in there. In this one I have the monster walking with the wolf man, and in the script I have the wolf man say, "You know, I change to a wolf at night." And the monster looks at him and says, "You're kiddin'!" They didn't notice it till the last minute—then they threw it out.

It was a job. They were fairy tales. It was always implied horror. You didn't show someone with the guts pouring out.

You returned to novel writing about this time. Can you tell me about how you came to write *Donovan's Brain*?

I was dumped out in Devil's Hot Springs. Henrietta wanted to get me away from my brother because he interfered with my writing. It was a strange place in the desert. Wild boars come out at night. Nobody lives there but the old women with arthritis. There are holes in the

Advertisement for *The Wolf Man* (1942).

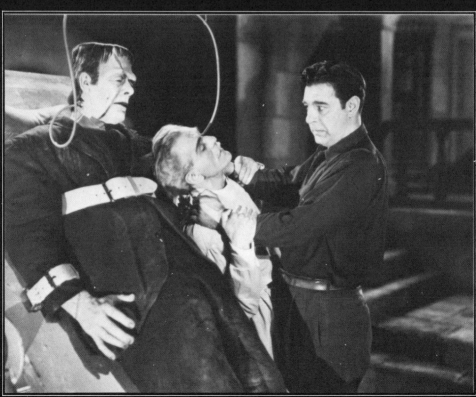

Glenn Strange, Boris Karloff, and Lon Chaney, Jr., in *House of Frankenstein* (1944).

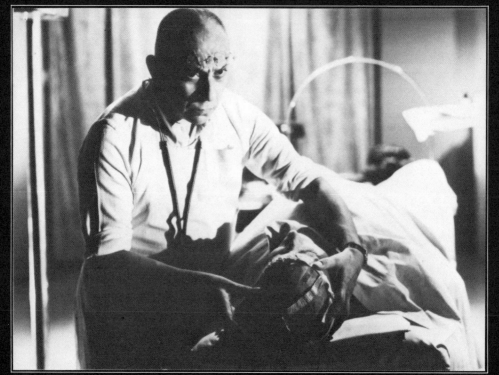

Erich von Stroheim in *The Lady and the Monster* (1944).

Publicity still for *Earth vs. the Flying Saucers* (1956).

ground and the stream comes out. You put your food in there and it cooks it. So I had the idea and I lived there and wrote a book.

I was at the B unit at Columbia. I told the idea to Irv Briskin. He says, "That's the most idiotic thing I've ever heard in my life." I tried other studios. Couldn't sell it. I sold the book to *Black Mask* magazine. And still couldn't sell it. Finally, I sold the picture rights to Yates at Republic Studios, for $1,900. Then the book was published by Knopf, and it's sold about 5 million copies. Humphrey Bogart called me, and Laird Cregar, they wanted to do it. But I had sold it already. Later, United Artists wanted the television rights, for $1 million. But I'd sold it. For $1,900. And they must have made $3 million with it by now. . . . But it doesn't matter. I look at the credits—those guys are dead, I'm alive. Who's winning?

Three times they filmed *Donovan's Brain*, and three times they fucked it up. Never got it right. I got a call from Yates after he bought it. He said, "You're crazy with this book you wrote. Don't you know that a scientist lives in a castle, not in a hut? We have to change it." And they had von Stroheim in it running through the halls like an old bat. And Yates said, "And I have the new title for you: *The Lady and the Monster*." The lady would be Vera Hruba Ralston, his girlfriend, an ice skater. I didn't write the script. And then they did it again, used my title this time, and God destroys the brain with a thunderbolt. I didn't see it. And then they did it in England, called *The Brain*, and there's a cancer cure in it, and I didn't see it.

You did one of Val Lewton's classics, *I Walked with a Zombie*. Did you work closely with Lewton?

He left me alone. They always leave me alone. With George Waggner, I only talked with him every Thursday. He didn't want to talk with me. He'd say, "I want your ideas, not mine." When I went in to see George, I always gave him so much honey, tell him what a big man he was. I thought he must know that I was kidding. He never knew.

But Lewton was a very erudite man, much better than any other producer I worked for. Oh, yes, a very educated man. But cold. There was something very cold about him. He told me he liked to sit in his garage with a bow and arrow, wait for coyotes to come down at night and look in the garbage. Then he'd shoot them. He had worked for Selznick. Selznick's right-hand man. Selznick would ask him about things, all sorts of questions. And Lewton, very erudite, would reply something, even if it wasn't true at all. Selznick was happy.

On *I Walked with a Zombie* Lewton gave me a short story, but I never used it. My idea was that a man is very much in love with this woman, but she can't stand the little island where they live. And so he takes her to Paris every year. And he knows that, next time, she won't come back. Then there is fever on the island and she gets the fever, and it burns out her brain. So now she has a beautiful body but no reactions. And it went from there. Lewton worked on it a little bit afterward with a woman I never met, Ardel Wray. But it was mostly mine, and I got the credit.

The film proceeds very subtly, almost in vignettes.

All my stories are in vignettes. All my books, if you read them, vignettes. You build the story in pieces. It's a theory of writing. You find a way to tell your stories. George Waggner—he wrote scripts, too—would say, "Curt, when you write 'dissolve to,' where do you dissolve to?" He couldn't figure my style of writing. For me, it was easy.

How about *The Beast with Five Fingers*?

Yes, that was a short story, too. But I didn't use it. And I actually wrote the character for Henreid, Paul Henreid. And then Paul says, "I'm not wild to play against a dead hand." He was wrong. It would have been much better with Henreid than with Peter Lorre. A good-looking man like Henreid, it's a shock when you see that he's deranged at the end. With Lorre it was so obvious that he was crazy.

You made your debut as a director rather late in life. Had you always wanted to direct?

I directed a few pictures. I didn't pay much attention to it. I did it to show Robert I could direct, too. My stuff is running forever on TV, anyhow.

Did you enjoy directing?

I loved it. You know yourself as a writer—you get up and you don't feel good in the morning, how can you work? You cannot. But the director can come in like that and everyone says, "Good morning, sir. How did you sleep?" And the machinery, the filmmaking machinery, is all there. The actors can do their lines; the cameraman, the camera. And so the director can lie down and wait till he feels better. The movie takes care of itself. Directing is highly overrated. The directors only have such standing because they spend the money. Anybody can direct. Shoot one million feet of film like George Stevens. Have good actors, have a good script. What do you need a director for? The cutter puts the picture together. You need a certain understanding of story values, technique, to be any good. But most of them are just set decorators. Writing is something else.

You went up the Amazon to shoot _Curucu_?

I went up the Amazon for seven months. I did two pictures together—I left and came right back again—_Curucu_, and they gave the second one a terrible title, _Love Slaves of the Amazon_. But it was an interesting story. I was up above Manaus, in the Brazilian rain forest for months. A Portuguese crew. I learned Portuguese fast to understand what the sons of bitches were saying behind my back . . . Just kidding. For the whole thing, $155,000. And they're still running on TV. I have nine-tenths of a percent of the screenplay rights. Not even _one_ percent. And I get money for the last twenty-six years on the thing. Can you imagine how I could collect with one percent? I would become a Republican and vote for Reagan!

   You know, I joined the original Screen Writers Guild when I came here in '38. It was a bad situation then. I remember when I came to Paramount and they told me to write a script, but I couldn't get any credit. They had already decided, Grover Jones, Talbott Jennings would get the credit. So the picture was done, _Spawn of the North_, my script, without my name on it. Or there would be a girl's name on the script—the girlfriend of the producer, paid off with her name on the screen. But no more of that after the Guild. And we fought for things, percentages, other things. We fought for thirty years. Now they get it. We didn't.

You're listed as a story source on the James Bond film, _Moonraker_.

Yes. They bought _City in the Sky_, my book. Here's why. The girl is floating in space and Roger Moore goes floating up there with her and they have sex. That's the end of the picture. They needed that gag. So they paid me $70,000 for the book, for that one bit. But it's nothing to them, believe me. A minute's shooting on that picture cost $225,000. So, from their budget, they paid me for twenty seconds of their time. Besides, they bought the book and it's interesting, so maybe someday they will make a film of that.

You referred to your old horror films as fairy tales. What do you think of the present-day films in the genre?

It's outrageous now. The Screen Writers gave a Halloween show, and invited me, Robert Bloch, and two other writers, to talk about horror. There was an audience, about a hundred people.

Well, there is a world of difference. We are story writers. We write a real story with so-called horror in it, but we never showed anything bloody. But here, these younger men, all they talked of was mattresses that bust open and 250 gallons of blood comes out. That's what they write. One guy says, "Fuck 'em and kill 'em." But this is not *writing*.

You see, there are only a few people in Hollywood who could make their living without writing for motion pictures. They sit the whole day thinking, "How do I get a movie job?" I say to them, "If you just want to make money, sell condoms to China." Don't say you are a writer. Assignment, money, how much can they get. Hacks. I can be a hack, too. If I get an assignment today, I'll do it, too, for money. But real writers write. They are driven people, compulsive. Writing is a sickness and a cure at the same time. For me, it is easier to write than not to write. I have to strain myself not to write. I have to express myself. It's tough to be married to a writer, believe you me.

Most of your work has been horror or science fiction. I know you believe in science, but do you have any belief in the supernatural?

We are in a three-dimensional world—height, width, length. Everything is a cube. All the laws of physics we *invent*, actually, to explain the three dimensions to us. So if you go into outer space, there might be other laws—time shrinks, light bends, antimatter, we don't know. The fourth dimension I can explain to you; the fifth, I cannot.

Since we have three pounds and two ounces of brains—nobody has more—we will never understand two things: what was before the beginning, and what is after the end? And in this void we put our symbols, religion, philosophy—whatever fills the unexplainable. If someone says a white onion created the world and you believe in it, be happy with it. So we try to find out the unexplained to explain it to ourselves in order to live. . . . But we never find out.

You've heard about the two goldfish swimming in their bowl, and one says, "If you don't believe in God, then tell me, who's changing the water?"

Overleaf: Jack Carson and Joan Crawford in *Mildred Pierce* (1945).

12 · CATHERINE TURNEY

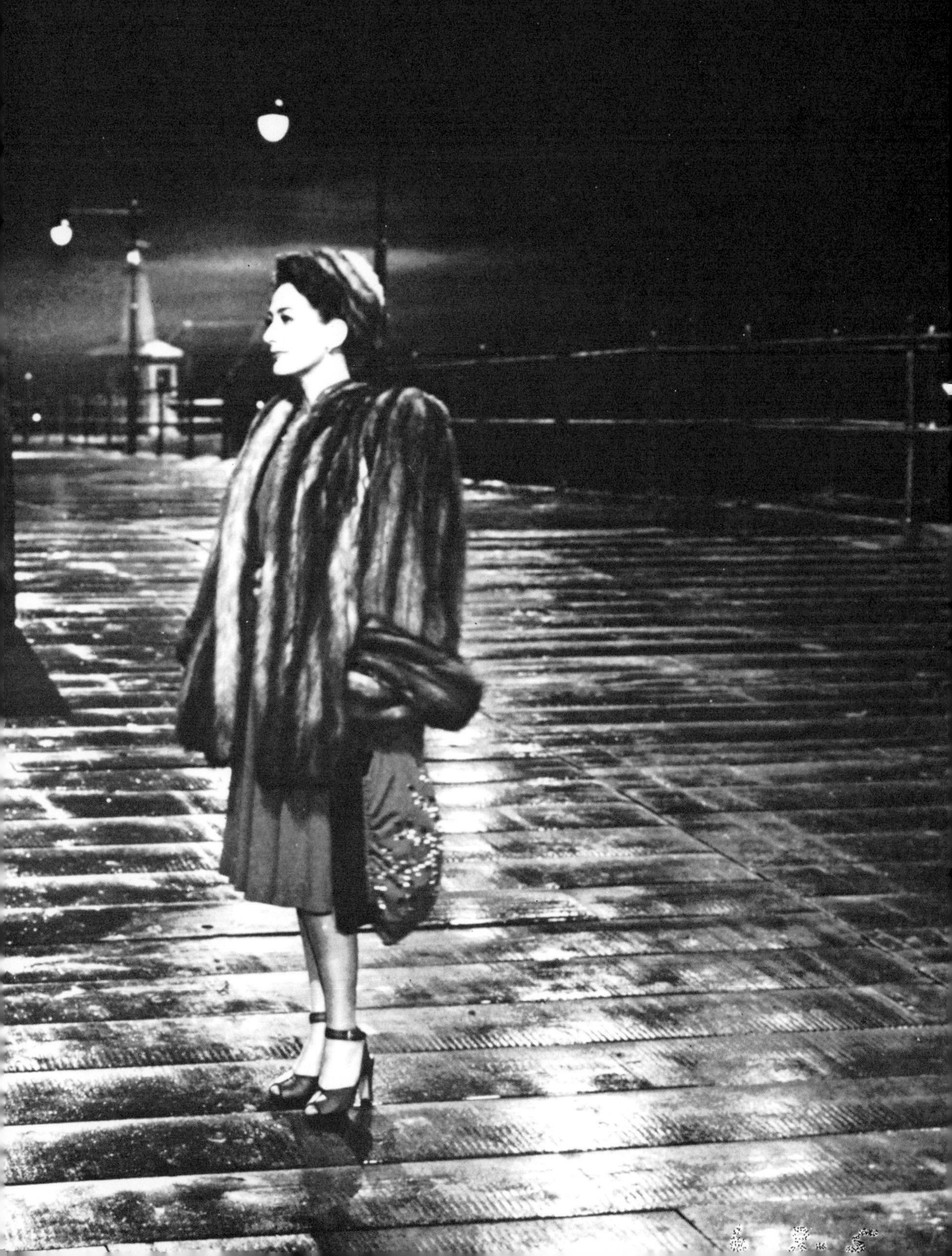

Catherine Turney.

Catherine Turney was a specialist in what were commonly, and no doubt condescendingly, known as "women's pictures." In the '40s, Warner Bros., formerly dominated by street-tough male stars, found itself with a roster of strong leading ladies under long-term contract: Bette Davis, Joan Crawford, Barbara Stanwyck, Ida Lupino, Ann Sheridan, Eleanor Parker, Jane Wyman. Catherine Turney wrote for all of them— passionate vehicles in which the female stars had plenty of room to suffer nobly or claw their way to happiness, to fall in and out of love, usually with disreputable smoothies in tuxedos and pencil-thin moustaches. While the "hard-nosed sports writers" she sat next to in the studio commissary may have looked down on Turney's women's pictures, the huge audience of home-front females gave films like *Mildred Pierce* and *A Stolen Life* an undeniable endorsement.

In any case, Turney's films differed from the standard Fannie Hurstian weepies of the 1930s. Her women characters tended to be more independent (Joan Crawford's restaurateur in *Mildred Pierce*, Ida Lupino's stoic saloon singer in *The Man I Love*), and more talented (Bette Davis's painter in *A Stolen Life*, her poetess in *Winter Meeting*), and while she accepted the usual soap-opera elements of tragic love affairs and domestic strife, Turney explored more complex family and romantic relationships, adding a dollop of sexual sophistication and a Freudian insight or two, and heightened the atmosphere with the neuroses and moody violence of *film noir*.

She began as a playwright, her work produced first in California, then New York,

London, and around the world. Her play *My Dear Children* (1939), provided John Barrymore with his Broadway swansong. It was a notorious production, not for Turney's words but for Barrymore's antics (at one performance he reportedly urinated across the front row) and the irredeemable vanity of his co-star and then-wife, Elaine Barrie. Turney returned to California after the show's closing, and in the early '40s began her second stint as a screenwriter, working for Warners till the end of the decade. By then an era had ended, the studio's *grandes dames* having lost their box office appeal and then their contracts.

The women's picture as a genre, as a staple of American moviemaking, is a thing of the past now, as surely as the musical and the western. Unlike those genres, however, the women's picture has received relatively little critical attention. Still, Catherine Turney is not without her fans, young people who seek her out to discuss feminist readings of *Mildred Pierce* or *The Man I Love*. Her lack of pretension may stymie them—she claims no subversive intent, only to have written of things she knew and understood, and to have tried "to please the boss, Mr. Warner."

She is a bright, cheerful, and modest woman. She is quick to give credit to her collaborators and is equally hesitant to speak badly of any of them, no matter how badly they may have behaved. One senses in her, even from a short meeting, a very generous spirit.

Nowadays, you may find Turney working in the research department of the Huntington Library in San Marino, California. The library is a popular tourist attraction in the summertime, people coming to stroll through the lush gardens and to see Gainsborough's *Blue Boy* hanging in the gallery. It's not far from Pasadena, where Turney's first play was produced, or from Glendale, where Mildred Pierce baked her first pie. We go outside to talk, to a bench in the garden, under the shade trees.

I got my first movie job after having written a play. I worked at the Pasadena Playhouse for a long time. I was in the first class of the school's theatre, from 1926 or so to 1930. I had gotten to enjoy writing while I was there, and I wrote a play called *Bitter Harvest*. It was about Lord Byron and his marriage and his relationship with his half-sister. A friend of mine sent it over to someone he knew in England, a man with considerable connections in the theatre. He submitted it to the Stage Society, and they decided to produce it.

The Stage Society was composed of people involved in the theatre who liked to do very *outre* things. There was a lot of censorship at the time, the lord chamberlain still censoring away. And because of the nature of this play, in which there was an incestuous relationship, why, the lord chamberlain refused to give it a license. He demanded a lot of changes. But we went ahead and did it at the Stage Society. Eric Portman played Byron, and it was his first important role. After the Stage Society performance—it had gone over very well—Gilbert Miller and Daniel Laird decided to produce it on the West End at the St. Martin's Theatre. It went on in 1936, and it was quite a critical success.

It didn't have a very long run, unfortunately, coming on just weeks after the death of King George. The Court was in mourning and . . . it just wasn't the time. But I did get glowing notices, and, on the strength of the notices, my agent received a call from MGM wanting to interview me. I went there with the agent, Nat Goldstone, and I was signed to a contract.

The first day I arrived at MGM, I was sent to see Joe Mankiewicz. He had just been made

Joan Crawford and Robert Yo

a producer. We met and he said, "I understand you've written a play about Byron. I've always been very interested in Byron myself." And then he said, "Now that you'll be rooming here, we'll have to arrange for you to meet some people since you don't know anybody." And I said, "Well, I love to meet people." I thought he was talking about people at the studio, but, as the conversation went on, I realized he was talking about *Americans*. He'd somehow thought that I had just come here from England, and since I came from Pasadena, I thought it was kind of a funny mixup.

The interview ended, and I stayed at MGM for a year.

It was a strange place for a new writer at MGM in those days. Thalberg was genuinely interested in getting new writers into the studio. But there was an entrenched group of writers there, established and with great credits, and that didn't make it easy for newcomers. You were gauged, your talents were gauged, by how much money you made, to a great extent. A $500-a-week writer sat at one place at a table and a $1000-a-week writer sat at another. It was a pecking system. And this policy kept the new writer from getting a fair share of the credits. This was before the Writers Guild got teeth and forced through arbitration on this problem.

The older writers didn't exactly steal your credit, but they would be put onto a script after you'd done much of the work and broken the back of the story. The tried-and-true writer would put the finishing touches on the thing, and then he or she would end up getting the main credit.

I was assigned to work on an unproduced play by Molnar called *The Girl from Trieste*. It was not a very good play. They teamed me up with Waldo Salt. He was one of what they called their "junior writers," and he had just come down from college. I was supposed to show him how to write scripts, but I didn't know too much, either. Later, of course, he learned to write them very well.

So Waldo and I flew around on this Molnar thing for I don't know how long. Finally, they got Joan Crawford interested in it. At that time Mr. Mankiewicz was seeing quite a bit of Miss Crawford, and he took the script and went off somewhere to rewrite it to her specifications. The picture was made, and it turned out to be an awful turkey called *The Bride Wore Red*. Terrible. We didn't get a screen credit, Waldo and I, only Academy credit.

And that was all I really got done out at MGM in that year. You spent a lot of time just sitting around waiting for them to give you something. You'd go day after day and finally get a call from a producer to go up. Sometimes it would be a month. Then you'd turn in something, and the producer never got around to reading it or kept putting off getting together for a conference. They had a lot of writers and a lot of money at that time, at MGM, and so they could afford to keep you around till they needed you. And the newer writers weren't getting that much money.

You were recruited into the Screen Playwrights, the company union.

Yes. Well, I had just begun to work in Hollywood, and John Lee Mahin and Howard Emmett Rogers were the two who recruited me. They told me they were the ones to join with, that all the big writers were signed with them. I didn't realize at the time all of the ramifications, about what they were trying to do to the Guild and so forth. John just made it sound like a good career move. I would get all the big assignments.

Then one of the Hacketts, Frances Hackett, called me, saying, "How could you sign with them? They're in it with the producers." And Phil Dunne came to see me and explained the situation. So I told Mahin I was resigning from the Screen Playwrights. I realized I had sloughed badly with that one.

Much later John Mahin became a loyal member of the Guild. He became very much involved. I remember during the strike several years back when we were out for five weeks, I went over to serve on the strike committee, and there was old John working away. He was thinking more about the Guild by then than about politics. But the Screen Playwrights and the things that happened later caused a great deal of bitterness. Those wounds were never healed. There are still people who, when they're invited to dinner, ask who's coming. They don't want to mix with their old enemies. It's very sad. A painful experience for everybody, and I'm sorry it had to happen.

I don't know what happened to the other man who recruited me, Howard Emmett Rogers. I think he's been dead for many years.

What did you do after you left MGM?

I wrote a play called *My Dear Children*. It went on in New York in '39 and starred John Barrymore. It ran for a year in Chicago, and then it ran five months in New York. It also had a big run down in Buenos Aires, oddly enough, where the leading man, a matinee idol down there, made himself up to look like Barrymore, with the nose and all. It played for many months.

I collaborated with my then-agent, Jerry Horwin, and we were with the thing all through the rehearsal period. We had all kinds of problems actually getting the show on the road. Mr. Barrymore was chronically broke and had to work, but it was his wife, Elaine, who really wanted to do the play. It was something nice for her, and she was the one who really wanted to go on Broadway with the play. But we had an awful time with rehearsals.

Barrymore was difficult to work with?

I was a great admirer of his. I loved him dearly, we all did. He was extremely intelligent when he wasn't drinking, and he really wasn't drinking as much as people thought he was at that time. He couldn't anymore. He had a wet brain. He was down to drinking Dubonnet and water. He had a male nurse who was always with him. In the main he was a nice man. But he could be awfully difficult at times.

There were the star ego things. He could suddenly turn on someone when doing a scene. And he had the ability to pull the rug out from somebody if he wanted to. He was a real master at that. I remember he had a crush on Dorothy McGuire, who was in the company and very good in her part. But she wasn't interested in Barrymore. So he got back at her. She had a big scene, a long climactic speech, and at the climax he was supposed to come in and top her. Instead, very often he would let it all drop deliberately so that it took the scene away from her and turned it to him.

Like most of the really top stars, he had a keen sense of his own persona. He could be the hail fellow well met until you were dumb enough to overstep the bounds, and then he let you know it.

But if you respected him—and I always did—he could be quite friendly. He was a good friend to me. And in rehearsals, while all the other actors would say, "Oh, this is no good, I can't read this line," he would never do that. Once in a while he would come to me and say, "What about this? Do you mind if we say it this way?" The really top people seldom quibbled about lines. And when those people did want to change a scene, you listened, because they had pretty good ideas. Someone like Bette Davis, and to some extent Crawford—yes, because Crawford

John Barrymore and Elaine Barry.

was a very professional actress—respected the writer, and once you gained their respect it was not hard to get along with them. In my experience, I found that the bigger the star, the easier they were to work with.

So I stayed with that play for some time. I was engaged to one of the members of the cast, and I was making good money, so I stayed with it. It was an interesting experience.

The play opened at the MacArthur Theatre in December of '39 and closed in, oh, May of '40. Then I spent some time working on something else, and I was back at the Playhouse.

The war came on, and by this time I had a new agent. He called and said, "You ought to be working in the movies. I've set up a meeting with Jim Geller at Warner Bros." Warners had not been particularly predisposed in favor of women writers. They were a male-oriented studio. But now a lot of the men were in the armed services, and they had all these big women stars—Bette Davis, and Joan Crawford, and Ida Lupino, any number of them. And so Warners was looking for women writers.

I was very lucky at Warners in that I got to work almost immediately with Henry Blanke, the producer. He was a top producer, and he was doing the kinds of things that I was able to do. He liked me and took me as a kind of protégée of his. He would spend hours in my room going over things I had written, explaining things, teaching me how to write for films. Because, in the beginning, I would have the camera doing some very strange things.

What was your first assignment at Warners?

They gave me *Mildred Pierce* to do. That was a very big novel, about 600 pages, and you had to break it down to, at most, ninety minutes. Mr. Warner was absolutely adamant about not having long movies. That meant that you had to do an awful lot of maneuvering and cutting and dovetailing to fit a story of that magnitude and that many people into a comparatively small space. I call that breaking the back of the thing—taking a novel and breaking it down so that it's a play. This requires in itself a certain amount of skill. I think that playwrights generally do this better than, say, novelists. William Faulkner, for instance, was a great novelist, but he never really did a particularly good job as a screenwriter. They used him often, particularly at Warners, but he never handled screenwriting the way he did prose writing. Either you can do it or you can't. I don't say it's a great gift, but you had to be able to understand how it was done.

As I said, a playwright may have been better suited than a novelist, but there were also things unique to screenwriting. Often, for instance, the less you say, the better. I remember when I was first at Warners and I'd tell Henry Blanke, "I don't know how to say this." And he'd say, "Have you ever tried saying nothing?" He taught me to let the camera say it instead. He showed me all sorts of tricks about storytelling on the screen—how to make a point, or to bring out a detail, with the camera instead of describing it or talking about it.

But to get back to *Mildred Pierce*, I had to compress it quite a bit, but I wanted to stay with the novel the way it was as much as possible. I liked the novel very much. But the property went on the shelves for a time because nobody wanted to do a movie about a housewife who made pies. It wasn't very glamorous or interesting to people at the studio. No actress wanted to play it, no director wanted to do it, period. It was finally Jerry Wald who revived the project and talked Joan Crawford into doing it. She also did not want to do the picture at first. She was in her mid-thirties at the time and didn't want to play the mother of a sixteen-year-old daughter who stole the man from her. And then Wald wanted to turn the thing into a murder mystery.

There was no murder in Cain's novel.

No. The novel is very different from the movie. In the book, Veda, the bitchy daughter, really does have a good voice, and she comes through in the end, so you have the feeling that she's really going to go on and accomplish something. Which makes Mildred's sacrifices for her and belief in her worthwhile. But Jerry didn't want that. He wanted the murder. And then, the flashback structure was his idea as well.

I think Wald was quoted as saying that, after seeing *Double Indemnity*, he was going to use flashbacks in all his movies.

Yes? I didn't think that particular movie needed the flashback technique, and that is one of the reasons why I didn't get along too well with Jerry Wald. The flashbacks took up an awful lot of footage and took away from the story itself. I thought that another murder story was not as interesting as Mildred's story, of her gradual move from Glendale housewife to somebody fighting and clawing her way in the restaurant, making good, her relationship with her daughter, and so on.

I also think his approach had something to do with the censorship that was in force. If a girl transgressed, she had to be punished, according to the framework of the Johnson-Hays office. You were absolutely in a straitjacket about morality. You couldn't say "damn," or "oh my God," or anything like that. Husbands and wives could not sleep in the same bed. You couldn't have horizontal kissing, and any kiss could only last a certain amount of time. If a woman had an extramarital affair, she had to suffer for it. She certainly couldn't have a good time doing it.

I wrote a remake of *The Animal Kingdom* called *One More Tomorrow*. It was a pretty good picture, but nothing like the original. The Philip Barry play had to do with a man with a lovely woman for a mistress but who decides to marry a socialite. The woman he marries turns out to be an awful, venal woman, and in the end he walks out on her and returns to his mistress. Well, in order to get the idea of a man walking out on his wife for his mistress past the Hays office, I had to have the wife say, at three different times in three different scenes, that she *refused to have children*. Then the situation was acceptable.

It was so silly. When I look back on it now, I think some of the stories I worked on, if we didn't have so much harnessing, would have made much more interesting pictures.

You were taken off *Mildred Pierce* when Wald asked for changes?

Bette Davis had asked for me to do *A Stolen Life* with Curt Bernhardt, and Wald got Randy MacDougall. Randy had done a great many things for Wald, and Wald liked him—and they both went along with the flashback technique.

Bette liked Curt and me as a combination. We did *My Reputation* together, which starred Barbara Stanwyck, and was a big hit, and was quite an adult thing considering the strictures of the Hays Code. It was not always easy to work with him, though. A lot of people had trouble with Curt. He was a German Jew who got out of Germany by the skin of his teeth. He was very Germanic and difficult at times. He was a product of the Berlin school of filmmaking, and they were quite sophisticated, those early German movie directors. And he thought Americans were hopelessly naïve at that time.

But it was a good experience working with him. I learned. For one thing, both he and Henry Blanke taught me a valuable lesson: never attack a scene head on, always do it obliquely, if

Glenn Ford and
Bette Davis in
A Stolen Life (1946).

Advertisement
for *A Stolen Life*.

possible. Never have anything on the nose. It makes the audience more curious if you approach your points sideways. Another thing Bernhardt made me do was avoid sentimentality. I generally wrote about women's problems, emotional things, and I had a tendency to be sentimental in my writing. He was a stickler for staying away from sentimentality. Keep away from it, keep away from it! Give it a hard edge.

A *Stolen Life* was where Bette Davis played identical twins.

Yes. They did a lot of things with the special effects that they'd never done before. Went way out on a limb. It was difficult. They had to be very precise in the staging of scenes with both sisters. Bette would play one sister, and they would have another actress about her size and height playing opposite her. Then, on Stage Five, where they had the special effects, they would remove the head of the actress and substitute Bette's head. And I remember the first time we were all sitting there watching as her head came off. I remember Bette saying, "I don't like that! Why do we have to do that?" It was the only time I saw her lose her cool.

They did do some outstanding things in that. She would pass a cigarette to herself, and you really believed it. But I had written it without any thought of the effects and what was possible. Curt had said, "Write it as two characters. Forget that Bette is playing both. Don't get involved in that or it will inhibit you." And it would have, too, wondering what could be done and what couldn't.

Many people found Bette Davis very difficult to work with, but you two became good friends, didn't you?

I admired her very much. I was always fond of Bette. We're still friends. I hear from her occasionally. I liked Joan pretty well, too. I didn't particularly like Barbara Stanwyck. I admired her a great deal as an actress, but I never could get close to her. I don't think she liked women very well. She was polite, but I never felt any warmth there. I don't think there is a lot of warmth in her. If you think back on her performances, there isn't much warmth there.

But Bette I worked very closely with on *A Stolen Life*. I was on the set all the time with that, and very much against the will of the studio.

Why?

Because I was under contract and they wanted me working on something else. But Bette kept asking me to go down on the set. We would have big discussions, and everybody would be standing around waiting. It drove some of the stage crew crazy.

You see, Bette was the producer on *A Stolen Life*. At that time, the studio was making deals with some of the big stars so they wouldn't have to give them raises in salary. They would make them producers in name only, and it allowed them to get capital gains, something taken off their income tax. They did this with Errol Flynn, for instance, on another picture I did, *Cry Wolf*. He was the producer on that, but he never functioned in any way. He couldn't have cared less. But when they set up this deal with Bette, to their astonishment and dismay she took it completely seriously. She would attend all meetings and would call for endless meetings in her portable dressing room on the set.

For what sort of problems would she call you to the set?

I remember one time she called a big discussion about the kind of dog to be used in a scene.

There was a scene after she takes on the other sister's life, and the dog gives her trouble, not recognizing her. Well, there was a tremendously long discussion about what kind of dog the girl would have. A chihuahua, for instance? What would that signify? Or maybe it should be a Belgian wolfhound? It took almost half a day discussing what kind of dog. It got a little out of hand. We finally ended up having people bring a whole bunch of dogs of all sizes and shapes and parade them around. I believe we picked a wire-haired fox terrier.

But Bette did give her all to that picture. I remember when they did the scene with the shipwreck. They did it at night in the tank, where you could simulate these tremendous waves. They would hit with a tremendous splash. I don't think a real storm at sea could have been any stronger when they let loose those tons of water through the chute. And Bette was in there, doing all those shots herself. The water would knock her right out of the boat, and sometimes she'd get waterlogged in the boat and somebody would have to jump in and pull her out. But she wouldn't use a double. I guess she thought that in this picture there was already *enough* doubling. How many doubles can you have?

That reminds me of a funny thing that occurred a little later. It so happened that Randy MacDougall went down on a trip to Mexico and saw this Mexican picture about two twin sisters. It was called *La Otra*. He reported it to Warner Bros. and said, "There's this marvelous movie you must buy, and we'll remake it in Hollywood." And Warners bought the movie. Then Michael Curtiz got involved. He was intrigued by the story and wanted to set it in New Orleans. They showed me the Mexican movie, and, as I was watching it, I said to them, "This is an awful lot like *A Stolen Life*." And they said, "No, no, it isn't."

But it was. It was the same movie as *A Stolen Life*—right to the dog. No one else seemed to make the connection, though. Michael Curtiz didn't want to know anything about *A Stolen Life*. I eventually heard from Preston Foster—I think it was—who had come back from working in Mexico, what had gone on. The people who made *La Otra* had someone sitting in the back of a theatre in Mexico where *A Stolen Life* was playing, taking down all the dialogue and everything in shorthand. They then went ahead and made their own Mexican movie from it.

And so Warner Bros. had bought the rights to something stolen from one of their own movies. At least they never ended up making it, I don't think. I got out of it, anyway. I told them I didn't want to spend any more of my life writing about identical twins.

You mentioned *Cry Wolf*. That was an unusual part for Flynn to take, wasn't it? The focus was more on the woman.

Yes. They got the property for Barbara Stanwyck. She had read the book and thought it was a good part for her. Flynn's part was basically supporting her. And when he read the script, he said, "I'm playing support to Barbara Stanwyck." But he said, "It's kind of an interesting character. I don't mind doing it, really." But this was after we had to talk him into it a little bit. I was told he wanted to talk to the writer about the script, so we were invited to lunch. We went over and had a pleasant lunch. We had martinis and a very pleasant lunch. I found him very easy to work with, very charming. And he was always very agreeable with me on the set. And it turned out to be a pretty good picture.

Can we talk about *The Man I Love*?

Originally they bought that one for Ann Sheridan. There was a scene with a black woman

Barbara Stanwyck and Errol Flynn in *Cry Wolf* (1947).

who ran a whorehouse or something. Ann didn't want to play that scene, so she turned it down. We ended up taking that scene out, anyway.

I'm not going to take full credit for breaking the back of that story because someone else had done a treatment on the thing. But we worked on it and made changes, and it turned out to be a pretty good picture. It was not at all what I regarded as my kind of story, actually. Although the woman played a big part in it, it was basically the man's story. The gangster, the Robert Alda character, was the key character in that one. But Ida Lupino was good in that and she liked her part.

There again I had to break the back of a huge novel, 900 pages or so. It was called *Night Shift* and there were thousands of characters all over the place. I think we used the whole Warner Bros. stock company on that one.

There was another case where the picture would have been more interesting if there was less censorship and we could have been more outspoken and frank. There was a big scene with Ida Lupino's sister and the lover, Bruce Bennett, a rape scene not unlike the Fatty Arbuckle case. And we really had to pussyfoot around that to get anything by.

Did Raoul Walsh have any input on the script?

No. It wasn't the kind of thing they generally gave him. But I really think Walsh quite liked it, and he enjoyed working with me. He was an interesting man, a tough guy, you know, with that patch over his eye, rather inarticulate and pretty basic in his language. But he was helpful. He knew what he was doing with the camera. It was just a job for him, but he did know how to put a scene together. I learned a lot from him.

Your last film for Warners was *Winter Meeting*.

This was a project of Blanke's for Bette Davis. It was not a successful movie. It looks a little better now on the small screen. It's better suited for television. But it was much too talky. It was the director Bretaigne Windust's first movie. He had made quite a name for himself on Broadway and came out with a big fanfare. But he directed it like a stage play. And we had an actor, Jim Davis, who was not right for the part at all. So that was kind of a disaster. And Bette was starting to lose her box-office appeal. Television was coming in.

You moved on to Paramount.

I moved on to Paramount for *No Man of Her Own*. It was from a Cornell Woolrich novel, *I Married a Dead Man*. And that was a very unpleasant assignment all the way through.

Why?

It was not unalloyed joy working with Mitchell Leisen. It was not just me. I don't think anybody had any joy working with him as far as I could make out. He drove the producer, Richard Maibaum, absolutely crazy. He aced him out of the thing and just went ahead and did what he pleased.

He wanted to be a writer, and he joined the Writers Guild so he could start getting writing credit. He would take the *No Man of Her Own* material home with him at night and come back the next day with all his own changes. I'm not saying that they were all bad, but I could see that what he wanted was to get enough material in so he could get a writing credit. He was very wily. I think he did have a certain ability to direct. He had flair—he used to be a costume designer. But he acted very unfair. And there was a very rough time with him when the final credits came through and he didn't get a writing credit. He called an arbitration and the arbitration went against him. He was furious and I understand that he fell apart, screaming and yelling.

He had, I believe, a problem with alcohol.

Mitchell later wrote a book, taking credit for everything.

He said he had to rewrite Wilder and Brackett. . . .

Oh yes, he claimed he rewrote everybody! A lot of people fell in love with themselves, particularly the directors.

How often did you feel that you were the "author" of the scripts you wrote, in the sense that you were the author of your plays?

I was usually adapting someone else's book or story, and I tried to be true to the material as much as possible. I tried to use as much dialogue as was possible out of the book. But very often a book doesn't lend itself to being spoken aloud. And so I would have to create a lot of original dialogue. And the more of your own material you put in, the more the characters become your own. And any writer, even adapting someone else's material, finds herself responding more to certain characters and scenes than to others.

There is a recurring theme of family rivalries in your scripts—mother and daughter, sisters, wife and mistress. Was this conscious?

Well, these relationships interested me. I did feel that women's relationships were interesting. I don't know how conscious I was of a theme.

Did you object to being categorized as a writer of "women's pictures"?

Well, I couldn't have done the other things. The majority of Warner movies were men's movies, *Action in the North Atlantic, Destination Tokyo,* that sort of thing. That was their specialty at the time I came there. When I arrived, I think Lenore Coffee was the only woman writer they had. The roster of writers was primarily pretty hard-nosed guys, a lot of newspapermen, sports writers. They were inclined to be condescending with me, at the beginning. They used to say, "What are you working on?" and then, "Oh yeah, a woman's picture." And they dismissed it. But they didn't after some of those pictures went out and made a lot of money. And they recognized the fact that a woman could handle a story about a woman's troubles better than most men could. Anyway, you can rest assured that if the studio didn't think the woman did a better job, she wouldn't have been there for very long.

So, no, I didn't feel constricted by women's pictures. It was the sort of thing I felt simpatico with. If I was pigeonholed, it was with something that I really liked doing.

Filmography

CHARLES BENNETT

1929 *Blackmail* (co-adaptation of his play)
1930 *The Last Hour* (screenplay)
1931 *Deadlock* (co-screenplay)
　　 Number Please (co-screenplay)
　　 Two-Way Street (co-screenplay)
1932 *Partners Please* (screenplay)
1934 *The Man Who Knew Too Much* (co-story, co-screenplay)
1935 *The Clairvoyant* (co-screenplay)
　　 The Thirty-Nine Steps (adaptation, co-screenplay)
　　 King of the Damned (co-screenplay)
1936 *Sabotage* (screenplay)
　　 Secret Agent (screenplay)
1937 *King Solomon's Mines* (co-screenplay)
1938 *The Girl Was Young* (co-screenplay)
　　 The Young in Heart (co-screenplay)
1939 *Balalaika* (co-screenplay)
1940 *Foreign Correspondent* (story, co-screenplay)
1941 *They Dare Not Love* (co-screenplay)
1942 *Joan of Paris* (co-screenplay)
　　 Reap the Wild Wind (co-screenplay)
1943 *Forever and a Day* (co-screenplay)
1944 *The Story of Dr. Wassell* (co-screenplay)

1947 *Ivy* (screenplay)
　　 Unconquered (co-screenplay)
1948 *The Sign of the Ram* (screenplay)
1949 *Black Magic* (screenplay)
1950 *Madness of the Heart* (screenplay, director)
　　 Where Danger Lives (screenplay)
1951 *Kind Lady* (co-screenplay)
1952 *The Green Glove* (screenplay)
1953 *No Escape* (screenplay, director)
1954 *Dangerous Mission* (co-screenplay)
1956 *The Man Who Knew Too Much* (co-story of remake)
1957 *Night of the Demon* (U.S. title *Curse of the Demon,* screenplay)
　　 The Story of Mankind (co-screenplay)
1959 *The Big Circus* (co-screenplay)
1960 *The Lost World* (co-screenplay)
1961 *Voyage to the Bottom of the Sea* (co-screenplay)
1962 *Five Weeks in a Balloon* (co-screenplay)
1965 *War Gods of the Deep* (co-screenplay)

A.I. BEZZERIDES

1940 *They Drive by Night* (from his novel *The Long Haul)*
1942 *Juke Girl* (screenplay)
1943 *Action in the North Atlantic* (co-screenplay)
1947 *Desert Fury* (co-adaptation)
1949 *Thieves' Highway* (screenplay, from his novel *Thieves' Market)*
1950 *On Dangerous Ground* (screenplay, adaptation)

1951 *Sirocco* (co-screenplay)
1952 *Holiday for Sinners* (screenplay)
1953 *Beneath the Twelve Mile Reef* (screenplay)
1954 *Track of the Cat* (screenplay)
1955 *A Bullet for Joey* (co-screenplay)
　　 Kiss Me Deadly (screenplay)
1959 *The Angry Hills* (screenplay)
　　 The Jayhawkers (co-screenplay)

IRVING BRECHER

1937 *New Faces of 1937* (co-screenplay)
1938 *Fools for Scandal* (additional
       dialogue)
1939 *The Wizard of Oz* (additional
       dialogue, uncredited)
       At the Circus (story, screenplay)
1940 *Go West* (story, screenplay)
1941 *Shadow of the Thin Man*
       (co-screenplay)
1943 *Du Barry Was a Lady* (screenplay)
       Ship Ahoy (co-screenplay)
       Best Foot Forward (co-screenplay)
1944 *Meet Me in St. Louis* (co-screenplay)
1945 *Ziegfeld Follies* (co-screenplay)
       Yolanda and the Thief (screenplay)
1948 *Summer Holiday* (adapatation)
1949 *The Life of Riley* (story, screenplay,
       producer, director)
1952 *Somebody Loves Me* (story,
       screenplay, producer, director)
1961 *Cry for Happy* (screenplay)
1963 *Bye Bye Birdie* (screenplay)

JOHN BRIGHT

1931 *Public Enemy* (co-story, co-
       screenplay, from his novel *Beer
       and Blood*)
       Smart Money (co-story,
       co-screenplay)
       Blonde Crazy (co-story,
       co-screenplay)
1932 *The Crowd Roars* (co-screenplay)
       Taxi (co-screenplay)
       Union Depot (co-screenplay,
       uncredited)
       Three on a Match (co-story)
       If I Had a Million (co-screenplay)
1933 *She Done Him Wrong* (co-screenplay)
1936 *Girl of the Ozarks* (co-story)
1937 *The Accusing Finger* (co-screenplay)
       John Meade's Woman (co-screenplay)
       San Quentin (co-story)
1939 *Back Door to Heaven* (co-screenplay)
1940 *Glamour for Sale* (story, screenplay)
1942 *Broadway* (co-screenplay)
       *Sherlock Holmes and the Voice of Ter-
       ror* (co-screenplay)
1945 *We Accuse* (narration; documentary)
1948 *Close Up* (co-screenplay)
       A Palooka Named Joe (screenplay)
       I Walk Alone (co-adaptation)
       Open Secret (additional dialogue)
1949 *The Kid from Cleveland* (co-story,
       co-screenplay)
1951 *The Brave Bulls* (screenplay)
1954 *Rebellion of the Hanged* (screenplay)
1955 *Mexican Trio* (screenplay)

PHILIP DUNNE

1933 *Student Tour* (co-screenplay)
1934 *The Count of Monte Cristo*
       (co-screenplay)
1935 *The Melody Lingers On*
       (co-screenplay)
1936 *The Last of the Mohicans* (screenplay)
1937 *Breezing Home* (co-story)
       Lancer Spy (screenplay)
1938 *Suez* (co-screenplay)
1939 *Stanley and Livingstone*
       (co-screenplay)
       The Rains Came (co-screenplay)
       Swanee River (co-screenplay)
1940 *Johnny Apollo* (co-screenplay)
1941 *How Green Was My Valley*
       (screenplay)
1942 *Son of Fury* (screenplay)
1947 *The Late George Apley* (screenplay)
       Forever Amber (co-screenplay)
       The Ghost and Mrs. Muir (screenplay)
1948 *Escape* (screenplay)
       The Luck of the Irish (screenplay)

1949 *Pinky* (co-screenplay)
1951 *David and Bathsheba* (story, screenplay)
      Anne of the Indies (co-screenplay)
1952 *Lydia Bailey* (co-screenplay)
      Way of a Gaucho (screenplay)
1953 *The Robe* (screenplay)
1954 *Demetrius and the Gladiators* (story, screenplay)
      The Egyptian (co-screenplay)
1955 *The View from Pompey's Head* (screenplay, director)

1956 *Hilda Crane* (screenplay, director)
1957 *Three Brave Men* (screenplay, director)
1958 *Ten North Frederick* (screenplay, director)
1959 *Blue Denim* (co-screenplay)
1965 *The Agony and the Ecstasy* (screenplay)
1966 *Blindfold* (co-screenplay)

WILLIAM LUDWIG

1938 *Love Finds Andy Hardy* (screenplay)
      Out West with the Hardys (co-screenplay)
1939 *The Hardys Ride High* (co-screenplay)
      Stronger Than Desire (co-screenplay)
      Blackmail (co-screenplay)
1941 *Love Crazy* (co-story, co-screenplay)
1942 *Journey for Margaret* (co-screenplay)
1943 *The Human Comedy* (co-screenplay, uncredited)
1944 *An American Romance* (co-screenplay)
      Andy Hardy's Blonde Trouble (co-story, co-screenplay)
1946 *Boys Ranch* (story, screenplay)
      Love Laughs at Andy Hardy (co-screenplay)
1948 *The Hills of Home* (story, screenplay)

      Julia Misbehaves (co-screenplay)
1949 *The Sun Comes Up* (co-screenplay)
      Challenge to Lassie (screenplay)
1950 *Shadow on the Wall* (screenplay)
1951 *The Great Caruso* (co-story, co-screenplay)
      It's a Big Country (co-screenplay)
1952 *The Merry Widow* (co-screenplay)
1954 *The Student Prince* (co-screenplay)
      Athena (co-story, co-screenplay)
1955 *Hit the Deck* (co-story, co-screenplay)
      Interrupted Melody (co-screenplay)
      Oklahoma (co-screenplay)
1957 *Ten Thousand Bedrooms* (co-story, co-screenplay)
      Gun Glory (screenplay)
1961 *Back Street* (co-screenplay)

NAT PERRIN

1931 *Monkey Business* (co-screenplay, uncredited)
      Sidewalks of New York (co-screenplay)
1933 *Duck Soup* (co-screenplay)
      Roman Scandals (co-screenplay)
1934 *Kid Millions* (co-story, co-screenplay)
1936 *Rose of the Rancho* (co-screenplay)
      Dimples (co-screenplay)
      Stowaway (co-screenplay)
      Pigskin Parade (co-story)
1937 *Don't Tell the Wife* (screenplay)

      New Faces of 1937 (co-screenplay)
      On Again Off Again (co-screenplay)
1939 *The Gracie Allen Murder Case* (screenplay)
1940 *Alias the Deacon* (co-screenplay)
      Hullabaloo (screenplay)
1941 *Hellzapoppin'* (story, co-screenplay)
      Keep 'em Flying (co-screenplay)
      The Big Store (co-story)
1942 *Pardon My Sarong* (co-story, co-screenplay)
      Whistling in Dixie (screenplay)

1943 *Swing Fever* (co-screenplay)
Whistling in Brooklyn (story, screenplay)
1945 *Abbott and Costello in Hollywood* (co-story, co-screenplay)
1947 *Song of the Thin Man* (co-screenplay, producer)
1949 *Miss Grant Takes Richmond* (co-screenplay)

Tell It to the Judge (screenplay)
1950 *The Petty Girl* (screenplay, producer)
1965 *I'll Take Sweden* (story, co-screenplay)
Frankie and Johnny (co-story)
1968 *Wicked Dreams of Paula Schultz* (co-screenplay)

ALLEN RIVKIN

1932 *Is My Face Red?* (co-story)
The Devil Is Driving (co-adaptation)
Madison Square Garden (co-screenplay)
Night World (co-story)
70,000 Witnesses (co-dialogue)
1933 *Dancing Lady* (co-screenplay)
Picture Snatcher (co-screenplay)
1934 *Cheating Cheaters* (co-screenplay)
1935 *Black Sheep* (screenplay)
Our Little Girl (co-screenplay)
Bad Boy (screenplay)
1936 *Champagne Charley* (screenplay)
Half Angel (co-screenplay)
1937 *Love Under Fire* (co-screenplay)
This Is My Affair (co-story, co-screenplay)
1938 *Every Day's a Holiday* (co-screenplay, uncredited)
Straight, Place and Show (co-screenplay)
1939 *It Could Happen to You* (co-screenplay)
Let Us Live (co-screenplay)
1940 *Typhoon* (screenplay)
Dancing on a Dime (co-screenplay)
1941 *Behind the News* (co-story)

Singapore Woman (co-screenplay)
Highway West (co-screenplay)
1942 *Kid Glove Killer* (co-screenplay)
Joe Smith, American (screenplay)
Sunday Punch (co-screenplay)
1946 *Till the End of Time* (screenplay)
The Thrill of Brazil (co-story, co-screenplay)
1947 *Dead Reckoning* (adaptation)
Guilt of Janet Ames (co-screenplay)
The Farmer's Daughter (co-screenplay)
1949 *My Dream Is Yours* (co-adapatation)
1950 *Tension* (screenplay)
1951 *Gambling House* (co-screenplay)
Grounds for Marriage (co-screenplay)
The Strip (story, screenplay)
1952 *It's a Big Country* (co-screenplay)
1953 *Battle Circus* (co-story)
1954 *Prisoner of War* (story, screenplay)
1955 *Timberjack* (screenplay)
The Road to Denver (co-screenplay)
The Eternal Sea (screenplay)
1958 *Girls on the Loose* (co-screenplay)
Live Fast, Die Young (co-screenplay)
1959 *The Big Operator* (co-screenplay)

WELLS ROOT

1928 *Varsity* (co-screenplay)
1930 *The Storm* (co-screenplay)
1931 *Politics* (screenplay)
Prodigal (co-screenplay)
1932 *Bird of Paradise* (co-screenplay)
Tiger Shark (screenplay)
1933 *I Cover the Waterfront* (screenplay)

1934 *Black Moon* (screenplay)
Paris Interlude (screenplay)
1935 *Public Hero Number One* (screenplay)
Pursuit (screenplay)
Shadow of Doubt (screenplay)
1936 *Bold Caballero* (screenplay)

Beloved Vagabond (co-screenplay)
Sworn Enemy (screenplay)
1937 *The Prisoner of Zenda* (adaptation, co-screenplay)
1939 *Man of Conquest* (co-story, co-screenplay)
Sergeant Madden (screenplay)
Thunder Afloat (co-screenplay)
1940 *Flight Command* (co-screenplay)
1941 *Bad Man* (screenplay)
The Getaway (co-story, co-screenplay)

1942 *Mokey* (co-screenplay, director)
Tennessee Johnson (co-screenplay)
1943 *Man from Down Under* (co-screenplay)
Salute to the Marines (adaptation)
1952 *Stronghold* (screenplay)
1954 *Magnificent Obsession* (co-screenplay)
1957 *Hell Ship Mutiny* (co-story, co-screenplay)
1961 *Secret of Deep Harbor* (co-screenplay)
1966 *Texas Across the River* (co-story, co-screenplay)

ALLAN SCOTT

1933 *Goodbye Again* (from his play)
1934 *By Your Leave* (screenplay)
1935 *Village Tale* (screenplay)
Top Hat (co-screenplay)
Roberta (co-screenplay)
In Person (screenplay)
1936 *Follow the Fleet* (co-screenplay)
Swing Time (co-screenplay)
1937 *Quality Street* (co-screenplay)
Shall We Dance (co-screenplay)
Wise Girl (co-story, screenplay)
1938 *Carefree* (co-screenplay)
Joy of Living (co-screenplay)
Man About Town (co-story)
1939 *Fifth Avenue Girl* (story, screenplay)
1940 *Primrose Path* (co-screenplay)
Lucky Partners (co-screenplay)
Honeymoon for Three (from his play)
1941 *Skylark* (screenplay)
Remember the Day (co-screenplay)
1943 *So Proudly We Hail* (story, screenplay)

1944 *Here Come the Waves* (co-story, co-screenplay)
I Love a Soldier (story, screenplay)
1946 *Blue Skies* (adaptation)
1949 *Tell It to the Judge* (co-screenplay)
1950 *Let's Dance* (screenplay)
1951 *The Guy Who Came Back* (screenplay)
1952 *The Four Poster* (screenplay, co-producer)
Wait Till the Sun Shines, Nellie (co-adaptation, screenplay)
1953 *The 5,000 Fingers of Dr. T* (co-screenplay)
1959 *Imitation of Life* (co-screenplay)
1973 *Don't Look Now* (co-screenplay)
1974 *The Girl from Petrovka* (co-screenplay)
1979 *The Awakening* (screenplay)

CURT SIODMAK

In the mid-1920s Siodmak translated and wrote German title cards for imported Mack Sennett comedies.

1928 *Sudsee-Abenteuer* (co-screenplay)
1929 *Flucht in die Fremdenlegion* (screenplay)
Menschen am Sonntag (story, co-screenplay)

Mastottchen (co-screenplay)
1930 *Der Kampf mit dem Drachen* (screenplay)
1931 *Der Mann, der seinen Mörder sucht* (co-screenplay)
Der Ball (co-screenplay)
1933 *F.P. 1 (Does Not Reply)* (co-screenplay)
1934 *La Crise est finie* (story, co-screenplay)

1935 *The Tunnel (Transatlantic Tunnel)* (story, screenplay)
1936 *I Give My Heart* (co-screenplay)
1937 *Non-Stop New York* (co-screenplay)
I, Claudius (co-screenplay; un-completed production)
1938 *Her Jungle Love* (co-story)
Spawn of the North (co-screenplay, uncredited)
1940 *The Invisible Man Returns* (co-story, co-screenplay)
Black Friday (co-story, co-screenplay)
The Ape (co-screenplay)
1941 *Pacific Blackout* (co-story)
The Invisible Woman (co-story, co-screenplay)
Aloma of the South Seas (co-screenplay)
1942 *Invisible Agent* (story, screenplay)
London Black-Out Murders (story, screenplay)
The Wolf Man (co-story, co-screenplay)
1943 *Son of Dracula* (co-screenplay)
Frankenstein Meets the Wolf Man (story, screenplay)
I Walked With a Zombie (co-screenplay)
The Purple V (co-screenplay)
The Mantrap (screenplay)
False Faces (story, screenplay)
1944 *The Lady and the Monster* (from his novel, *Donovan's Brain)*
House of Frankenstein (story)
The Climax (adaptation, co-screenplay)

1945 *Shady Lady* (co-story, co-screenplay)
Frisco Sal (co-story, co-screenplay)
1946 *The Return of Monte Cristo* (co-story)
1947 *The Beast With Five Fingers* (screenplay)
1948 *Berlin Express* (story)
1949 *Tarzan's Magic Fountain* (co-story, co-screenplay)
Four Day's Leave (co-screenplay)
1951 *Bride of the Gorilla* (story, screenplay, director)
1953 *Donovan's Brain* (from his novel)
The Magnetic Monster (co-story, co-screenplay, director)
1954 *Riders to the Stars* (story, screenplay)
1955 *Creature With the Atom Brain* (story, screenplay)
1956 *Earth vs. the Flying Saucers* (story)
Curucu, Beast of the Amazon (story, screenplay, director)
1957 *Love Slaves of the Amazon* (story, screenplay, director)
1962 *Sherlock Holmes und das Halsband des Todes* (English version, *Sherlock Holmes and the Deadly Necklace,* 1968) (screenplay)
The Devil's Messenger (screenplay)
1963 *Das Feuerschiff* (screenplay)
1966 *Ski Fever* (co-screenplay)
1969 *Hauser's Memory* (from his novel)
1977 *Der Heiligenschein* (from his novel *Variation of a Theme)*
1978 *Moonraker* (in part from his novel *Skyport)*

CATHERINE TURNEY

1936 *The Bride Wore Red* (co-screenplay, uncredited)
1945 *Mildred Pierce* (co-screenplay, uncredited)
1946 *One More Tomorrow* (co-screenplay)
Of Human Bondage (screenplay)
My Reputation (screenplay)
A Stolen Life (screenplay)

1947 *The Man I Love* (co-adaptation, screenplay)
Cry Wolf (screenplay)
1948 *Winter Meeting* (screenplay)
1950 *No Man of Her Own* (co-screenplay)
1952 *Japanese War Bride* (screenplay)
1957 *Back from the Dead* (from her novel *The Other One)*

Bibliography

CEPLAIR, LARRY and STEVEN ENGLUND. *The Inquisition in Hollywood: Politics in the Film Community, 1930–1960.* Garden City, N.Y.: Anchor Press/Doubleday, 1980.

COLE, LESTER. *Hollywood Red.* Palo Alto, Calif.: Ramparts Press, 1981.

COOK, BRUCE. *Dalton Trumbo.* New York: Scribner's, 1977.

CORLISS, RICHARD. *Talking Pictures: Screenwriters in the American Cinema.* Woodstock, N.Y.: The Overlook Press, 1974.

CURTIS, JAMES. *Between Flops: A Biography of Preston Sturges.* New York: Harcourt Brace Jovanovich, 1982.

DUNNE, PHILIP. *Take Two: A Life in Movies and Politics.* San Francisco: McGraw-Hill, 1980.

FETHERLING, DOUG. *The Five Lives of Ben Hecht.* New York: New York Zoetrope, 1980.

FORDIN, HUGH. *The Movies' Greatest Musicals.* New York: Frederick Ungar, 1975.

FROUG, WILLIAM. *The Screenwriter Looks at the Screenwriter.* New York: Macmillan, 1972.

GOLDMAN, WILLIAM. *Adventures in the Screen Trade: A Personal View of Hollywood and Screenwriting.* New York: Warner Books, 1982.

HECHT, BEN. *A Child of the Century.* New York: Simon & Schuster, 1954.

HIGHAM, CHARLES. *Warner Brothers.* New York: Scribner's, 1975.

KAEL, PAULINE. *The Citizen Kane Book.* Boston: Little, Brown, 1971.

LASKY, JR., JESSE. *Whatever Happened to Hollywood?* New York: Funk & Wagnalls, 1973.

LOOS, ANITA. *Kiss Hollywood Goodbye.* New York: Viking Press, 1974.

MARX, SAMUEL. *Mayer and Thalberg: The Make-Believe Saints.* New York: Random House, 1975.

McBRIDE, JOSEPH. *Hawks on Hawks.* Berkeley, Calif.: University of California Press, 1982.

MERYMAN, RICHARD. *Mank: The Wit, World, and Life of Herman Mankiewicz.* New York: William Morrow, 1978.

RIVKIN, ALLEN and LAURA KERR RIVKIN. *Hello, Hollywood.* Garden City, N.Y.: Doubleday, 1962.

ROOT, WELLS. *Writing the Script.* New York: Holt, Rinehart and Winston, 1979.

SARRIS, ANDREW. *The American Cinema.* New York: E.P. Dutton, 1968.

SCHWARTZ, NANCY LYNN. *The Hollywood Writers' Wars.* New York: Alfred A. Knopf, 1982.

SPIGELGASS, LEONARD, ED. *Who Wrote the Movie and What Else Did He Write?* Los Angeles: Academy of Motion Picture Arts and Sciences and Writers Guild of America (West), 1970.

SPOTO, DONALD. *The Dark Side of Genius.* Boston: Little, Brown, 1983.

TRUMBO, DALTON. *Additional Dialogue.* New York: M. Evans, 1970.

ZOLOTOW, MAURICE. *Billy Wilder in Hollywood.* New York: Putnam, 1977.

Index

251